WISDOM FROM THE LATE BRONZE AGE

Society of Biblical Literature

Writings from the Ancient World

Theodore J. Lewis, General Editor

Associate Editors

Billie Jean Collins
Daniel Fleming
Martti Nissinen
William Schniedewind
Mark S. Smith
Emily Teeter
Terry Wilfong

Number 29
Wisdom from the Late Bronze Age

WISDOM FROM THE LATE BRONZE AGE

by Yoram Cohen

Edited by Andrew R. George

Society of Biblical Literature
Atlanta

WISDOM FROM THE LATE BRONZE AGE

Library of Congress Cataloging-in-Publication Data

Cohen, Yoram.
Wisdom from the late Bronze Age / by Yoram Cohen.
p. cm. — (Writings from the ancient world ; no. 34)
Includes bibliographical references and index.
ISBN 978-1-58983-753-9 (paper binding : alk. paper) — ISBN 978-1-58983-754-6 (electronic format) — ISBN 978-1-58983-775-1 (hardcover binding : alk. paper)
1. Assyro-Babylonian literature. 2. Wisdom literature—Criticism, interpretation, etc. 3. Akkadian language—Texts. 4. Assyro-Babylonian literature—Translations into English. I. Title.
PJ3941.C64 2013
892'.1—dc23

2013004614

Printed on acid-free, recycled paper conforming to ANSI/NISO Z39.48-1992 (R1997) and ISO 9706:1994 standards for paper permanence.

CONTENTS

Series Editor's Foreword

Writings from the Ancient World is designed to provide up-to-date, readable English translations of writings recovered from the ancient Near East.

The series is intended to serve the interests of general readers, students, and educators who wish to explore the ancient Near Eastern roots of Western civilization or to compare these earliest written expressions of human thought and activity with writings from other parts of the world. It should also be useful to scholars in the humanities or social sciences who need clear, reliable translations of ancient Near Eastern materials for comparative purposes. Specialists in particular areas of the ancient Near East who need access to texts in the scripts and languages of other areas will also find these translations helpful. Given the wide range of materials translated in the series, different volumes will appeal to different interests. However, these translations make available to all readers of English the world's earliest traditions as well as valuable sources of information on daily life, history, religion, and the like in the preclassical world.

The translators of the various volumes in this series are specialists in the particular languages and have based their work on the original sources and the most recent research. In their translations they attempt to convey as much as possible of the original texts in fluent, current English. In the introductions, notes, glossaries, maps, and chronological tables, they aim to provide the essential information for an appreciation of these ancient documents.

The ancient Near East reached from Egypt to Iran and, for the purposes of our volumes, ranged in time from the invention of writing (by 3000 B.C.E.) to the conquests of Alexander the Great (ca. 330 B.C.E.). The cultures represented within these limits include especially Egyptian, Sumerian, Babylonian, Assyrian, Hittite, Ugaritic, Aramean, Phoenician, and Israelite. It is hoped that Writings from the Ancient World will eventually produce translations from most of the many different genres attested in these cultures: letters (official and private), myths, diplomatic documents, hymns, law collections, monumental inscriptions, tales, and administrative records, to mention but a few.

Significant funding was made available by the Society of Biblical Literature for the preparation of this volume. In addition, those involved in preparing this volume have received financial and clerical assistance from their respective institutions. Were it not for these expressions of confidence in our work, the arduous tasks of preparation, translation, editing, and publication could not have been accomplished or even undertaken. It is the hope of all who have worked with the Writings from the Ancient World series that our translations will open up new horizons and deepen the humanity of all who read these volumes.

Theodore J. Lewis
The Johns Hopkins University

Preface

This book presents a collection of Mesopotamian wisdom literature compositions and proverbs recovered in archaeological excavations of the Late Bronze Age sites of Ḫattuša, Emar, and Ugarit (ca. 1500–1200 B.C.E.). Among the compositions included here are some of the major works of Mesopotamian literature of this period, such as The Ballad of Early Rulers, *Šimâ Milka* (Hear the Advice), The Righteous Sufferer and The Date Palm and the Tamarisk, as well as some shorter compositions and proverbs. The final chapter of the book is dedicated to proverbs and aphorisms appearing in contemporary or near-contemporary letters.

Many of the wisdom pieces brought together in this book are attested almost exclusively in the archives and libraries of Ḫattuša, Emar, and Ugarit, yet they are Mesopotamian creations. If not for the copies recovered at these sites, these wisdom compositions would have almost completely disappeared from the record, their only trace their titles, preserved in Mesopotamian literary catalogues. Hence Late Bronze Age manuscripts of Mesopotamian wisdom literature—or to put it more simply, Late Bronze Age wisdom compositions, a term we will use throughout this book—are crucial in our reconstruction of Mesopotamian literature. Specifically they further our understanding of the content, scope and distribution of Mesopotamian wisdom literature.

These compositions, generally thought to have been composed during the Post Old Babylonian period or the early Kassite period (the sixteenth–fourteenth B.C.E.), constitute a missing link between wisdom literature of the Old Babylonian period (twentieth–seventeenth centuries B.C.E.) and wisdom pieces that were composed at the end of the second millennium or the beginning of the first millennium in Mesopotamia. To explicate, Late Bronze Age wisdom compositions complete for us a literary sequence (although at times still poorly represented) that begins with the Old Babylonian wisdom literature corpus in Sumerian and ends with well-known Akkadian wisdom compositions, such as *Ludlul Bēl Nēmeqi* (I Will Praise the Lord of Wisdom) or The Babylonian Theodicy, of the Kassite and post-Kassite periods. As will be demonstrated throughout this book, Late Bronze Age wisdom compositions stand as witnesses to a long and complex process of transmission and reception of Mesopotamian literature, wisdom literature included, in Babylonia and the surrounding regions (those west of Babylonian collectively referred to as the western periphery).

Part 1 of the book is an introductory essay that discusses definitions, key themes and approaches for understanding the form and function of wisdom literature. It introduces the sources and briefly discusses current scholarly views of what constitutes Mesopotamian wisdom literature. It then offers a few approaches through which wisdom literature will be explored. It continues by examining the archival and archaeological contexts where Late Bronze Age wisdom literature manuscripts were found. On this basis it evaluates the role of wisdom literature in the curriculum of cuneiform scribal schools. The aim of part 1 is to expose readers to a variety of compositions situated within particular historical and social contexts in order to sharpen their appreciation of wisdom literature and highlight the position of this genre within Mesopotamian literary and scholarly creativity.

Part 2 consists of eight chapters devoted either to single works or to a few sources that together constitute a single subject. The wisdom compositions are presented in their original languages (mostly Akkadian and occasionally Sumerian or Hittite). Each composition is provided with an introduction to the main theme of the work and its sources. Then come the text edition and its translation, followed by an extensive discussion. An appreciation of the relationship between Late Bronze Age wisdom compositions and the wider circle of Mesopotamian literature is given throughout. Since most of the manuscripts presented in the book were found outside the Mesopotamian core areas (i.e., Babylonia and Assyria), at times the degree of local influence upon the Late Bronze Age wisdom compositions is questioned. In this respect the ways in which Akkadian and Sumerian compositions were understood and occasionally translated by local scribal circles are also considered.

Late Bronze Age cuneiform texts deviate from the Old Babylonian or Standard Babylonian Akkadian dialect with which nonspecialist students of Akkadian are usually familiar. For example, they make use of a different syllabary from that encountered in Old Babylonian compositions. They are also full of aberrant spelling, textual errors, and nonstandard vocalization of Babylonian Akkadian (and sometimes Sumerian). This requires a careful reworking of the primary sources that leads to a certain degree of compromise. Thus the transcribed or normalized texts presented here cannot be considered full critical editions. However, the outcome, so it is hoped, is the presentation of lucid and yet reliable text editions that readers can navigate without great difficulty. These editions allow readers to appreciate the literary and at times the poetic quality of the compositions, enabling them to assess the choice of vocabulary by recourse to the standard dictionaries (such as the *Chicago Assyrian Dictionary*, *Concise Dictionary of Akkadian*, *Akkadische Handwörterbuch*, *Chicago Hittite Dictionary*, and the *Electronic Pennsylvania Sumerian Dictionary*). For those seeking more detailed editions of the primary sources I have provided relevant bibliography at the end of each chapter.

The editions and translations in this book derive from my own textual reconstruction based on autograph copies and photographs (where available) of the original tablets. I have benefited from previous editions, discussions, and translations. Mention is to be made here of one of the important recent publications used in this collection: Arnaud's 2007 book *Corpus des Textes de Bibliothèque de Ras Shamra—Ougarit (1936–2000)*, which includes improved text editions of wisdom works from Emar and Ugarit. Among its pages are also found two previously unpublished manuscripts of *Šimâ Milka* from Ugarit. These new manuscripts allow a reconstruction and translation of this composition that are fuller than any published before.

On occasions where I adopted the readings and translations of Andrew R. George, the academic editor of this book, I have acknowledged his contributions (noted as ARG in the textual notes). Throughout the discussion I have made reference to individual studies or editions, but because of the format of this series, I have avoided the use of footnotes. As a consequence, one runs the risk of conveying the impression that one is the author of certain ideas when one is not; certainly that was not my intention, therefore apologies are extended in advance to those who may feel they have not been given sufficient or adequate credit. And contrariwise, when I have tried to articulate my own ideas and conclusions, I have attempted to make clear that responsibility for the contents expressed lies with me. My hope is that I have not falsely attributed to anybody ideas not his or hers.

Travels to fields other than Assyriology have been ventured here and there. The occasional comparisons to biblical verses or the citation of a proverb or two from the Sayings of Ahiqar, however, are merely illustrative, neither critical nor comprehensive in their scope. Hopefully more competent scholars than myself will see in this study an opportunity to continue and explore the relations between Mesopotamian wisdom literature and other wisdom corpora.

This book will have more than fulfilled its purpose if it succeeds in writing a chapter in the history of Mesopotamian literature that secures a place for Late Bronze Age wisdom compositions alongside better known works, such as The Instructions of Šuruppak found in Alster's magisterial *Wisdom of Sumer* (2005) or The Dialogue of Pessimism made famous by Lambert's classic *Babylonian Wisdom Literature* (1960).

ACKNOWLEDGEMENTS

This book started as a collaborative research project "Wisdom Literature of Israel and Ancient Syria" conducted with Ed Greenstein and supported by the Israel Science Foundation (Grant no. 621/08) during the years 2008 to 2010. My thanks to Ed for his continued support, encouragement, and guidance throughout our research project and in years since. It was he who suggested that the outcome of my part of the research be published as a book in the SBL Writings from the Ancient World series and for that I am also grateful. The research fellows of our collaborative project deserve my gratitude: Shirly Yulzari for collecting the research materials and preparing the databases for this book; and Sivan Kedar for administrating the project.

I was very fortunate to have Andrew George as the academic editor of this book. His commitment to the success of this endeavor was without compromise. It is due to his meticulous reading and observant comments that the book is in its present form; it is also my duty to acknowledge his crucial contribution to the understanding of this book's major composition *Šimâ Milka*.

Special thanks are offered to Takayoshi Oshima for sending me a preprint version of his book on prayers to Marduk; and to Amir Gilan and Itamar Singer for the precious time they spent reading with me the Hittite materials in the book and offering numerous improvements on my translations. To my great sorrow Itamar passed away on September 2012. My colleagues Abraham Winitzer and Shai Gordin commented on particular parts of the manuscript and for that I am in their debt.

Large parts of this book were written in London during sabbatical leave (2010–2011). I thank Mark Geller and Andrew George for hosting me in their institutes, respectively, the Department of Hebrew and Jewish Studies, UCL, and the Department of the Languages and Cultures of the Near and Middle East, SOAS. I was fortunate to have Mark Weeden and Martin Worthington as close friends who were willing to discuss many an obscure proverb during lunch breaks in the SOAS cafeteria.

The introduction to the book was written during summer 2012 at the Institut für Alterumswissenschaften, Würzburg, and the Bibliothèque d'Assyriologie, Collège de France, Paris. Warm thanks are offered to Daniel Schwemer and Jean-Marie Durand for ensuring that I enjoyed smooth and productive research periods. Annie and Daniel Attia are to be thanked for their hospitality in Paris.

Financial support for the formatting and editing of the book was graciously offered by the Israel Science Foundation, the Young Foundation, The Faculty of the Humanities, and the Sonia and Marco Nadler Institute of Archaeology, Tel Aviv University.

The formatting and indexing of the manuscript were expertly provided by Sivan Kedar.

My sincerest gratitude goes to Theodore Lewis and the editorial board of the Writings from the Ancient World series for accepting my manuscript for publication and to Billie Jean Collins for her care and concern throughout the production process from manuscript to printed volume.

Tel Aviv
September 2012

Abbreviations

A.	Tablet signature of texts from Mari
ABD	*Anchor Bible Dictionary*. Edited by D. N. Freedman. 6 vols. New York, 1992
ABL	*Assyrian and Babylonian Letters Belonging to the Kouyunjik Collections of the British Museum*. Edited by R. F. Harper. 14 vols. Chicago, 1892–1914
AfO	*Archiv für Orientforschung*
ANESSup	Ancient Near Eastern Studies Supplement
AnOr	*Analecta Orientalia*
AnSt	*Anatolian Studies*
AOAT	Alter Orient und Altes Testament
AoF	*Altorientalische Forschungen*
ARG	Andrew R. George
ARM	Archives royales de Mari
ARMT	Archives royales de Mari, transcrite et traduite
AS	Assyriological Studies
ASJ	*Acta Sumerologica*
AuOr	*Aula Orientalis*
AuOrSup	Aula Orientalis Supplementa
BWL	Wilfred G. Lambert, *Babylonian Wisdom Literature*. Oxford, 1960
CAD	*The Assyrian Dictionary of the Oriental Institute of the University of Chicago*. Chicago, 1956–2010
CHANE	Culture and History of the Ancient Near East
CM	Cuneiform Monographs
CUSAS	Cornell University Studies in Assyriology and Sumerology
EA	*El-Amarna Tablets*. According to the edition of J. A. Knudtzon. *Die el-Amarna-Tafeln*. Leipzig, 1908–1915. Reprint, Aalen, 1964. Continued in A. F. Rainey, *El-Amarna Tablets*, 359–379. 2nd revised ed. Kevelaer, 1978

ETCSL	The Electronic Text Corpus of Sumerian Literature; online at http://etcsl.orinst.ox.ac.uk
FAOS	Freiburger altorientalische Studien
FRLANT	Forschungen zur Religion und Literatur des Alten und Neuen Testaments
GMTR	Guides to the Mesopotamian Textual Record
HANE/M	History of the Ancient Near East: Monographs
HO	Handbuch der Orientalistik
HSCP	Harvard Studies in Classical Philology
HSS	Harvard Semitic Studies
JANER	*Journal of Ancient Near Eastern Religion*
JANES	*Journal of the Ancient Near Eastern Society*
JAOS	*Journal of the American Oriental Society*
JCS	*Journal of Cuneiform Studies*
JMC	*Le Journal des Médicines Cunéiformes*
JNES	*Journal of Near Eastern Studies*
JSOTSup	Journal for the Study of the Old Testament, Supplement Series
KAR	*Keilschrifttexte aus Assur religiösen Inhalts*. Edited by E. Ebeling. Leipzig, 1919–1923
KBo	*Keilschrifttexte aus Boghazköi*. WVDOG 30, 36, 68–70, 72–73, 77–80, 82–86, 89–90. Leipzig, 1916–1923, Berlin: Gebr. Mann, 1954–.
KUB	Keilschrifturkunden aus Boghazköi. Berlin: Akademie, 1921–.
LAPO	Littérature Ancienne du Proche-Orient
MAOG	Mitteilungen der Altorientalischen Gesellschaft
MARI	*Mari, Annales de Recherches Interdisciplinaires*
MC	Mesopotamian Civilizations
MRS	Mission de Ras Shamra
NABU	*Nouvelles Assyriologiques Bréves et Utilitaires*
OBO	Orbis biblicus et orientalis
OIS	Oriental Institute Seminars
OLA	Orientalia Lovaniensia Analecta
OLP	*Orientalia Lovaniensia Periodica*
Or	*Orientalia*
ORA	Orientalische Religionen in der Antike
PIHANS	Publications de l'Institut historique-archéologique néerlandais de Stamboul (Leiden)

RA	*Revue d'Assyriologie et d'Archéologie Orientale*
RlA	*Reallexikon der Assyriologie und vorderasiatischen Archäologie*
RS	Ras Shamra (excavation number)
SAA	State Archives of Assyria
SAACT	State Archives of Assyrian Cuneiform Texts
SBLSymS	Symposium Series
SBLWAW	Writings from the Ancient World
SBLWAWSup	Writings from the Ancient World Supplement Series
SEL	*Studi Epigrafici e Linguistici sul Vicino Oriente Antico*
SMEA	*Studi Micenei ed Egeo-Anatolici*
StBoT	Studien zu den Boğazköy-Texten
THeth	Texte der Hethiter
TUAT	Texte aus der Umwelt des Alten Testaments
UF	*Ugarit-Forschungen*
VT	*Vetus Testamentum*
VTSup	Vetus Testamentum Supplement Series
WO	*Die Welt des Orients*
wr.	written
WVDOG	Wissenschaftliche Veröffentlichungen der deutschen Orientgesellschaft
ZA	*Zeitschrift für Assyriologie und Vorderasiatische Archäologie*

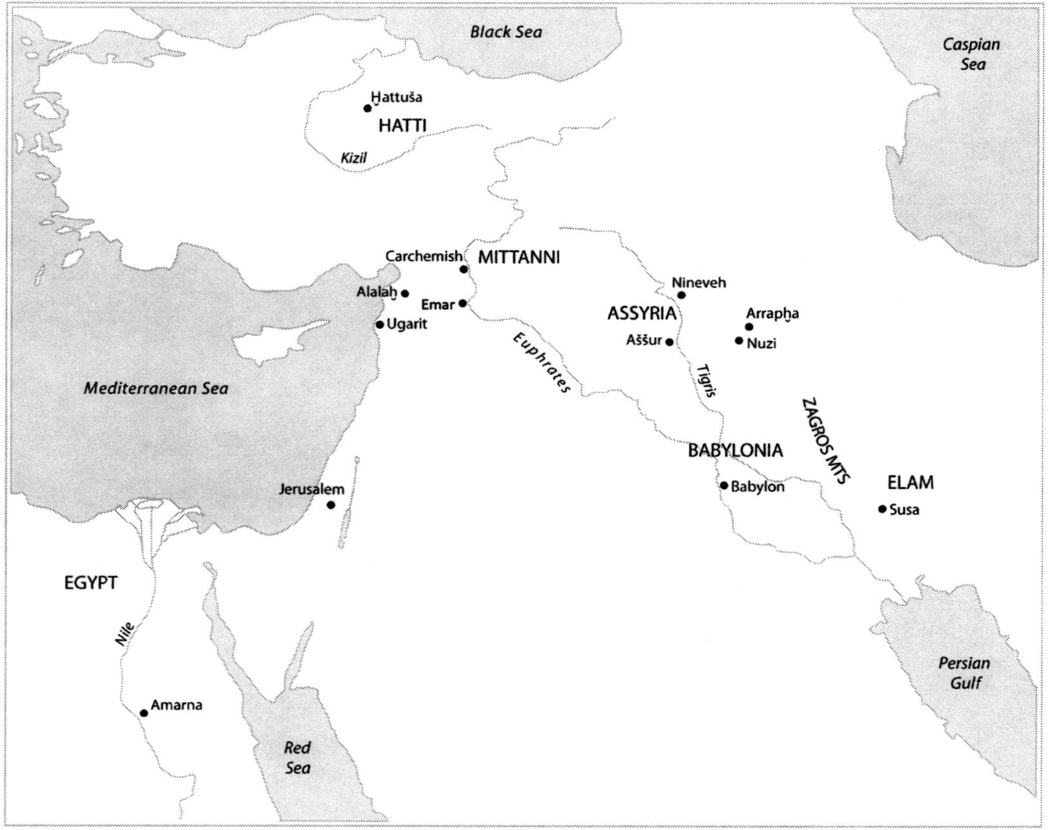

Fig. 1. Map of the ancient Near East in the Late Bronze Age

Part 1
Introduction

1.1
A General Overview of the Compositions and Their Sources

This study includes five major wisdom compositions, three shorter works of proverbs (that lack any narrative frame), and a selection of proverbs deriving from letters. They are briefly described here so that the reader can appreciate from the very start of the book the nature and scope of the corpus. The numbers given below to each composition or group of proverbs will continue to designate these works throughout the book. First to be surveyed are the major wisdom compositions:

1. *Šimâ Milka* or Hear the Advice (sometimes called The Instructions of Šūpê-amēli) is the longest composition in the book, with over 150 lines. It deals with the two themes present in Late Bronze Age wisdom compositions, namely, practical wisdom and skeptical wisdom. The first theme is presented by a person called Šūpê-amēli, and the second theme, in the form of a reply to the first, is delivered by his son, who is not named in the composition.
2. The Ballad of Early Rulers is a composition extending a little over twenty lines. A string of sayings about the futility of life opens the composition. It then goes on to list early rulers of the past, such as Gilgameš and Etana, who, in spite their glorious deeds, are now dead.
3. Enlil and Namzitarra is a short story concerned, like The Ballad of Early Rulers, with the futility of life. The theme is introduced in a dialogue between the god Enlil and a priest called Namzitarra. Once the main composition ends, a string of proverbs, very poorly understood, follows.
4. The Righteous Sufferer from Ugarit is a prayer to the god Marduk. Although in and of itself it is not a wisdom composition, it deals with one of the chief concerns of Mesopotamian wisdom literature, namely, divine retribution. This prayer is usually considered to be in one form or another a forerunner of the great Babylonian wisdom composition,

Ludlul Bēl Nēmeqi, "I will Praise the Lord of Wisdom," also known as "The Babylonian Job."

5. The Date Palm and the Tamarisk is a debate poem, a subgenre of wisdom literature. The two contestants, the date palm and the tamarisk tree, engage in a lively debate as to who is more beneficial to civilization.

The other materials lack narrative frames (as far as can be judged from the remains of the compositions today; the only exception is 6 B, for which see below), but are simply collections or assemblages of proverbs without a connecting thread between one saying and the next.

6. Proverb collections from Ḫattuša include two (unconnected) sources. The first source (6 A) is a collection of Akkadian proverbs, some of which are in very poor condition. There is no apparent relation between one proverb and the next. The second source (6 B) is written in Hittite (it is a translation of an Akkadian column, now mostly broken away). It includes a proverb followed by a short speech discussing the importance of the study of wisdom. The speech perhaps offered a summation of a longer composition, now lost.
7. The Akkadian-Hurrian proverb extract is an exercise tablet containing two proverbs in Akkadian provided with a Hurrian translation.
8. The last chapter in this book is dedicated to proverbs and colloquial sayings found in the Mari letters and Late Bronze Age correspondence including the famous Amarna letters. Over twenty-five proverbs and sayings from various social and historical contexts are presented.

The languages represented in our corpus are Sumerian, Akkadian, Hittite, and Hurrian. The Akkadian language features in all our compositions, either alone (in 1 [the Emar and Ugarit sources], 4, 5, 6 A, and 8), as a translation or paraphrasing of the Sumerian (2 and 3), or as the language translated into the target languages Hittite and Hurrian (1 [the Ḫattuša source] and 6 B into Hittite; 7 into Hurrian).

The sources at our disposal derive mainly from three sites—Ugarit, Emar, and Ḫattuša. They are occasionally supplemented by sources deriving from elsewhere and dating to different periods. The richest site in wisdom-literature finds is Ugarit, followed by Emar and then Ḫattuša. The count of manuscripts from each site results in the following figures: Ugarit boasts of ten manuscripts, Emar seven, and Ḫattuša three; note that some manuscripts are very fragmentary. The distribution of the manuscripts according to wisdom compositions is as follows (included within this count are fragmentary manuscripts of wisdom compositions that are not treated in this book; see further below).

		Ugarit	Emar	Ḫattuša
1.	*Šimâ Milka*	3	1	1
2.	Ballad of Early Rulers	3	2	–
3.	Enlil and Namzitarra	1	1	–
4.	The Righteous Sufferer	1	–	–
5.	Date Palm and Tamarisk	–	2	–
6.	Proverbs from Ḫattuša	–	–	2
7.	Akkadian-Hurrian Extract	1	–	–
(other)	(The Fowler)	–	1	–
	(The Fable of the Fox)	1	–	–
	TOTAL	10	7	3

Only one composition, *Šimâ Milka*, was found at all three sites. In spite of its popularity in the Late Bronze Age, it has not been recovered in the Mesopotamian core areas. Two compositions, The Ballad of Early Rulers and Enlil and Namzitarra are known from two sites each—Ugarit and Emar. The rest of the works were recovered at only one site.

As noted above, sometimes our sources can be supplemented from manuscripts from elsewhere. Perhaps the most popular piece, to judge by its distribution (although this might be coincidental), is The Date Palm and the Tamarisk. Recovered from only one Bronze Age site (Emar), it is however represented in addition by two fragmentary Old Babylonian manuscripts (of the same tablet) from Tel Harmal in Babylonia, two Assyrian manuscripts from Assur (one dated to the Middle Assyrian period, the other possibly to the early Neo-Assyrian period), and a fragment from Susa.

Next comes The Ballad of Early Rulers. It is not represented at sites other than Ugarit and Emar during the Late Bronze Age, but is known from a Neo-Assyrian fragment. A Sumerian version of the composition dating to the Old Babylonian period is represented by a few manuscripts.

Enlil and Namzitarra is known in its bilingual version only from Ugarit and Emar, but it is found in seven monolingual Sumerian manuscripts dating to the Old Babylonian period.

The Righteous Sufferer was found only in Ugarit. However, its literary heritage is indirectly reflected in *Ludlul Bēl Nēmeqi*, known from later Mesopotamian sources. The rest of the works we will encounter are known only in Late Bronze Age manuscripts.

Proverbs are quoted in letters from Mari, El Amarna (but written in the cities of Canaan and Lebanon), Ḫattuša, and elsewhere. They do not attest directly to the spread of wisdom literature in learned contexts, that is, schools and archives, but they may reflect something of the spread of wisdom throughout the region in more or less the time period we are interested in.

I have specified what this book includes but a word is needed on what was excluded and on what grounds. Three wisdom compositions were left out of this collection mainly because of their poor preservation. The Fowler and His Wife is a wisdom piece or Sumerian morality tale (following Alster's definition; see Alster 2005: 371–72) known from chiefly Old Babylonian sources; it is represented by two very poorly preserved fragments from Emar (Arnaud 1985–1987, no. 768). Not enough of the piece remains to merit its reproduction here and afford it a suitable discussion. It does however feature in 1.5 where I discuss wisdom literature and its role in the Emar curriculum.

Another piece excluded is a fragment of unknown provenance of The Instructions of Šuruppak. It is a bilingual piece written in two columns, Akkadian and Hurrian. It has been suggested that the fragment comes from Emar but this cannot be verified. It is in a rather pitiful state, but nonetheless sense can be made out of it by comparing the remains to parallel passages in the Sumerian version. Since a commendable result has been achieved by B. Alster and G. Wilhelm (for the Hurrian column), the reader is referred to their work (in Alster 2005).

The final wisdom work excluded is The Fable of the Fox, represented by two pieces from the House of Urtenu in Ugarit (Arnaud 2007, no. 51; Yon and Arnaud 2001, no. 29). Because the remains are not well preserved and the composition itself is only poorly known elsewhere (see Kienast 2003; *BWL* 186–209; Vanstiphout 1988; Alster 2005: 346–51), I decided to omit it. It deserves additional investigation much beyond the scope of this book. I will briefly mention it when I assess the remains from the House of Urtenu in 1.4.

1.2
Definitions and Approaches

When dealing with a collection of works brought together under the rubric of wisdom literature, there is no escape from the question, what is wisdom literature? Since the compositions in this book originated in Mesopotamia (regardless for the present of whether or not they underwent any editorial changes or modifications on their transmission route to or reception at Late Bronze Age sites), I will revise the question to, what is Mesopotamian wisdom literature? In the first part of this chapter, I will try to examine the different ways in which scholars have responded to this question in the past. As we will discover, the question revolves around the issue of genre. The changing understanding of what genre is and whether it is useful in discussing ancient literature has affected the definition of Mesopotamian wisdom literature. The second part of this chapter will introduce three methodological approaches by which our question can be addressed: examining the Mesopotamian view of wisdom literature, re-evaluating key themes in the compositions, and adopting a contextual approach in the study of wisdom literature.

I will focus here primarily on the opinions of ancient Near Eastern scholars who have studied wisdom literature extensively, for a review of the whole range of opinions on what Mesopotamian wisdom literature is and whether genre is a useful category in the discussion of ancient Near Eastern literature is beyond the scope of this short presentation. Likewise, it must be made clear from the outset that this short introduction does not pretend to redefine the genre of wisdom literature, but rather to present in a critical way already existing definitions and offer a few approaches for its further investigation.

Definitions

Like many studies concerned with wisdom literature, this book begins by briefly sketching how wisdom literature has been defined and redefined, categorized, and studied in modern scholarship; and like many studies, it too will begin with Lambert's now classic 1960 magisterial edition, translation, and commentary of Babylonian wisdom compositions known at that time. We will see how Lambert attempted to define Babylonian wisdom literature in his book; then observe how, with the spate of new Mesopotamian literature compositions from the mid-twentieth century onwards, a reevaluation of Mesopotamian wisdom literature was required; and, finally, consider the questioning by recent scholarship of the very usefulness of such a literary category or genre as wisdom.

"'Wisdom' is strictly a misnomer as applied to Babylonian literature." Thus the first sentence in Lambert's introductory chapter to *Babylonian Wisdom Literature*. As Lambert explains, wisdom as a literary genre is applied to the Biblical wisdom books, Proverbs, Job, and Qohelet. He stresses that, "though this term (i.e., wisdom literature) is thus foreign to ancient Mesopotamia, it has been used for a group of texts which correspond in subject-matter with the Hebrew Wisdom books, and may be retained as a convenient short description." Hence the implication is, if one chooses to recognize an apologetic tone in Lambert's words, that although Babylonian wisdom literature shares its subject matter with biblical wisdom books, "real" wisdom is inherent in biblical literature. The unease Lambert felt in using the term "wisdom" was because this category, taken from biblical studies, defines a group of books that are in essence very different from ancient Near Eastern sources in their theological view of wisdom, if one takes, as an example, Proverbs 1 or 8.

But perhaps more than apologetic—if one may venture to read deeper in to Lambert's pronouncement—in a sense his view was a reaction against the strained relationship between biblical studies and Assyriology, which continues to this day (a heritage of pan-Babylonianism and the Babel-Bibel controversy; Holloway 2006; Chavalas 2002). To illustrate this claim, one may look at Langdon's *Babylonian Wisdom* of 1923. In its introduction it is said to bring together "fragments of the books of Babylonian Wisdom," including an edition of *Ludlul Bēl Nēmeqi*, recognized almost since its initial publication at the end of the nineteenth century C.E. to be of special relevance for the book of Job. Langdon's treatment of *Ludlul Bēl Nēmeqi* was, so he himself writes, "inspired by a desire to complete the profound system of Sumero-Babylonian theology in its ethical aspects." Langdon spoke of the "books" of Babylonian wisdom, which he held to be as profound as the wisdom found in the biblical books and which were a crucial ethical component in Mesopotamian theology. However, Lambert asserts that the term wisdom when applied to Mesopotamian writing should be used with caution lest it be abused: Babylonian culture should be studied on its own merit.

For lack of a better criterion by which to include compositions under the title of wisdom literature, Lambert borrowed (with some apparent unease) a definition foreign to Mesopotamian categories. He chose works that were deemed to be within the sphere of "what has been called philosophy since Greek times though many scholars would demur to using this word for ancient Mesopotamian thought" (Lambert 1960: 1).

That is as far as Lambert was prepared to go in defining Babylonian wisdom literature. The rest of his introduction avoids any discussion of the form or structure of the genre. However, although the book on the whole refrains from providing an explicit definition of the genre, Lambert's collection de facto defined the genre (Clifford 2007: xii). Surely, his choice and arrangement of the materials were individual and consciously subjective, because, in his words, "there is no precise canon by which to recognize them (i.e., wisdom compositions)." Nonetheless, it is obvious that his collection of compositions was influenced, like van Dijk's book *La Sagesse suméro-accadienne* (1953), by earlier compilations of ancient Near Eastern literature, such as *Altorientalische Texte zum alten Testamente* (Gressmann 1909), *Cuneiform Parallels to the Old Testament* (Rogers 1912) and the first edition of *Ancient Near Eastern Texts Relating to the Old Testament* (=*ANET*; Pritchard 1950). They all included "wisdom" literature within their pages.

Whatever the influences on Lambert, *ANET* in its third edition (1969) was already citing his *Babylonian Wisdom Literature*. Lambert's book instantly became canonical: it is an exemplary work of Assyriological philology; it remains one of the most read books in the field of ancient Near Eastern studies; its influence on Bible studies was immeasurable; and, most importantly for the present discussion, it is the yardstick by which all anthologies of wisdom literature are measured—it was and still is *the* canon. However, the usefulness of Lambert's loosely defined genre of wisdom literature was soon questioned, as change was on the horizon.

After the Second World War, serious efforts, spearheaded by Samuel Kramer and Edmond Gordon, were made to collect and better understand Sumerian literature. Since then, the corpus of Sumerian literature has grown significantly, constantly augmented by a flow of editions and studies by Bendt Alster, Miguel Civil, Jacob Klein, Herman Vanstiphout, and the ETCSL team led by Jeremy Black, as well as others.

In addition, the corpus of mostly Akkadian literature found outside of Mesopotamia also substantially expanded, with new discoveries at Ḫattuša, and particularly at Ugarit (published by Nougayrol 1968), and later Emar (published by Arnaud 1985–1987).

In short, Mesopotamian literature vastly expanded in the number of new compositions and in their scope. For lack of a precise generic definition, a multitude of new works, which were difficult to define, differing in structure as well as in form, themes, style, and language, jumped on the "wisdom literature" bandwagon: Sumerian proverbs, debate poems, school compositions, humorous or satirical works, and others were placed in the category of "wisdom." The strain on Lambert's (as well as others') loose definition of wisdom literature was beginning to be felt. The result, many scholars thought, was a genre that had become so broad that it lost any useful meaning (see George 2007a). In the words of the Assyriologist Niek Veldhuis (2003: 29), wisdom literature had become "a mixed bag."

Perhaps awareness of this problem is what drove Hallo and Younger to choose a new category in which to place wisdom literature with all its new Sumerian and Akkadian compositions. As editors of *The Context of Scripture* (a three-volume book that successfully replaced *ANET* as a modern anthology of ancient Near Eastern texts in English; 1997–2003), they included in the first volume (Canonical Compositions) *Ludlul Bēl Nēmeqi* and The Babylonian Theodicy under the header "Individual Focus" (one of three such categories, the other two being "Divine" and "Royal"). But under the same category as *Ludlul Bēl Nēmeqi* and The Theodicy came proverbs, instructions, disputations, and even Sumerian School Dialogues, which are short humorous works describing life at the scribal school. It seems that Lambert's definition of wisdom literature was simply replaced by another definition even broader than his. Was Hallo and Younger's "Individual Focus" to have any meaning if works as profound as *Ludlul Bēl Nēmeqi*, dealing with the concept of divine retribution, were included under the same category as the Sumerian School Dialogues, which are concerned with students skipping school and lazy pupils not preparing homework?

The all-inclusive approach adopted by *The Context of Scripture* was one alternative. Exclusion of compositions from the genre of wisdom was another. One of the major wisdom compositions I will deal with here is The Ballad of Early Rulers (2.2). In Foster's *Before the Muses* (2005, 3rd edition) it is relegated to a lesser rank. The Ballad, one of the most-widely distributed compositions in the ancient Near East, can boast of a long literary history ranging from the Old Babylonian to the Neo-Assyrian period. And yet it is placed under the nondescript header "Miscellaneous Expressive Compositions," together with The Monkey Man, a rather insignificant spoof of a legal document of no known literary history. (Later, we will see what a distinguished position the Mesopotamians themselves gave to The Ballad of Early Rulers: It was considered to be a part of series of wisdom compositions compiled by a Mesopotamian sage; see 1.5.) Excluded from the genre of wisdom literature, The Ballad of Early Rulers, according to Foster, is considered no more than an "Akkadian drinking song," pushed far away from Lambert's anthology of texts belonging to "what has been called philosophy." As expected, however, *Ludlul Bēl Nēmeqi*, as well as its "forerunner," The Righteous Sufferer from Ugarit (2.4), and other wisdom compositions are collected in *Before the Muses* under the heading "Wisdom and Experience"; but so are minor wisdom compositions, as well as proverbs retrieved from letters. How do these lesser works fare in comparison to The Ballad of Early Rulers?

In the book *Akkadian Literature of the Late Period* (2007), meant to serve as an annotated guide to the Mesopotamian textual record, Foster located wisdom literature under the general header "Human Experience" and then rather thoughtfully placed one or several compositions in subcategories such as Ancient Wisdom, Human Plight, Fables, Debates, Humorous Stories, Parody and Satire, and so on. The Ballad of Early Rulers, a work surely within the timeframe of Foster's Late period (since it is known from the Late Bronze Age as well as the Neo-Assyrian period), is however not mentioned at all. Was it because this work was already considered trivial in Foster's *Before the Muses*?

All of this is meant neither to offer a critique of Foster's choices (although I disagree with them) nor to defend the place of The Ballad of Early Rulers with the Mesopotamian tradition of wisdom literature (I will do this later in the book). The intention is to demonstrate how genre very much defines our understanding of an ancient text, its meaning, purpose, and importance in Mesopotamian literary history (and see here Longman 1991: 16–19; George 2007a).

As the examples of *The Context of Scripture* and *Before the Muses* demonstrate, genre as a category was breaking down. However, this breakdown was not only caused by too many new compositions that nobody knew what to do with; it was a sign of the times. The last two decades of the twentieth century saw a sustained and prolonged attack intent on the disintegration—or deconstruction if one prefers this term—of canon and genre. Western canon, including the Classics and the Bible, was understood as an oppressive political and social mechanism whose aim was to appropriate, colonize, and marginalize non-Western cultures (among, so to speak, its many other victims). *Wisdom* in Mesopotamian wisdom literature, a loaded term taken from biblical studies, simply became too difficult to employ: Using the term wisdom foreign to ancient Near Eastern categories implies an appropriation of ancient Near Eastern literature and, implicitly, its eventual marginalization in comparison to the biblical canon (and see here the remarks of Annus and Lenzi 2010: xxxv). As discussed, real wisdom was thought to lie within the books of Proverbs, Qohelet, and Job. Was wisdom not after all a misnomer in Lambert's words because only the biblical books contained revealed wisdom? The terms *genre* and even *literature* were now deemed inadequate, imposed by a modern western system of thought, foreign to the Mesopotamians who themselves had no definitions of such categories. In Andrew George's words (2007a:53), the notion of wisdom literature in ancient Mesopotamia had come under attack.

Some views were reductionist to the extreme, others more moderate. Buccellati (1981) denied outright any identification of a literary genre with wisdom. Vanstiphout (1999a; 1999b), although much informed about Mesopotamian literature, and as a consequence more willing to recognize a Mesopotamian understanding of genre, even if not explicitly defined, nonetheless concluded his evaluation of our genre with the words: "Exit 'Wisdom Literature'" (1999a: 713). In his eyes, there is simply too much of it for "wisdom literature" to have been meaningful to an ancient Mesopotamian scribe, hence, as a category meant to designate a group of texts, it is worthless.

Alster (2005), to conclude this brief survey, was perhaps less harsh, although he too wished to abandon the category of wisdom as genre. Like others, he saw "wisdom literature" as a harmful, outdated, and unusable genre designation. Alster (2005: 25) writes in the conclusion to the introduction of his monograph *The Wisdom of Sumer*:

> It must be admitted that "wisdom" can be regarded as a relic from the early days of oriental scholarship, when the wisdom of Zarathustra had already become a common cliché. "Wisdom," indeed, was one of the literary topics that first aroused interest when Babylonian and Assyrian literature started to become available to scholarship around the turn of the twentieth century. Today, using the designation "wisdom" would make sense only if this is refined and restricted to a much narrower group of texts.

How ironic that Alster critiques the use of the term wisdom in Mesopotamian wisdom literature as something not far removed from orientalism, only to call his own book *The Wisdom of Sumer*, in the same pattern of the topical "*The Wisdom of...*" book title, common, as he points out, in the early days of scholarship.

In the next section (under Key Themes) I consider how Alster, like others, tried to redefine and restrict the corpus of wisdom literature.

Approaches

As we have seen, recent scholarship came to regard Mesopotamian wisdom literature as an empty literary category. This was the result of two trends, the first the ever-growing accumulation of different types of works all conveniently dumped under the rubric of wisdom literature, the second the result of postmodern intellectual trends at the end of the twentieth century. Despite, or perhaps as a reaction to, such a hypercritical evaluation, scholars attempted to reconsider the worth of Mesopotamian wisdom literature as a useful independent category of genre from different points of view.

I use three different approaches that I believe can contribute to this study. The first approach examines closely the Mesopotamian view of the literary genre of wisdom; the second reevaluates key themes in wisdom literature; and the third adopts a contextual approach to the study of wisdom literature. I will briefly elaborate on all three because they are the methodological underpinnings upon which this book is based (note however that fuller presentations of the data will be found in the rest of part 1 and throughout the book). As we will see, these approaches do not solve all the problems I have identified. At best, they allow a renewed appreciation of wisdom literature and point out the significance of key themes or intellectual trends found in wisdom compositions and additional Mesopotamian literature.

The Mesopotamian View of Wisdom Literature

Many scholars writing on Mesopotamian literature and specifically contending with Mesopotamian wisdom literature face a rather frustrating situation. Outside of technical genres such as omens or incantations, and other than performative designations, such as *song*, *lament*, Mesopotamian literature lacks explicit native categories of genre. The result is first and foremost an absence of a defined or regulated canon of compositions, as Lambert was already aware. However, we are not totally in the dark regarding the Mesopotamians' understanding of genre, including wisdom literature. As will be discussed in greater detail here and throughout this study there are a few clues that permit us to gather indirectly how wisdom literature was understood by its ancient students and compilers.

Recent scholarship has looked carefully at the way Old Babylonian student exercises were compiled. It was seen that they consisted of a few consecutive texts, which arguably were studied one after the other. When individual wisdom compositions are found together in such a way on *Sammeltafeln* or collective or compilation tablets, it can be implied that some connection (thematic or other) was understood to exist between them.

Another group of texts that has been under the spotlight recently are the so-called Old Babylonian library catalogues. Regardless of the various opinions about their exact function, the catalogues provide us with groupings of various texts. Sometimes, the reasoning for grouping particular texts together escapes us, but it is clear that when wisdom compositions are arranged thus, some type of connection is to be assumed between them. With all due reservations, it can be argued that the connection is one of genre, even if not explicitly defined as such by the ancient compilers.

A more explicit definition of wisdom literature can be reconstructed from loose strings of related data, such as catalogues, commentaries, and other learned texts, mostly dated to the Kassite or post-Kassite period. By piecing this information together, it can be demonstrated that wisdom literature as such was understood by Mesopotamian scholars to be a select corpus (like other textual corpora such as omens). This corpus transmitted a written legacy that was valuable because of its antiquity. It was considered to have been compiled or composed by learned figures of old, who were associated with famous kings. More will be said at the close of 1.5 about the importance of these sources for appreciating the Mesopotamian definition, or at least the understanding of, wisdom literature.

Key Themes

A major contribution of Alster's *The Wisdom of Sumer* (2005) to the questions discussed here is his identification and elucidation of two basic key themes, which bring about a sharpened appreciation of a particular group of wisdom compositions. Alster studies a group of wisdom compositions (comprising the bulk but not all of his book), which he divides into two categories: a traditional or conservative outlook and a critical approach. In the steps of the biblical scholar Michael Fox, one can term these categories as *positive* wisdom and *negative* wisdom. Fox (2011) uses these terms to define wisdom in two of the biblical wisdom books, namely, Proverbs (positive) and Qohelet (negative).

Positive, or traditional, wisdom offers a model for attaining success in life, either material or ethical. The preservation of one's wealth, marrying properly, behaving adequately in the company of others, acting with fairness will provide one with a good and fulfilled life. This view is articulated in some Sumerian proverbs found in the Sumerian Proverb Collection (Alster 1997), and notably in The Instructions of Šuruppak, a wisdom composition already known from mid-third millennium manuscripts but mainly reconstructed on the basis of Old Babylonian sources (Alster 2005). There, father instructs son on how to achieve a proper life.

This kind of wisdom is also seen in our collection. In the first part of *Šimâ Milka* (2.1), the sage Šūpê-awīli offers this kind of practical or positive wisdom to his son, telling him for example, how to behave in a tavern, whom to marry, and where to avoid digging a well in order to ensure the success of one's field.

Similar attitudes inform the collection of proverbs from Ḫattuša (2.6) and the Akkadian-Hurrian proverb extract (2.7). Many of the proverbs found in letters (2.8) also convey positive instructions, hence they share the same attitude in regards to wisdom.

The reversal of this key theme is negative wisdom, or to use Alster's definition, a critical approach. It expresses two intertwined notions: 1) nothing is of value, hence 2) enjoy life while you can before eternal death. These ideas are reflected in several short Old Babylonian Sumerian compositions beginning with the lines "Nothing is of value, but life itself should be sweet-tasting." The first sentence is defined by Alster as the vanity theme and the second the *carpe diem* theme.

In the Late Bronze Age collection of wisdom compositions, we find negative wisdom in The Ballad of Early Rulers (2.2) and Enlil and Namzitarra (2.3), and again in *Šimâ Milka* through its second part—the son's response to his father. The son tells his father that instructions such as his (i.e., positive wisdom) are worthless because life is short and beyond it there is only death. Worth pointing out in relation to our discussion about genre is that both key themes are found in the same text, *Šimâ Milka*. Their presence shows that the Mesopotamian scribe who wrote this piece consciously recognized the two distinct wisdom traditions. Ingeniously he combined them both in one single composition. This is certainly something important to think about when coming to evaluate the Mesopotamian sensitivity to genre or literary type even when not openly declared.

As Alster clearly demonstrated, both positive and negative key themes are common to many literary works. The positive key theme finds expression, as seen, already in the very first wisdom literature available—the mid-third millennium manuscripts of The Instructions of Šuruppak. The negative key theme or critical approach also boasts of a long history, beginning in the Old Babylonian period.

Wherein lie the origins of the critical perspective in wisdom compositions? It is not necessary to assume that this critical view arose as a result of a particular social or political event. It simply may be looked upon as part of a literary trope that began to be articulated more and more forcefully from the Old Babylonian period onwards, as part of an intellectual trend that had come to reflect on the limits of mortal life as opposed to the gods' eternal life. Such a trend is seen in a variety of epic stories about mortals that end in disaster, failure, or irresolution (see the observant remarks of George 2007a: 50). In wisdom compositions, this intellectual trend finds its articulation in the vanity theme, which is always expressed by mortals and not divine beings. How could the immortals ever understand death?

The tension between positive wisdom or traditional values and negative wisdom or critical values existed not only within the domain of wisdom compositions such as The Ballad of Early Rulers or *Šimâ Milka*. It can also be recognized, for example, in The Epic of Gilgameš, which underwent a development from a story concerned with a hero's glorification to one reflecting on the futility of life. According to George (2007a: 54; 2003: 32–33), it was the achievement of Sin-lēqi-unninni (traditionally considered as the author of the Standard Babylonian version of the epic) to reinforce the pessimistic tone in the epic, following the literary fashion of the day, as seen in the Kassite and post-Kassite pessimistic or critical poems. The vanity theme, however, was already present in the Old Babylonian versions of the epic. Here it is expressed by Gilgameš who encourages Enkidu to do battle with Huwawa:

mannu ibrī elû šam[*ā'ī*]
ilūma itti šamšim dāriš uš[*bū*]
awīlūtumma manûma ūmūša
mimma ša īteneppušu šāruma

Who, my friend, is the one to go to the sky?
Only the gods dwell forever in the sunlight.
As for mankind—its days are numbered.
Whatever it will chose to do—it is but the wind.
(The Epic of Gilgameš, Yale Tablet, col. iv, ll. 140–143; George 2003: 200–201)

Contextualizing Wisdom Literature

Adopting a contextual approach to the study of wisdom literature demands that the search for an all-inclusive or precise definition of wisdom literature be put aside while wider issues concerned with the historical, social, and intellectual background of these compositions are brought to the fore. A temporary position may consciously be adopted, such as viewing wisdom literature as *philosophical* (George 2007a, following Lambert), *existential*, or *intellectual* (so Alster 2005). This study prefers to avoid such loaded terms and recommends (following Beaulieu 2007) an intuitive understanding of wisdom literature based on common humanistic traditions; this will suffice to allow readers to recognize elements current in ancient Near Eastern literature that mark out certain compositions as wisdom literature, even if on a provisional basis.

A contextual approach, although not defined as such at the time, was at the heart of Lambert's introduction to *Babylonian Wisdom Literature*. Surely a source of disappointment for many, the introduction refrained from speaking at all about formal characteristics of Babylonian wisdom literature but moved on to discuss in a somewhat general way the development of thought and literature in ancient Mesopotamia. The introduction, apart from the opening section (which we have discussed above), is rather ignored nowadays because it is long outdated, its historical and social observations questioned if not dismissed. However, what is worth noticing is Lambert's attempt to speak of the social and political contexts out of which the texts he studied emerged.

An updated social and partly political approach, inevitably more sophisticated and subtle, is undertaken also by Beaulieu (2007). Taking for granted the existence of the genre of wisdom literature, he moves on to examine its intellectual milieu (especially in the Kassite and post-Kassite periods). He discusses the growing role of the professional exorcist, who becomes involved as a protagonist in wisdom compositions and whose own area of expertise in composing prayers or incantations comes to be reflected in wisdom compositions (see 2.4). He demonstrates the connections sought by these professional scholars between wisdom, Mesopotamian kingship, and the learned world of sages from before the flood. This was the outcome of an intellectual movement that sought to grant to scholars more standing in the sociopolitical world of their times, thus granting them a superior status. As Beaulieu concludes, wisdom literature was one particular form of scholarly expression, relatively minor amongst others of much greater importance (chiefly omens and rituals), but all relating to a broader theological purpose, that is, understanding the will of the gods so that the king's fate be divulged.

Beaulieu refrains from generic definitions but understands that especially after the Old Babylonian period wisdom literature was a form of expression within a larger system of thought. I have spoken above of some of such intellectual trends and am tempted to see a connection between the development of the critical or negative wisdom on the one hand and the rise of scholars to prominence in court on the other, as has been suggested repeatedly in the scholarly literature, but this is a topic beyond the purposes of our study.

Another, somewhat similar, contextual approach, although narrower and more focused in its investigation, has been advocated by Niek Veldhuis (2004). He suggests that Mesopotamian literature (and for that matter wisdom literature) should be viewed from a social-functional approach, which looks at literature from the "perspective of the institutional context in which literary texts were produced and consumed" (2004: 43). Hence, wisdom literature should be seen in the context of additional compositions that then should all be assessed with respect to where, by whom, and for what purposes they were produced, copied, and studied. Naturally Veldhuis was thinking about the Old Babylonian scribal school, students and teachers included, as the setting in which this comprehensive investigation is to be conducted. We have to shift however to another timeframe and geographical area, for the focus here is wisdom compositions of the Late Bronze Age. With all due limitations of the data, as will be seen, I will try to form questions similar to those put forward by Veldhuis.

The rest of my introduction will be devoted to examining in greater detail the historical and social contexts of Late Bronze Age wisdom compositions (1.3). I will then proceed to discuss the archaeological and archival contexts (1.4), and finally the curricular context of Late Bronze Age wisdom literature, namely, how it was used in schooling environments and for what educational purpose (1.5). In doing so, I will apply some of the approaches I have introduced here for the study of wisdom literature.

The understanding of what is wisdom literature has gone through many twists and turns since Lambert's canonical *Babylonian Wisdom Literature*. The influx of new compositions, Akkadian as well as Sumerian, challenged Lambert's loose definition, stretching the limits of the genre beyond what the label could bear. The result as we saw was almost a complete rejection of *wisdom* from Mesopotamian wisdom literature. But the stream of new compositions also brought about a renewed interest in the genre, especially with the publication of Akkadian wisdom literature from Ugarit and Emar. All these works have greatly expanded our view of ancient Near Eastern wisdom literature and with it, biblical wisdom. Let us just look briefly at two significant examples from the Late Bronze Age.

Šimâ Milka fills in a gap in the father-to-son instructions tradition which stretchs from The Instructions of Šuruppak to The Sayings of Ahiqar (although properly speaking the latter is an uncle-to-nephew instruction) and even Proverbs (e.g., 23:19). And The Ballad of Early Rulers highlights the continuity of the vanity theme from its rise in the Old Babylonian period to its fullest expression in the great pessimistic works of the late Kassite or Isin II period, later to become fully developed in The Dialogue of Pessimism (Lambert 1995). The relationship of these works to biblical wisdom has long been noted.

In his return to the subject of wisdom literature many years after the publication of *Babylonian Wisdom Literature* Lambert (1995) again made no direct attempt at defining Mesopotamian wisdom. According to his article's title "Some New Babylonian Wisdom Literature," in a volume dedicated to wisdom in ancient Israel, he seems to have been satisfied with the genre he himself did much to establish and define. One may also claim that Lambert felt more at ease to offer a place of honor for Babylonian wisdom literature side by side with biblical wisdom literature, without any qualms or disclaimers. After all, to paraphrase Lambert (41), Qohelet was only presenting in an Israelite garb the old old Mesopotamian vanity theme found in The Ballad of Early Rulers and other works. In this respect, is *wisdom* in Mesopotamian wisdom literature indeed a misnomer? I leave it for the reader of this book to decide.

1.3
The Historical and Social Contexts

In this chapter I examine the historical and social contexts of wisdom compositions of the Late Bronze Age. First, a very general overview will provide a basic picture of the geopolitical situation during the Late Bronze Age. Then I consider the unique scribal environment of the period. The second part of the chapter will gauge the social setting of the materials. I will look at the scribal schools of the period and try to understand by whom they were populated: who were the teachers, supervisors, and students of these institutions. Consideration will also be given to associating Late Bronze Age wisdom literature manuscripts with individual scribes or scribal circles and providing an approximate date for their copying in Emar, Ḫattuša, and Ugarit.

The Geo-Political Setting

The Late Bronze Age (ca. 1500–1200 B.C.E.) is characterized as a historical, but in a sense also a cultural, period of internationalism—of close political and economic cooperation between several territorial states, or kingdoms. Several peer kingdoms participated in a "regional system," which saw the travel of diplomatic emissaries between the courts of the great kings of the day, the exchange of luxury goods (thinly veiled as greeting gifts) between kings and royals, international marriage arrangements, and long distance trade. Hostilities between the parties were kept to the minimum by either overt or implicit international agreements and codified procedures of proper behavior, although from time to time serious confrontations did occur.

The chief political players during this period were Kassite Babylonia, the Hurrian kingdom of Mitanni, the Hittite Kingdom, New Kingdom Egypt and somewhat later, the Middle Assyrian Kingdom. The city-states located at the border zones were subjected either partly or fully to the rule of the great powers: the land of Canaan and the Lebanon fell under Egyptian influence while northern Syria up to the western bank of the Euphrates felt the rule of Mitanni, although not for long. In the second-half of the fourteenth century, the Hittite king Šuppiluliuma conquered northern Syria and with it Ugarit and Emar, two cities that, together with Ḫattuša, stand at the center of this book.

Ugarit, previously under Egyptian influence, came under Hittite control. A written treaty between Šuppiluliuma and King Niqmaddu and a tribute settlement with the city ensured that Ugarit, although under vassalage, remained a relatively independent entity. Emar, although enjoying periods of independence, was controlled in a much more direct fashion by Hittite officials from the provincial capital Carchemish, the seat of the Hittite viceroy who was responsible for all of northern Syria.

Close contacts were maintained between the capital Ḫattuša and its vassal city-states. Within the larger framework of the Hittite Empire, Ugarit and Emar traded with one another; by virtue of a marriage between a Hittite princess and the king of Ugarit the courts of Ḫattuša and Ugarit were family; and at Emar Hittite festivals were celebrated. The list of examples of the intimate cooperation between these centers could be continued.

Most of the information regarding the international political history of the times comes to us from the archives of El Amarna (for the fourteenth century) and after its desertion, mainly from the archives of Ḫattuša, Ugarit, and Emar (for the thirteenth and the beginning of the twelfth century). Additional information comes from the Middle Assyrian sites on the east side of the Euphrates and the Habur triangle. Information from Babylonia itself regarding international relationships is very sparse for this period, as most of its textual deposits deal with internal affairs; they have been only partly published.

The Scribal Environment of the Late Bronze Age

During the Late Bronze Age, almost all written communication between international parties (that is, between great kings) and between interregional parties (that is, between great kings and their vassals, or between vassal kingdoms themselves) was conducted by the exchange of letters written in the cuneiform script and the Akkadian language. The distribution of cuneiform writing and the Akkadian language was probably the most intensive, if not the widest ever, to be witnessed, the result no doubt of the political circumstances, which demanded that communication channels be made available. Among peoples speaking a variety of tongues, including Hurrian, Hittite, West Semitic languages such as Ugaritic and Canaanite, and Egyptian, Akkadian became the vehicle of written communication.

Akkadian was certainly the language of prestige in international and interregional circles, but it was also used in more mundane environments. Its best clients were the royal palace and temple, which used the language for administrative and cultic purposes. Private citizens also benefitted: they hired scribes to document in Akkadian their businesses (in the form of contracts or letters) and family affairs (e.g., wills, adoptions, etc.). The cuneiform script was also used to write other languages, Hittite predominately, but also other Anatolian languages (Hattic, Luwian, and Palaic), and Hurrian and Canaanite (to a much lesser extent). The only place where cuneiform did not take root at this period is Egypt, which had its own centuries-old writing system. There it was only used for diplomatic purposes—sending and receiving letters from the great kings and the rulers of the Canaanite vassal city-states.

As in Babylonia, the acquisition of writing skills was acquired in an institution called the Edubba, "scribal school" (literally, the "tablet house," although other explanations and translations have been offered for this Sumerian term). The scribal materials studied in the Late Bronze Age schools for achieving literacy in Akkadian came from Babylonia (even if not directly). Although in my reconstruction of the Late Bronze Age curriculum I will concentrate on Ḫattuša, Emar, and Ugarit, it can confidently be assumed that scribal schools existed in many other places. In almost every place where cuneiform tablets have been found, schooling materials were also recovered. This fact demonstrates that writing was not simply "out there" but had to be acquired through the schooling institution.

The archive of El Amarna, famous for its letters, also yielded remains of Mesopotamian school texts—lexical lists and Babylonian mythological narrative poems (such as Adapa)—a clear sign of a scribal-school environment. The city-states of Canaan (e.g., Ashkelon, Aphek, Megiddo, and Hazor) also provide us with evidence, meager as the remains are, to the same effect. A few lexical lists, liver model omens, a mathematical tablet fragment, and a fragment of The Epic of Gilgameš demonstrate that some kind of educational system was in place in Canaan. Sites in the Lebanon and Syria (e.g., Kumidu, Qatna, and Alalah) also have their share of Mesopotamian materials, which were used for the study of cuneiform script and Akkadian. We are not certain how Babylonian schooling materials arrived at all these places—some of the works were probably in circulation among local schools since the Old Babylonian period, others brought later by wandering teachers from Babylonia.

Although data are sparse and very varied from one place to the next, the overall picture that emerges is of a unified Babylonian literary culture transmitted from various places (such as the Middle Euphrates area, Mitanni, and Assyria, and of course Babylonia) to the Late Bronze Age scribal schools and the literate elites. No doubt this contributed to the spirit of internationalism characteristic of the period. However, it should be observed that Babylonian cultural hegemony was superficially superimposed on different cultures each with its own language, traditions, and literary legacy. Hence, when assessing the wisdom compositions from Emar, Ḫattuša, and Ugarit, we must remember that although these are Babylonian works, they were copied and studied by scribes whose native tongue was most likely not Akkadian, and whose cultural background was not Mesopotamian.

Nonetheless Babylonian literary culture created a conscious sense of belonging among the elite class of scribes who populated the scribal schools. This class of scribes viewed itself as privileged and distinct, part of a virtual scribal community bridging centuries. Scribes living very far away from Babylonia adopted Babylonian names as their *noms de plume,* a clear sign of prestige associated with their trade. Hittite, Ugaritian, and Emarite scribes evoked in their colophons the Mesopotamian patron gods of writing, Nabû and Nisaba, or mentioned in letters the god Ea, king of wisdom. One scribe, probably from Emar, even titled himself *apkallu* "sage," a venerated epithet in Mesopotamian scholarly traditions. Scribes may have written their own names with rare and obtuse signs in order to show off their knowledge, implying that they belonged to this privileged class. Living hundreds of miles from each other, on occasion scribes greeted one another in short postscripts appended to the letters exchanged between the great kings of the day, a sure sign of their shared cultural world.

At the end of the thirteenth century, the Late Bronze Age polities, great kingdoms and vassal states alike, were about to experience a full-scale catastrophe. First to disappear from the textual record is Ḫattuša around 1200, although its regional capital Carchemish continued to hold on unaffected for some time. In 1185 Ugarit and Emar disappear from view. All these cities were totally destroyed, their sites remaining desolate for many years. Other sites along the Lebanon coast were equally affected, as were the cities of Canaan, although to a lesser extent. Even Assyria and Babylonia suffered a serious regression.

This total system collapse was formerly attributed to the Sea Peoples or to other invaders but nowadays scholars understand that the breakdown cannot be attributed to a single cause but rather to a variety of reasons. Regardless, this collapse was so deep that the entire region entered a dark age. When the light turns on again in the first centuries of the first millennium, the political and cultural landscape is completely new. For our purposes, cuneiform writing vanishes from the region, as a relatively new writing system, the alphabet, becomes widespread. Akkadian is no longer the international language, and is replaced by Aramaic.

Ironically, it is thanks to this catastrophe that such rich textual materials are now at our disposal. Although many tablets are badly broken and hardly a complete one is to be found, it is because many of the Late Bronze Age sites were abandoned for such long periods that their textual materials remained buried and relatively safe from the ravages of time.

The Late Bronze Age Schooling Phenomenon

Here I look in greater detail at the schooling institutions from the three sites at the center of our study, namely, Emar, Ugarit, and Ḫattuša. I begin however with a short overview of the Old Babylonian scribal institutions, for they were the blueprint upon which Late Bronze Age schools were modeled.

The Old Babylonian Scribal Schools

The scribal schools of the Late Bronze Age, with all their differences, were based on the model of the scribal schools of the Old Babylonian period, Ḫattuša perhaps being an exception. These were long gone of course as functioning institutions, but their intellectual traditions were still very much retained in ancient Near Eastern scribal circles. For one, the Late Bronze Age curriculum, although different, nonetheless relied on the structure of the Old Babylonian curriculum (this issue will be dealt with in 1.5). Secondly, the social structure of Late Bronze Age schools, as far as we understand, depended on Old Babylonian models.

What do we know about the Old Babylonian school? In order to reconstruct its social makeup, previous scholarship has very much relied on the Sumerian School Dialogues and the literary Edubba Letters, which described life in the Edubba in order to reconstruct its social makeup. However, recent studies have stressed the fictional and generally nonreliable nature of these sources. It has been convincingly argued that these literary works may tend to exaggerate actualities in the school for the sake of humor, or alternatively, reflect a distant reality—the scribal schools of the Ur III dynasty under the patronage of King Šulgi—much removed from Old Babylonian social setting.

Scholars therefore have turned to the raw materials rather than fictionalized accounts to understand better the curriculum and the social structure of schools (Robson 2001; George 2005).

The modern reconstruction of the school and its curriculum nowadays depends on the meticulous study and analysis of thousands of student exercise tablets and day-to-day documents. Most of these tablets were considered a waste product by the ancient scribe—used as building fill in the walls or floors of the houses where they were once studied and copied. (Only the more accomplished manuscripts were archived as library copies to serve in the education of a new generation). At the hand of modern scholarship however, these student "notebooks" have proven to be invaluable.

The long-held assumption that schooling was conducted under the auspices of the great royal and religious institutions of the ancient Near East, that is the temple or the palace, can mostly be dismissed as far as the Old Babylonian period is concerned. When the available evidence is scrutinized with more attention to detail, it emerges that schooling was conducted in private environments. We know that schooling took place not within the palace or temple but rather within houses belonging to private individuals. Some of these individuals indeed could have been employed by the city, palace or temple administration, but others could have depended on different means for making a living. Van Koppen (2011) draws a remarkable reconstruction of a scribal family from Old Babylonian Sippar, stretching over five generations: first as scribes drafting contracts, later functioning as witnesses to various contracts; some appointed as judges to serve the city administration; others merchants. Some family members had careers that spanned over forty years!

Mostly such individuals educated their own family members—a father teaching his own or his relatives' children. But there was an alternative: an instructor could come to the house to teach the pupil. Tanret (2011) argues that a teacher came in to teach young Ur-Utu at his house at Sippar-Amnānum; Ur-Utu then grew up to be a *galamāḫum* "chief lamentation priest" in succession to his father. Indeed the end goal in scribal education was to educate the children, always male but for special circumstances, so that they could start working first as apprentices and then take over their fathers' jobs. One can find scribes copying school compositions as dub.sar tur "junior" or "apprentice scribe," only to show up later in life as dub.sar "scribe." For example, Iqip-Aya, a junior scribe who copied Atrahasis as part of his studies, is known in his adulthood to have been a professional scribe active in Sippar and possibly Babylon. Iqip-Aya was educated by his own father, himself a scribe (van Koppen 2011).

It is known that schooling took place in the Edubba. But the Edubba, contrary to what one might think, was not an independent self-standing structure. Investigating where the Edubba was actually located on the basis of archaeological data from Ur, Nippur, and Sippar-Amnānum, reveals that it was located in the house, as part of the family dwelling space: perhaps a designated corner in a room or even outside in the courtyard, since reading and writing the cuneiform script demanded a strong directional light (in order to enhance the shadows created by the stylus' impression on the clay). In the courtyard stood the recycling bin into which exercise tablets were dumped and later fashioned anew. The upper floor of the house, or additional rooms, may have been dedicated to the storage of the family's business documents, exemplary schooling manuscripts for future study, or other scholarly compendia, such as omens or rituals, required in the course of the family members' professional duties.

How the school looked in the Kassite period is little more than a guess but there is some evidence that allows us to say with all caution that at least in Babylon schooling may have been conducted as before in private houses (Pedersén 2011; 2005: 69–108). The social setting of Kassite schools however is not yet properly understood.

I go on to discuss the Late Bronze Age schools in order to show how they resembled or differed from the Old Babylonian Ebubba. According to my aims specified above I will also be offering some background about the scribal circles and their places of operation to understand better the social background of Late Bronze Age wisdom literature. In this connection, I will try to see if our wisdom compositions can be linked to any specific scribe or shown to belong to a scribal circle operating with a certain timeframe. Emar is the first to be visited, because it offers far more materials for understanding the social structure of the school than any other place in the Late Bronze Age. It will be followed by Ugarit and then Ḫattuša.

The Social Background of Scribal Schools at Emar, Ugarit, and Ḫattuša

Emar

Although far smaller than Ugarit, let alone Ḫattuša, and of much less political power and wealth, Emar paradoxically provides us with more details of its scribes' social background than any other site. This is because of a remarkable textual deposit in a structure dubbed by the excavators of the site Temple M_1 or "The Temple of the Diviner." This structure (to which I will devote more attention later) housed the day-to-day documents, scribal exercises, and library copies of the scribes of Emar. Additional textual deposits from elsewhere in Emar leave us with over one thousand tablets and tablet fragments that provide the materials for a comprehensive reconstruction of scribal life in the city, notably of the so-called Zū-Ba'la family of diviners.

There are two scribal traditions in Emar, which, although once thought to be contemporaneous, are in fact consecutive: the older "Syrian" tradition (ca. the early-fourteenth century to the mid-thirteenth century B.C.E.), which was then replaced by the "Syro-Hittite" tradition (from the second half of the thirteenth century till the fall of the city in about 1185 B.C.E.). The importance of this distinction for the present purposes is that we can recognize two groups of scribes at Emar, the older Syrian group, and the younger Syro-Hittite group to which the Zū-Ba'la family belongs.

There are some thirty Syrian scribes known by name although their social background is obscure for the most part. They simply title themselves as dub. sar "scribe," when signing off or witnessing documents that they have written. As far as we know, the Syrian scribes held no administrative role. However one Syrian scribal family retained the title of diviner. Ba'al-bārû was a diviner, as was his son, Mašru-hamiṣ, who, as one remarkable document informs us, received a plot of land from the king of Emar; it is thanks to his divination skills that the city was saved from enemy attacks.

There are not many students that we can identify from this early period of scribal activity in the city, but one does stand out. Ribi-Dagan, a novice diviner, wrote this extraordinary colophon:

> The hand of Ribi-Dagan
> servant of Nabû and Nisaba.
> I w[rote] this tablet (when) I was placed
> in bronze chains for a period of [some days].
>
> (S^{a} Vocabulary, *Emar* 537 C = Cohen 2009: 129; after Civil 1989: 7)

Scribes are never forthcoming about their personal life in their colophons, so this is an exceptional statement. Why Ribi-Dagan was in chains is not clear but there are sources from elsewhere that report other cases of people imprisoned while copying tablets.

We are much more informed about the Syro-Hittite scribes, in particular the Zū-Ba'la family who lived and worked in Temple M_1. Members of the Zū-Ba'la family were the diviners of the gods of the city of Emar and in charge of running the religious life of the city, including the Hittite cult, with the help of Hittite officials from Carchemish. As a consequence, their economic and social status in the city was very high. The patriarch of the family, Zū-Ba‘la, and his son Ba‘al-qarrād, both diviners, left evidence neither of their scribal abilities nor of their involvement in the scribal school. However Ba‘al-qarrād's sons, Šaggar-abu and Ba‘al-mālik, were both students and later probably teachers at Temple M_1, their home. I quote here two colophons, one belonging to Šaggar-abu, as copyist of an advanced text although still a student; the other Ba‘al-mālik's, as a teacher of a family member (whose name is missing). Both colophons come from Temple M_1.

> [*ṭup*]-*pí* šu ^{md}30!-*a-bu* dub.sar [tur]
> [arad] ^{d}Ag *u* ^{d}Nisaba arad ^{d}[…]
> [arad ^{d}*É-a u* ^{d}]*Dam-ki-in-na* gáb.zu![.zu *ša* …]
>
> [Tab]let of the hand of Šaggar!-abu, [junior] scribe […]
> [servant of] Nabû and Nisaba, servant of […]
> [servant of Ea and] Damkina, stud[ent of…].
> (Celestial Omens, *Emar* 652: 83′–85′ = Cohen 2009: 168)

[šu o-o-o dumu ^{d}Im-*ma-li*]*k*	[The hand of so and so, son of Ba‘al-māli]k
l[ú.dub.sar lú.ḫa]l	s[cribe, divin]er
š[*a* dingir.meš ^{uru}] ⌜*E*⌝-*mar*!	o[f the gods of the city of] ⌜E⌝mar
x[…]	[…]
gáb.[zu.z]u	stu[den]t
ša ^{md}Im-*ma-lik*	of Ba‘al-mālik

(lú=*ša*, *Emar* 602AD = Cohen 2009: 177)

Šaggar-abu was the chief diviner but after his premature death, his youngest brother Ba‘al-mālik took over. On the basis of business documents, memoranda and letters, his business career can be reconstructed in quite some detail. We learn that he was in charge of the city cult and running the family affairs. The scribal colophons inform us of his responsibility over the scribal school, where he educated his own children. The life and times of Ba‘al-mālik's children, however, are hardly known, because they were young when the city was destroyed.

As at bigger scribal centers, the scribal school at Emar employed a foreign instructor. A person by the name of Kidin-Gula, who probably was a Babylonian, supervised members of the Zū-Ba'la family when copying lexical lists, an essential component in Mesopotamian education. Kidin-Gula himself lived elsewhere in Emar, in Area A, House 5, in the merchant quarter where he wrote documents for fellow foreigners.

In sum, the social setting of the Emar school very much resembles the Old Babylonian scribal schools: a family affair headed by the senior family member and conducted within the family house, with the occasional support of a teacher from elsewhere. The persons running the school, as in the Old Babylonian period, were not simply scribes, but had other duties—in the case of the Zū-Ba'la family, as diviners of the city and its gods.

Identifying the actual place where schooling took place is not as difficult as will be the case for Ḫattuša. All the evidence points to Temple M_1 as the central place for scribal education, although there exists the possibility that there were other schools located elsewhere in Emar. That such a Mesopotamian institution was recognized at Emar is clear. An offering list dedicates sacrifices to "Ea of the scribes" and to "Nabû of the schools."

The Zū-Ba'la family of scribes was active from the first decades of the thirteenth century B.C.E. to not long after 1185 B.C.E., the time when the city fell. Šaggar-abu lived in the last decades of the thirteenth century; since he is identified as the copyist of The Ballad of Early Rulers (2.2) in the colophon of the tablet, we know approximately when he copied this manuscript.

The colophon of The Ballad of Early Rulers is written cryptographically, that is to say using rare signs, and in an Old Babylonian calligraphic or monumental script not in use for everyday writing. Thus Šaggar-abu boasts of his erudition and sense of pride as belonging to the elite class of professional scribes. The colophon, partly broken, is restored after another colophon of his, appended to the wisdom composition The Fowler and His Wife (which because of its poor state of preservation is not included in our collection).

> *ṭup-pu an-nu-t*[*u_4* š]u ^{md}Šir-^{N}[^{U}-sig$_7$]-ad lú a.[zu]
> *ù* lú.zu.z[u a]rad ^{d}*Eš-tar* ^{d}Mùš *ḫa-ši*
> arad ^{d}Im … arad ^{d}Ag *u* ^{d}Nis[aba]
> … lú dub.s[ar lú.ḫal]

> Thi[s] is the tablet of [the ha]nd of Ša[ggar]-abu, divi[ner],
> and see[r, ser]vant of Ištar, Ištar of Ḫaši
> servant of Ba'al… servant of Nabû and Nis[aba]
> … scribe, and [diviner].

(Ballad of Early Rulers, *Emar* 767 = Cohen 2009: 169)

This is the only wisdom composition in our collection whose copyist can be confidentially identified. The other wisdom compositions from Emar, *Šimâ Milka* (2.1) and Enlil and Namzitarra (2.3), although having no preserved colophons, perhaps were also copied by Šaggar-abu, since they are written in the Syro-Hittite script and in very much the same style as the rest of the manuscripts of this prolific scribe. I will come back to Šaggar-abu when I discuss the Late Bronze Age curriculum.

UGARIT

The social setting of schooling at Ugarit can be reconstructed on the basis of the scribal colophons that accompany scholarly compositions. These are supplemented by everyday sources, which sometimes mention individual persons who are identified as scribes.

It has been demonstrated rather persuasively that the Ugaritic scribes mastered both the syllabic cuneiform script and the locally devised alphabet, for both scripts occasionally occur on the same practice tablets (Hawley 2008a: 63). Hence the scribes were bilingual or at the very least biscriptural (that is commanding both Ugaritic and Akkadian as written languages). Hurrian is also encountered in Ugarit, written either with the alphabetic script or in cuneiform, as seen in our collection (2.7). It has been argued that there is some likelihood that Hurrian was spoken by some of the city's religious personnel, among them the scribal class.

It seems that scribes inherited their positions from their fathers, so schooling was conducted in the family domain, although there was the intervention of teachers coming from outside the city, as will be seen. Once students finished their education, they moved on to serve the city administration, as far as can be gathered from the meager evidence. The scribes bore the title sukkal̆ (in cuneiform texts), its Ugaritic equivalent title *ṯ'y* (in alphabetic texts); teachers were called gal.sukkal. The title may have denoted some high administrative function but details are lacking (van Soldt 1988).

There are a few cases where scribal families can be reconstructed. Take the scribal family of Nuʻme-Rašap. Nuʻme-Rašap was the scribe responsible for the copy of Atraḫasis recovered from the *Maison aux tablettes*. Four of his sons followed in his footsteps as scribes. One of them, Gamir-Addu, also served as a teacher. Because Gamir-Addu is mentioned in three different archives, van Soldt (1995: 181) suggests that his job required him to move about from one Edubba to the next.

We know of a few other notable scribes in Ugarit. Ili-malku was the author of Ugaritic myths and epics but also apparently composed Akkadian contracts;

he was educated by Attenu the diviner. Yanḫānu was a scribe of lexical materials and other school texts; he names two of his teachers, who are otherwise unknown. It would have been useful to know if his two teachers taught different subjects. Most of this scribe's copies were kept at the House of Rapānu.

The owner of the House of Urtenu, Urtenu himself, was also probably a scribe, but more will be known about him and his social milieu once the full contents of his archive are published. For now, it certainly looks as if he was an influential person in the city, judging from the letters found in his archive, some addressed to the Ugarit royalty.

Unfortunately we know next to nothing about Šipṭu or Šipṭia. He is the scribe who copied one of the manuscripts of *Šimâ Milka* according to its colophon, recovered at the *Maison aux tablettes*. His father was Abdu-[...]; Šipṭu calls himself a gáb.zu.zu "a novice scribe" or "student," but reading the name of his teacher remains a problem because it is probably written with cryptographic logograms (see Arnaud 2007: 178).

There is some evidence that foreign scribes were employed in the service of businessmen at Ugarit and it is very likely that they were also active as teachers. An Assyrian called Naḫiš-šalmu perhaps instructed local students. He worked as a scribe for Yabnīnu, the owner of the House of Yabnīnu (also known as the Southern Palace). And on the basis of the schooling materials from the Lamaštu Archive it can be assumed that a Babylonian teacher was active at the place, probably as a teacher, although further evidence is lacking.

Schooling was concentrated in specific parts of private houses, as far as such residences can be defined as private (on many occasions their archives contained materials concerned with international affairs as well as with private matters). I discuss these places in greater detail in the next chapter but for now point out the House of Rapānu (the residence of an important official in the city), the Lamaštu Archive, and the House of Urtenu as places where schooling most probably took place.

Most of the scribes are documented as active around the mid-thirteenth century to the beginning of the twelfth century, which is when Ugarit was destroyed. For example, Gamir-Addu, son of Nu'me-Rašap, was active around the close of the thirteenth century. Since his name is associated with three archives, two of which include wisdom compositions, it can be cautiously suggested that these manuscripts were perhaps copied at around that time; these are the manuscripts of The Ballad of Early Rulers (2.2) and The Righteous Sufferer (2.4) from the complex of the Lamaštu Archive and the House of the Hurrian Priest; and *Šimâ Milka* (2.1), the manuscript copied by Šipṭu/Šipṭia from the *Maison aux tablettes*.

The same argument can be made concerning the two manuscripts of *Šimâ Milka* found in the House of Urtenu. Since Urtenu's and others' activities in the archive are dated to the close of the thirteenth century and the beginning of the twelfth century B.C.E., it is possible that this period is when the manuscripts were copied.

These suggestions must be taken as conjectural because the manuscripts may already have been archival. That is to say, they had been copied sometime before and then placed in these archives as library copies for future reference and study.

Ḫattuša

Understanding the social setting of Hittite schooling remains a problem. This is because the textual materials and the archaeological remains from Ḫattuša are very different from what was recovered in Ugarit and Emar.

There is hardly any circumstantial evidence regarding the scribes and their families, unlike in Ugarit and Emar. We lack business documents, such as contracts or wills, and private memoranda or letters that could tell us more about social class. This is of no great surprise considering that no clear-cut private domiciles have been found in the city. The architectural remains of Ḫattuša seem to be institutional, that is, under the domain of either the palace or the temple. Even the House on the Slope, suggested to have housed a scribal school, appears to have been an institutional structure rather than a private residence belonging to a certain individual or family. This state of affairs inhibits us from knowing much about the social setting of Hittite scribes, although recent studies have considerably advanced the reconstruction of the city's scribal circles.

There are about one hundred identifiable scribes from Empire period Ḫattuša. They are known according to their professional epithets (dub.sar "scribe," dub.sar tur "junior scribe," and gáb.zu.zu "student"). These epithets are found in Akkadian and Hittite compositions. As far as can be understood, at least some if not all scribes were bilingual or biscriptual in Akkadian as well as in Hittite (and possibly in a few other languages as well).

There are some indications that scribes had other posts, as in Emar and Mesopotamia. The chief scribe called Mittanna-muwa was probably also a physician, as were two other scribes. There are additional examples of scribes having other official or cultic duties. However, as van den Hout (2009a and 2009b) concludes, on the whole, other than in exceptional circumstances, the scribes working in Ḫattuša did not belong to the ruling elite of the Hittite Empire.

Some Ḫattuša scribal families or rather scribal circles who worked together, can be reconstructed mainly thanks to their colophons. Note these two examples.

Talmi-Teššub was a student of a certain teacher (the pronunciation of the name is not clear because it is written logographically), working under the supervision of his own father, Walwa-ziti. Walwa-ziti himself was a chief scribe, son of the chief scribe and physician Mittanna-muwa, whom I mentioned above.

Angulli, son of the scribe Palla, was supervised by Anuwanza, a well-attested scribe and official in the Hittite bureaucracy. Once Angulli finished his schooling under Anuwanza he himself became a supervisor of three students. One of these students was a certain Zuwa. Zuwa, presumably on finishing his education, went on to teach the student Aliḫḫini, himself a scion of a well-known family of scribes. The lineage of Aliḫḫini's family can be traced all the way back to the scribe Ḫanikkuili and his father Anu-šar-ilāni—the oldest attested scribal family in Ḫattuša dating to the pre-Empire period (ca. mid-fifteenth century).

The pre-Empire scribe Ḫanikkuili, ancestor of the above-mentioned Aliḫḫini, wrote the prism KBo 19.99, a piece of *narû*-literature about the Sargonic king Narām-Sîn, and drafted land grants. His father, probably responsible for his education, was one Anu-šar-ilāni, scribe and translator. Who this Anu-šar-ilāni was and where he came from remain unknown to us. However, on account of his non-Anatolian name and a few other considerations, it has been suggested that he was a scribe of Babylonian or perhaps Syrian origin (Beckman 1983: 104; Weeden 2011a: 24–25).

One may assume that, like Anu-šar-ilāni, other foreigners residing at the capital as diplomats or specialized professionals, like physicians, were also partially responsible for the education of Hittite scribes. Recently it has been demonstrated that the eminent physician from Babylon, Rabâ-ša-Marduk, who lived for a considerable time in Ḫattuša eventually to die there, was also a competent scribe responsible for copying medical compositions (Heeßel 2009). It stands to reason that he imparted some of his knowledge to trainee scribes and/ or medical students.

It remains at present difficult to identify the Edubba or Edubbas at Ḫattuša. However, there is no doubt that this institution was recognized by the Hittites because the Edubba, written as such, is found in a few disparate textual sources (Weeden 2011b: 119–22). Circumstantial evidence advocates two locations in the city as potential places where training of scribes took place: the House on the Slope and the House of Craftsmanship (É GIŠ.KIN.TI). Student colophons were found among the tablets excavated in the House on the Slope; and a person titled as Master of the House of Craftsmanship (EN GIŠ.KIN.TI) is understood to have been a teacher. Note that archaeologically speaking both structures are institutional, as will be discussed in greater detail later. Hence, it has been suggested that schooling in Ḫattuša, unlike in Emar and Ugarit, was conducted or supported by the palace or temple authorities. I will examine the archaeological remains and archival contexts of these locations and follow up this supposition in 1.4.

As in Ugarit and in Emar, most scribes were active in the thirteenth century, although some are known from earlier periods. Ḫanikkuili was probably operative in the mid-fifteenth century. Since he was the copyist of the *narû*-literature prism as we saw, there is some possibility that he was also the copyist of one of our compositions—a collection of Akkadian proverbs, also written on a prism and found at Ḫattuša (2.6, Text A). Because the piece lacks a colophon, further investigation into Hanikkuili's scribal habits is required to verify this suggestion.

The two other Ḫattuša wisdom composition manuscripts (2.1, the Ḫattuša manuscript; and 2.6, Text B) were found next to the House on the Slope. Viewed within the wider dating of manuscripts found there, a thirteenth century date can be tentatively argued for them. Currently, however, they cannot be linked to a scribe or a scribal circle. They derive from a secondary deposit, contain no colophons that would have given us the identity of the scribe, and are in a poor state of preservation.

Further Reading

For the political, social and intellectual settings of the Late Bronze Age, see Liverani 1990; van de Mieroop 2007; Singer 2011; Beckman 1999; Bryce 2003, 2005.

For the scribal environment of the Late Bronze Age, see Izre'el 1997; Horowitz, Oshima and Sanders 2006; Moran 1992.

For the Old Babylonian schooling institution, see Tanret 2011; Van Koopen 2011; Robson 2001; George 2005; Waetzoldt and Cavigneaux 2009.

For Emar scribes, see Cohen 2009.

For Ugarit scribes, see van Soldt 1991, 1995, 2012; Hawley 2008a, 2008b; Vita 2009.

For Hittite scribes, see Gordin in press; Hoffner 2009; van den Hout 2009a; Torri 2008; Weeden 2011a, 2011b.

1.4
The Archaeological and Archival Contexts

This chapter will consider the three sites from which all Late Bronze Age wisdom literature compositions derive: Ḫattuša will be introduced first, followed by the lesser-sized Ugarit, and then Emar, the smallest (by far). For each site a brief history of the excavations and general layout will be given; it will be followed by a more focused examination of the chief areas where archives or textual deposits were discovered. These will be described so that the reader will gain a picture of the rich textual world in which scholarly and schooling materials, wisdom literature included, are to be imagined. The location, size, and contents of the main textual deposits at each site will be examined and their function as either schools, archives, or libraries will be assessed.

The purpose of this chapter is to show that wisdom literature manuscripts are not only situated academically within the Mesopotamian schooling tradition (as will be shown in 1.5) but are physically to be found among, or associated with, collections of Mesopotamian schooling texts, such as lexical lists and other learned materials. It will be demonstrated that in some cases, when the full archaeological and archival contexts are studied, manuscripts of Mesopotamian wisdom literature compositions can be comfortably located within scribal training environments or, in other words, schools.

Ḫattuša

Excavations and General Layout of the City and Its Major Archives

The city of Ḫattuša, the capital city of the Hittites and the Hittite Empire, is located at Boğazköy—a very large hilly site with several steep rocky outcrops, some 150 km east of Ankara.

Fig. 2. Ḫattuša: The City. From S. Herbordt, *Die Prinzen- und Beamtensiegel der hethitischen Großreichzeit auf Tonbullen aus dem Nişantepe-Archive in Hattusa*, p. 6, Abb. 1 (Gesamtplan von Hattusa). Bogazköy-Ḫattuša 19 (Mainz: von Zabern, 2005).

Excavations at Boğazköy began in 1906 (although the site was known before and already cursively explored during the closing decades of the nineteenth century). They continued intermittently until the First World War. After the war excavations pressed on until the Second World War. Renewed in 1952, the excavations continue to this very day.

The site can be divided into two sections: the Lower City, which includes the temple complex; and the Upper City, which includes the citadel (called Büyükkale), within which is the royal palace. Numerous temples, significantly smaller however than the main temple in the Lower City and other installations, were also found in the Upper City, outside the citadel area.

The Lower City: Temple 1

Temple 1 is the largest single architectural complex in Boğazköy (fig. 2). At its core stands the temple structure dedicated to the two main deities of the Hittite Empire: the Storm God of Hatti and the Sun Goddess of Arinna. This temple is surrounded on all sides by magazines. In three store rooms of the eastern magazine many tablets were recovered at the very start of the Boğazköy excavations. Additional tablets have come to light in subsequent excavations of the area. The deposit of the tablets, as has been assumed by scholars, is secondary, and occurred following the destruction of the site, hence we are left in the dark with regard to where the tablets were originally stored (perhaps on a second story, now destroyed) or under what shelf system they were archived.

The type of tablets found in and about the storerooms around Temple 1 seem to provide us with a good indication that we are faced with an archive or an official administrative center. The center was busy with the registration of property or goods and people, as we learn from the array of administrative tablets and inventories. However, other types of tablets broaden the scope and consequently the purpose of this deposit. Rituals, festivals, mythological literature, state treaties, the Hittite Law Code, and Mesopotamian scholarly materials also make up an important part of this collection. It is obvious that these are not genres we associate with administrative archives. Copies of the Hittite state treaties, various rituals or the Hittite Law Code may have been stored in the temple rooms as archival copies. The scholarly materials that were used in the training of scribes, first and foremost the lexical materials as well as fragments of Mesopotamian *narû* literature, may speak for the existence of a scribal school at the site.

There is some circumstantial evidence, it has been argued, to locate an Edubba elsewhere in the temple complex itself (see recently Gordin 2011). Rooms of the southern area of the temple complex have been identified with a structure called in the texts the É GIŠ.KIN.TI, the House of Craftsmanship. This place, according to the texts, may have housed a school on its premises; writing implements found in the area—styli of bone and bronze (if the interpretation of these artifacts is correct)—may support this thesis, but note that school texts, the most substantial proof of the existence of a scribal school, are very few in number.

The Lower City: The House on the Slope

Leaving Temple 1 through the main gate on its eastern side, we advance some one hundred meters eastwards to the so-called *Haus am Hang* or the House on the Slope. This is a moderately sized building of around 30×30 m, an independent structure and therefore not part of a larger complex, unlike the store rooms of the eastern magazine of Temple 1 or the various buildings on top of Büyükkale (as will be discussed).

The textual finds from the House on the Slope are the result of two excavation phases: an earlier phase, at the start of the Boğazköy excavations, when texts were retrieved from Rooms 3, 4, and 5 of the structure; the exact find-spots of the excavated materials were not systematically noted; and a later phase during the 1960s, which saw the discovery of more than 1,400 tablet fragments; these however all come from secondary deposits, outside of the structure itself.

The types of texts found within and around the House on the Slope can be characterized as archival manuscripts, current copies, and schooling materials. As Torri (2008) suggests, such a mixture invites us to imagine the House on the Slope as a type of scriptorium in the broad sense of the word: a place where people were engaged in organizing materials to be archived, where they manufactured new copies of old texts and perhaps composed new compositions, and where they studied and taught in a scribal institution as either students or teachers. The textual finds from the House on the Slope, which include also two wisdom literature manuscripts, suggest the existence of a scribal institution at the site.

From Ḫattuša we have a total of three Mesopotamian wisdom literature manuscripts. The find-spot of one of our sources—a collection of proverbs (KUB 4.40; 2.6, Text A)—is unknown, because the tablet was found at the beginning of the Boğazköy excavations, hence its find-spot was not recorded. Fortunately we do know rather precisely from where the two other wisdom compositions were recovered. The fragment of *Šimâ Milka* (KUB 4.3 + KBo 12.70) and a tablet containing another set of proverbs (KBo 12.128; 2.6, Text B) were discovered in the vicinity of the House on the Slope. KBo 12.128 (the collection of proverbs) was found in the vicinity of some eight tablets and fragments of various rituals, a fragment of the Myth of Illuyanka, and an administrative list. The *Šimâ Milka* fragment was found together with ritual and oracle fragments, historical texts, cult inventories, and a few Mesopotamian divinatory materials, such as a fragment of the *šumma ālu* omen series. The wider archival context of the area outside the House on the Slope reveals more typical schooling materials: over a dozen fragments of lexical lists (such as the S^{a} Vocabulary lexical list), a copy of *narû* literature (*šar tamḫāri*) and a Mesopotamian hymn provided with a Hittite translation (the Trilingual Hymn to Adad). In addition to these schooling materials rituals and historical texts were also recovered.

THE UPPER CITY: BUILDINGS E, D, A, AND K OF THE CITADEL

The citadel of the city, Büyükkale, lies on top a partially artificial platform situated on a high and fortified rocky outcrop (fig. 3). Here was located the royal palace—an architectural complex of several monumental structures built around four courtyards. At the center of the platform stands Building D, the royal audience hall, opening onto a large courtyard; to its left and right it is surrounded by smaller buildings, Building A, E, and K. All contained rather substantial textual deposits but none that can be in particular associated with a schooling institution.

Building E is similar in size and ground plan to the House on the Slope; according to its textual finds (some 2,500 tablets and fragments) it does not appear to have been a private or noninstitutional archive. It held royal correspondence and state treaties, administrative documents, cultic texts, and oracle protocols. A collection of Mesopotamian scholarly materials that we would associate with schooling is lacking, although the occasional Akkadian fragment was found here.

Building D is the largest building on the citadel. It was suggested that this building was the royal audience hall, with which was associated an administrative archive. This identification is less clear nowadays. Some of the texts, such as land donations, indicate this function, but the varied contents of the tablet deposit present us, as in the other buildings on top of the citadel, with a more opaque situation. There are a few Sumerian and Akkadian incantations and other learned materials, but they are not the type associated with the initial phase of scribal training, and we can surmise that there was no school in this building.

Building A is a large magazine-like structure, similar to the magazines of Temple 1 in the lower city. Over four thousand tablet fragments have been recovered from its rooms. A cursory examination of the Mesopotamian scholarly compositions found in Building A shows us that these were not the basic materials of the first stage of scribal education, but more advanced compositions. For the most part, they were bilingual (Sumerian and Akkadian) incantations or magical texts, whose purpose was probably to serve professionals, such as incantation priests or *āšipu*s.

And finally, Building K, it has been suggested, functioned as an administrative center. However, its textual deposit of over two hundred tablets and fragments does not lend much support to such a notion: the textual finds are not administrative tablets, such as the ones found within the rooms of the Royal Palace archives at Ugarit, but rather a selection of rituals, festivals, Hit-

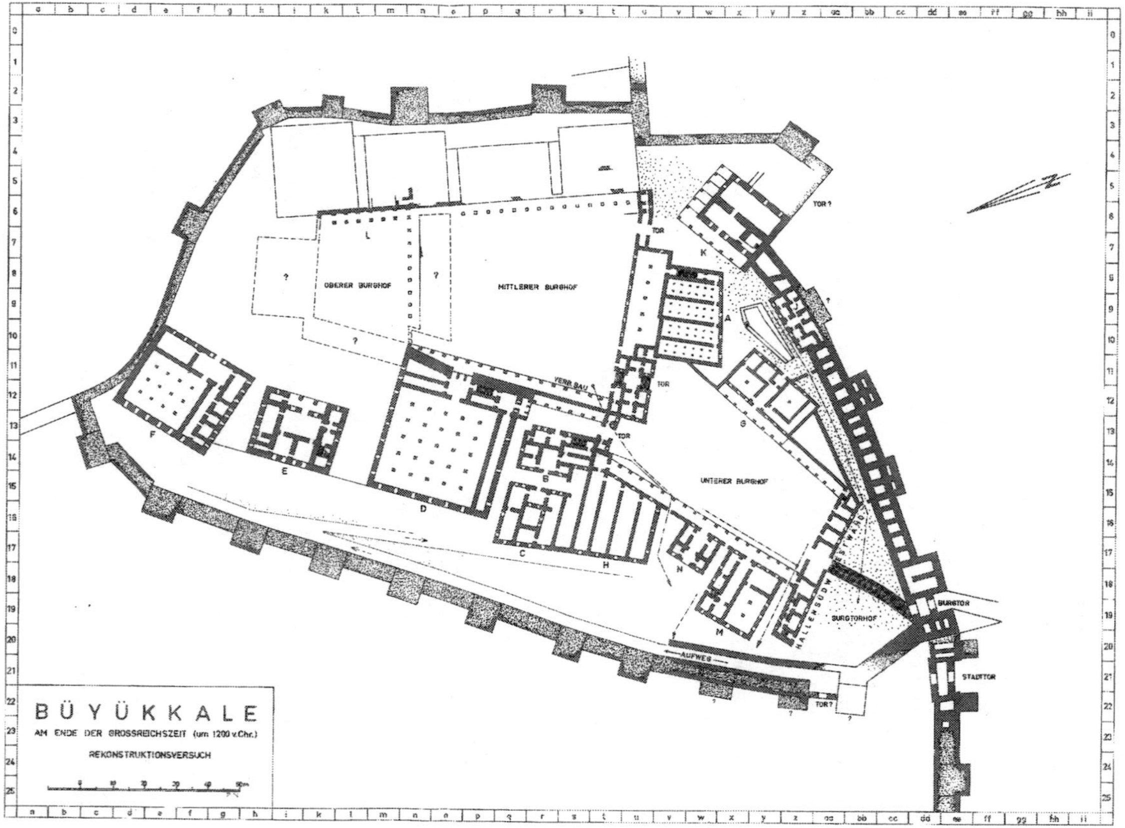

Fig. 3. Ḫattuša: The Palace. From Peter Neve, *Büyükkale die Bauwerke Grabungen 1954–1966*. Boĝazköy-Ḫattuša XII (Berlin: Gebr. Mann, 1982).

tite historical compositions, a few international letters, instructions and oaths, the Hittite Law Code, and a Hittite version of The Epic of Gilgameš.

Smaller deposits of textual materials were discovered outside of the citadel, inside some of the buildings uncovered in the Upper City. These buildings, identified by the excavators as temples (albeit much smaller than the main temple of the city, they exhibit the same ground-plan), included archival matter such as bullae and royal grants. Temple 15 and the much less-well preserved Temple 16 are worthy of mention. Both held fragments of the Hittite-Hurrian bilingual, The Song of Release, a composition that contains animal parables and therefore in a sense can be defined as a wisdom composition (see 2.7). Other nondocumentary materials, such as mythological fragments and rituals, were also discovered in one or two rooms. Temple 16 also included fragments of the Babylonian version of The Epic of Gilgameš.

To conclude, the overall archival context of the Mesopotamian wisdom manuscripts from Ḫattuša implies that they formed part of a larger group of Mesopotamian scholarly materials, some of which, such as the lexical lists, were used in schooling. Two manuscripts were found in the vicinity of the House on the Slope together with other Mesopotamian scholarly materials. It is perhaps telling that wisdom compositions have not been found in the citadel area in Building A or K: these depositories housed Sumerian and Akkadian compositions of a more advanced level, while the House on the Slope included elementary Mesopotamian scholarly compositions. Accordingly, we may cautiously suggest that the Mesopotamian wisdom compositions served in Ḫattuša in the instruction of scribes at the end of the first elementary stage of schooling, but more will be said about this in our discussion of the curricular setting of wisdom compositions (see 1.5).

Ugarit

Excavations and General Layout of the City and Its Major Archives

The ancient city of Ugarit is located at Tell Ras Shamra. The tell is situated about 1 km from the Mediterranean littoral and 10 km north of the modern city of Latakia in Syria. Excavations at Tell Ras Shamra began in 1929, led by a French expedition. But for short interludes and an hiatus during the Second World War the excavations continued into the first decade of the twenty-first century. I will consider the layout of the tell and its major archaeological and architectural remains and then move to discuss in greater detail some of the city archives (fig. 4).

The square-shaped tell is dominated by the royal palace lying at its northwest corner. The royal palace contains several tablet concentrations or archives. North of the royal palace are a few monumental buildings (such as the Hurrian Temple and the Pillared Building); on its southern flank, separated by a plaza, lies the House of Yabninu (also called the Southern Palace). East and southeast of the palace is the residential quarter: it includes houses, some with archives, of prominent people in the city. In the acropolis area further east of the palace and the residential area, two temples were excavated. They were apparently dedicated to the storm god Ba‘al (the chief deity of the city) and to the god Dagan. Between these two structures stands the House of the High Priest, from which the most important Ugaritic mythological compositions derive and on whose account the city of Ugarit became famous. South of the temple area two long trenches were opened, stretching in a north–south direction: they reveal an urban matrix containing concentrations of domestic structures, some with archives. In the South City trench, the *Maison aux tablettes* included cuneiform tablets in several of its rooms, forming the collection that gave the house its name. East of the South City trench is the South Acropolis trench. This is where the House of the Hurrian Priest and the Lamaštu Archive are located. In the South Central District at the south end of tell, the important House of Urtenu was found (Yon 2006, 1992).

The city archives can be divided roughly into two types: the institutional Royal Palace archives and noninstitutional private archives. As we will see when we examine more closely the content of these tablet collections, modern definitions that make a strong distinction between institutional and private domains of scribal activities fail to convey the true nature of ancient archives and libraries. In Ugarit, as in Emar, such categories melt away, since many of the so-called private archives contain textual remains of an institutional nature, such as letters dealing with affairs of state and international relations.

The Royal Palace Archives

The royal palace at Ugarit, the most prominent structure on the tell, is a large multiroom complex with six courtyards (fig. 5). It contained several archives, some held in a few rooms, others spread over a wing or two of a particular area of the complex. However, only in one archive was a manuscript of a wisdom composition retrieved. In Room 53 of the Eastern Archive in the Royal Palace a small tablet of Akkadian-Hurrian proverbs (RS 15.10; here 2.7) was recovered. It is the only literary Akkadian text from this archive. As we will see, this situation is not typical because other tablets of wisdom literature from Ugarit stem from contexts richer in scholarly materials. However, the tablet stands in isola-

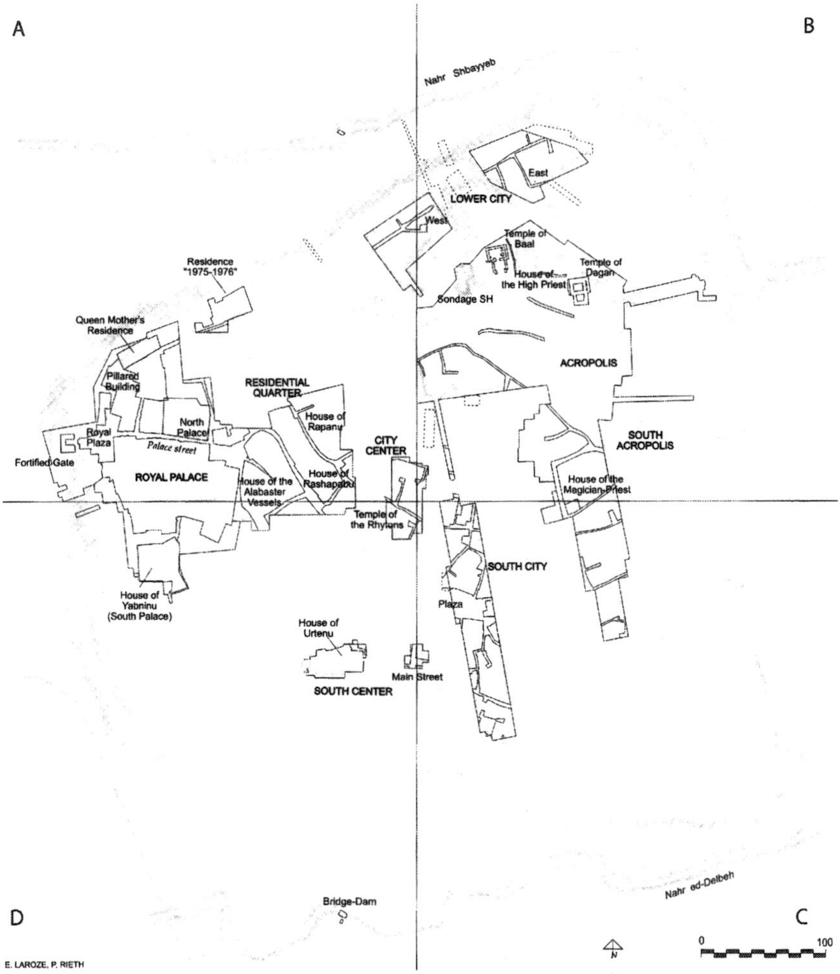

Fig. 4. Ugarit: Topographic map of the tell of Ras Shamra. From Marguerite Yon, *The City of Ugarit at Tell Ras Shamra* (Winona Lake, Ind: Eisenbrauns, 2006).

tion in this particular archive, which contains administrative documents in Ugaritic, as well as royal deeds, legal documents, and international correspondence.

Additional, although overall few, Mesopotamian scholarly texts were found in the Royal Palace archives. A list of incantations (Arnaud 2007, no. 21) comes from Room 30 of the Central Archive of the palace. The rest of the tablets in Room 30 and the adjoining rooms are administrative and legal documents, although across the courtyard, in Room 65 a copy of a lexical list was found. The entrance of the Western Archive of the royal palace yielded

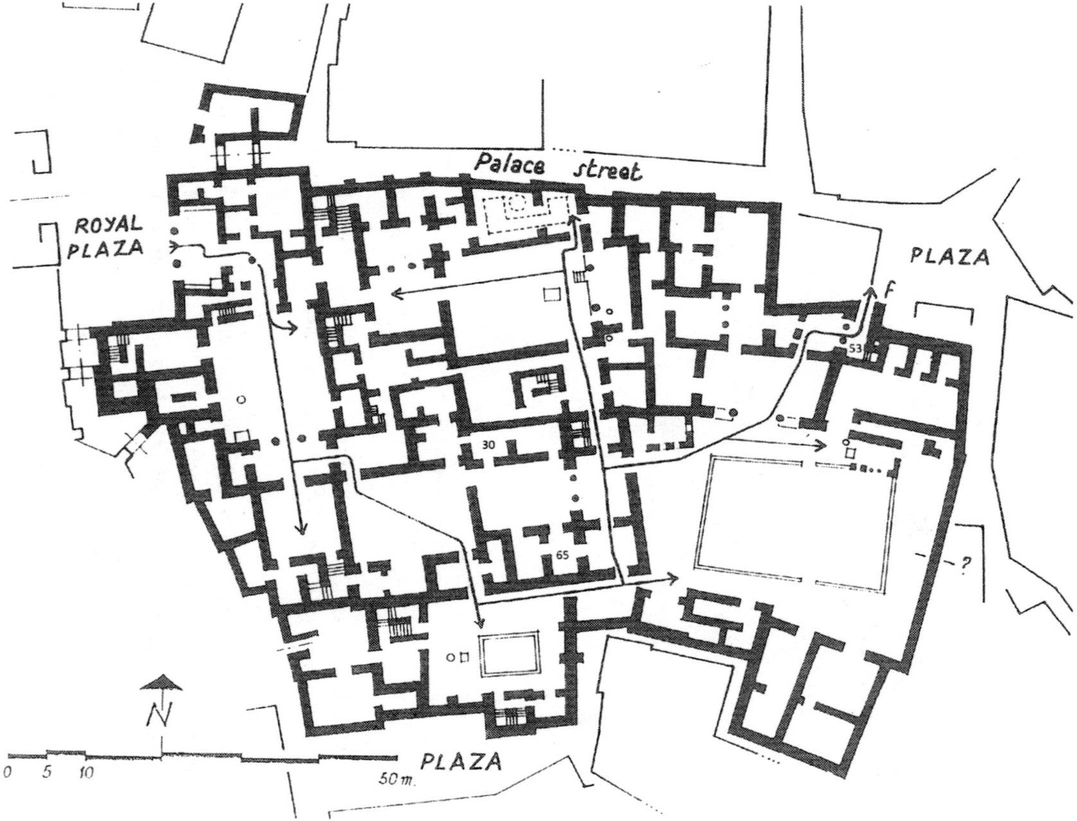

Fig. 5. Ugarit: Plan of the Royal Palace and its Passageways. After Marguerite Yon, *The City of Ugarit at Tell Ras Shamra* (Winona Lake, Ind: Eisenbrauns, 2006).

a copy of a grammatical text, a type of composition associated with scribal training. The Western Archive itself included mainly administrative texts in Ugaritic (utilizing the Ugaritic alphabet); some texts, however, were written in Akkadian. Also recovered is an Ugaritic translation of the treaty between Šuppiluliuma I and Niqmaddu and a copy of the tribute agreement between Ḫatti and Ugarit.

The Southwestern Archive of the royal palace includes a small library of twenty-five religious or literary texts of which twenty are in Hurrian; some of the Hurrian compositions include what are generally understood as musical notations. There are also three Ugaritic school texts in this archive. While this group is definitely not to be viewed as belonging to the corpus of Mesopotamian learning materials, recall that the wisdom tablet (2.7) in the Eastern Archive combines Akkadian proverbs and their Hurrian translations. Perhaps our wisdom tablet is somehow related to the Hurrian texts from the Southwestern Archive in spite of the different locations. Indeed, it becomes difficult to explain what this extract—for it is only a collection of two proverbs and not the entire composition—is doing in the archival context of the Eastern Archive, otherwise generally devoid of learning or scholarly materials.

The Southern Archive of the royal palace includes documents concerned with the relations of the city and its Hittite overlord, notably, a copy of the treaty between Šuppiluliuma and Niqmaddu, as well as other treaties. In addition there are documents concerned with the economic life in the city. It is devoid, however, of any Mesopotamian scholarly materials.

To conclude this survey of the textual finds from the royal palace, it can be said that its archives are characterized by documents concerned with city administration and the administration of the kingdom of Ugarit on both local and international levels. Although a few concentrations of nonadministrative tablets of religious or scholastic nature and a few abecedaries have been found in the palace, there is no clear-cut evidence of schooling (especially in the cuneiform script) anywhere in this complex. Evidence for schooling in Ugarit, as we will see, is found elsewhere.

Noninstitutional Archives

The rest of the textual remains from Ugarit were discovered in contexts that can be defined as private or better, noninstitutional. We find tablet collections or archives that were housed in structures much smaller than the palace, amid urban quarters that were identified by the excavators as residential. (This situation is in contrast with that of Ḫattuša.) Nonetheless, there is no doubt that these structures, mostly houses with a set of rooms opening to a courtyard, belonged to prominent citizens. The content of the documents within such houses reveals that their occupiers played important administrative roles: Yabninu, Rapānu, Rašap-abu, and Urtenu, persons in whose dwelling large archives were located, can be identified as leading administrators engaged in the affairs of the city of Ugarit, such as diplomatic relations and trade. It is also evident that in some of these houses scribal schooling took place. This conclusion is based on circumstantial but yet persuasive finds—schooling materials, such as lexical lists, discovered within the noninstitutional archives and a collection of scribal colophons. Let us dedicate the next few paragraphs to a closer look at some of these archives, four of which include wisdom literature manuscripts.

The archive located within the House of the High Priest is famous for its finds of the Ba'al cycle myth and other Ugaritic myths, such as Keret and Aqhat. It also contains a collection of Hurrian and mixed Hurrian-Ugaritic cultic texts in the alphabetic script, and a selection of Sumerian and Akkadian scholarly materials, such as lexical lists, which are indicative of schooling activities within this building.

The Southern Palace, also known as the House of Yabninu, south of the palace complex, was the administrative archive (of mainly Akkadian documents) of Yabninu, who was an important official in the city. An Assyrian scribe by the name of Naḫiš-šalmu worked in his house, and may have also functioned as teacher of novice scribes there.

In the residential quarter of the city we find an archive of legal and administrative documents in the House of Rašap-abu. Rašap-abu was another important official, perhaps in charge of the city's harbour. An archive of smaller proportions (which is probably linked to the House of Rašap-abu) is the so-called *Archive de Lettré*. It includes a number of Mesopotamian lexical lists and literary compositions. Mention can be made of a bilingual literary letter, typical of the Old Babylonian curriculum written in syllabic Sumerian and Akkadian (Arnaud 2007, nos. 54–55; Civil 2000; see further 1.5) and a collection of incantations (Arnaud 2007, no. 21).

The House of Rapānu is situated in the same residential quarter. The house is a large structure (about 300 m^2) that contained a somewhat eclectic archive of 343 tablets: two-thirds of this collection consists of lexical lists such as ḪAR-ra=*ḫubullu* and izi=*išātu* (and there is also an incantation against the evil eye, but no other Mesopotamian literary tablet). This speaks for scribal schooling within this house. The rest of archive of the House of Rapānu holds letters and administrative (some in Ugaritic) and legal documents concerned with the royal family and dealing with local and international affairs. Some of these letters and administrative documents are concerned with Rapānu himself.

The Lamaštu Archive is characterized by its collection of lexical materials and other Mesopotamian scholarly materials, such as omens, grammatical texts, and incantations against the demoness Lamaštu (from which the modern name of the archive). According to van Soldt (1991: 34; 2012), the building must have housed a school, its teachers probably Babylonian or at least trained by Babylonian scribes (see also 1.3).

One manuscript of The Ballad of Early Rulers (2.2; Version I = RS 25.130), was found in the Lamaštu Archive. Another (Version III = RS 25.424), was found some distance south of this archive; it probably was displaced from its original location in the archive itself.

North of the Lamaštu Archive is the House of the Hurrian Priest. It contains mainly tablets in Ugaritic covering magic, rituals, and mythology. An interest in divination is obvious because it houses a collection of inscribed clay models of sheep livers. It is assumed that such livers instructed the novice diviners in the art of divination. Also from this archive come a dozen texts in Hurrian. Overall, this archive contains a scholarly collection of cuneiform texts, although not solely in the Mesopotamian tradition.

One wisdom composition coming from this archive is a manuscript of The Righteous Sufferer (2.4). It is difficult to find an immediate connection between The Righteous Sufferer and the overall content of the archive. However, it may be that its religious character (for after all it is a prayer to Marduk) is what dictated eventually its inclusion in the archive of the House of the Hurrian Priest, which can be defined as a collection of learned compositions with a religious bent. One must also consider the possibility that The Righteous Sufferer was first copied in the adjacent Lamaštu Archive (which contains other prayers to Mesopotamian gods), and only transported to the House of the Hurrian Priest.

The archive of the *Maison aux tablettes* is characterized by Mesopotamian lexical, literary, and omen texts. Some of the tablets can be recognized as the efforts of novice scribes, but the full picture is missing because of the poor state of the colophons. As in other archives, such as the House of Rapānu and the House of Urtenu, this collection of scholarly materials does not stand in isolation: twelve letters and three legal documents in Akkadian, and some Akkadian and Ugaritic administrative lists are included in the archive.

A manuscript of *Šimâ Milka* (RS_1 = RS 22.439, written by the student Šipṭu/Šipṭia) was found in Room 4 of the archive, one of the five rooms of the north wing of this building complex where schooling probably took place. Another wisdom composition manuscript, although a mere fragment, that comes from the *Maison aux tablettes* is Enlil and Namzitarra (2.3). Outside of the archive itself, but probably originating from within its walls is another manuscript of The Ballad of Early Rulers (Version II = RS 23.34+). Also found outside was a fragment of Atrahasis (RS 22.421; written by Nuʿme-Rašap).

The House of Urtenu is the most important archive to have been discovered in recent years at Ras Shamra; and it is also the largest ever discovered at the site, holding over five hundred tablets. From the administrative documents and letters we learn that the archive probably belonged to a prominent citizen by the name of Urtenu, who had commercial dealings with the palace and conducted business with merchants outside of the city, some of them from Emar (Malbran-Labat 1995). The archive of Urtenu has not been published in full, but from preliminary descriptions it appears that it consisted of a variety of tablets, including royal letters; commercial transactions; administrative texts; and also school texts, such as lexical lists and literary compositions, among which are fragments of The Epic of Gilgameš (published by Arnaud 2007, nos. 42–45; but see now George 2007b) and omen literature (Yon and Arnaud 2001, no. 30).

Two manuscripts of *Šimâ Milka* (RS_2 = RS 94.2544 + RS 94.2548; RS_3 = RS 94.5028) were found in the excavation season of 1994. Full details concerning the find-spots of these tablets are still lacking but as far as can be understood from the preliminary publications, they derive from the archive of the House of Urtenu. According to Yon (2006: 87–88) the majority of tablets found in 1994 come from a single room. Some tablets were stored or placed in niche-like structures in the walls of the house. Those recovered on the floor of the building appear to have fallen from these niches. The wisdom composition The Fable of the Fox was also found inside this house (Yon and Arnaud 2001, no. 29).

Emar

Excavations and General Layout of the City and Its Major Archives

The city of Emar lies atop Tel Meskene on the west bank of the Euphrates in the province of Aleppo in modern-day Syria (fig. 6). Excavations were conducted during the early 1970s as part of several archaeological rescue missions that were intent on exploring as many sites as possible on the banks of the Euphrates. These sites were threatened by the Tabqa dam project, which eventually created an artificial lake that submerged all nearby ground. Excavations at Tel Meskene were renewed for a few seasons starting from 1999–2000 by a Syrian-German team, but parts of the site were already beneath the lake's waters. The

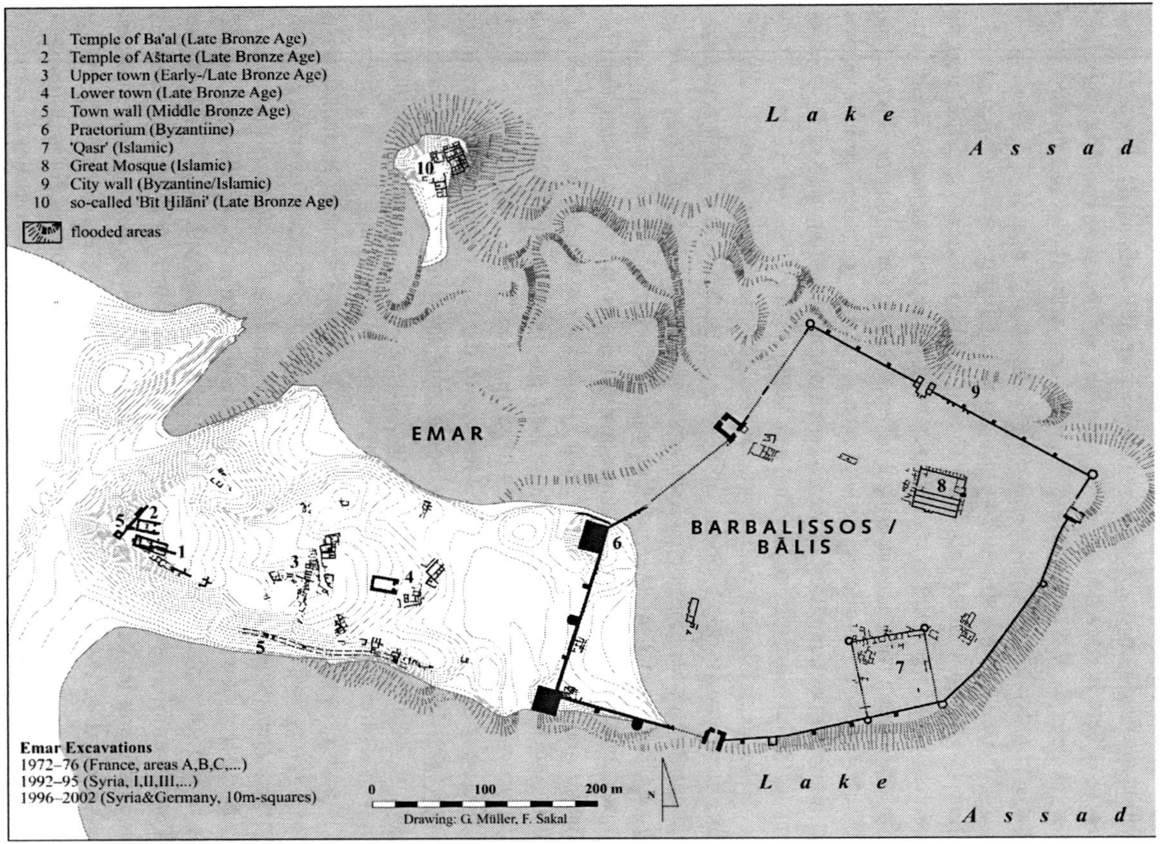

Fig. 6. Emar. From Uwe Finkbeiner. and Ferhan Sakal, eds., *Late Roman and Medieval Cemeteries and Environmental Studies* Vol. 1 of *Emar after the Closure of the Tabqa Dam: The Syrian-German Excavations 1996–2002* (Turnhout: Brepols, 2010). Courtesy of Dr. Sakal, Universität Tübingen. ©Project Emar.

northwestern tip of the site was then a small island, now almost vanished, as can be seen from the images on Google Earth.

It is now established with certainty that the city of Emar was inhabited since the Early Bronze Age, but most of its archaeological remains are from the Late Bronze Age. Several domestic quarters were revealed, as well as an acropolis area and three large temples.

The textual finds from Emar, all dating to the Late Bronze Age, were found dispersed unequally over the tell in several locations. The location richest in tablets is Area M (fig. 6, no. 4) at the southeast of the tell. I will first survey Area M and then proceed to the smaller textual deposits on the rest of the tell (which obviously demand less attention).

At Area M two structures were revealed: Temple M_1 and Temple M_2. Temple M_1, (sometimes called the Temple of the Diviner) yielded almost 90 percent of all the Emar textual finds. It is a large rectangular building with three adjoining rooms, measuring 15×7 m. Although considerably bigger than other houses in the city, its ground plan is similar to that of private houses common at contemporary or near-contemporary sites; in spite of its modern name, the building did not function as a temple.

The textual deposit of this structure includes materials that can be divided into three broad types: 1) documentary sources, such as letters and memoranda; administrative texts; property documents, such as sale and purchase of land or goods; land grants and other entitlements; testaments; and adoptions; 2) cultic or religious texts, which include seasonal ritual procedures and instructions for the installation of cult personnel; and 3) scholarly materials, including lexical lists, omen compendia, incantations, and Mesopotamian literature, in which category wisdom compositions are to be included.

The contents of these tablets lead us to the understanding that the main actors active in Temple M_1 were members of the Zu-Ba'la family, whom we met in 1.3 and will discuss again in 1.5. Temple M_1, it can be established, served as the family's home, scribal school, archive, and library. Because the final excavation reports of Emar and its most important textual depository, Temple M_1, have not yet been published, it is difficult to know how all these materials were organized within a single space. A study of the preliminary reports, nonetheless, reveals the following. The majority of what I termed here as documentary sources, along with some rituals, were found in Area I, or Room 3 adjoining the main hall of the Temple M_1. All the scholarly materials and the larger bulk of the ritual texts, with the remaining documentary sources, were found in Area III, the main hall of the building. These include the manuscripts of *Šimâ Milka*, The Ballad of Early Rulers, Enlil and Namizitarra, and The Fowler and His Wife. These tablets and many others may have originally been stored on a second floor, which collapsed with the structure's destruction. Thus, the distribution of the tablets may tell us less than seems to be the case at first sight.

Other areas around the tell have yielded considerably fewer tablets, hence only the more significant are briefly mentioned here. Near Temple M_1 is Temple M_2. This is a monumental building with massive walls, the largest structure in Emar. Despite its huge size, it has yielded a very small number of texts. Area A (fig. 6, no. 10) at the northwest tip of the site includes a large structure, which was at first considered to be the palatial quarter and royal residence housing its own archive. The complex was designated by modern scholarship as a *Bīt-ḫilāni*, a typical Syrian palace-like structure, thought to be the royal palace. However, this view has since been disputed and the complex itself is more likely to consist of residential units. There is nothing in the textual deposit of Area A that is indicative of a royal or institutional archive serving the palatial bureaucracy. International correspondence, such as was found in the archives of the royal palace at Ugarit and would be indicative of a royal residence or at least institutional bureaucracy, was not revealed in this complex.

South of the complex of Area A, House 5 is located. The house contains a small cache of documents (seven tablets) which represents the concerns of foreign merchants at Emar. I mention it here because it attests to the activities of a person called Kidin-Gula, a Babylonian teacher in the city in the service of the family of Zū-Ba'la.

At the highest point in the tell, in Area E (fig. 6, nos. 1 and 2), twin temples, presumably belonging to Ba'al and Aštarte, are located. The temples yielded around two-dozen tablets, which are mainly concerned with the management of the cult.

Other areas opened across the tell have revealed some small concentrations of tablets, most likely to have been originally housed in private archives of important individuals or prominent families of the city. All the tablets from these deposits are related to administrative or economic concerns of individuals, even if central authorities, such as the palace or the temple, are involved as buyers or sellers. Unlike in Ugarit, no learned texts, except for a few examples, were recovered among the textual deposits of these private archives.

The intention of this chapter was to provide the archaeological and archival contexts in which Late Bronze Age wisdom literature is situated, and from which point it is to be contextually interpreted. Our discussion of the location, size, and function of the many textual deposits, either as schools, libraries, or archives, has sharpened the social and functional contexts where wisdom literature was found. Looking more closely at the archaeological and archival contexts in which Late Bronze Age wisdom compositions were found shows us that their manuscripts are, for the most part, not scattered finds or chance remains. Exceptional is the isolated find, as most manuscripts come from well-defined archival contexts. For the most part they can be rather comfortably situated with additional scholarly materials, many of which served in the education of scribes. Hence it can be assumed, with all caution, that they, when contextually viewed, represent part of scribal training at the respective sites. In Ugarit and Emar, wisdom literature manuscripts can be located within the sphere of a scribal institution, or school; in Ḫattuša, the situation, as we have seen seen, is less clear. How wisdom compositions fitted within the school curriculum of the scribal schools during the Late Bronze Age will be the concern of the next chapter.

Further Reading

For the history of the excavations at Ḫattuša and the city's textual deposits, see Alaura 1998, 2001; Košak 1995; Torri 2008, 2009; van den Hout 2005, 2006, 2009b.

For the archaeology of Ugarit, see Yon 1992, 2006. A description of the structure and content of the Ugarit archives is found in van Soldt 1991, 1995, 1999; Dietrich and Mayer 1999 (the Hurrian texts); Pitard 1999 (the alphabetic texts); and Pedersén 1998: 68–80. For the Assyrian scribe, Naḫiš-šalmu, see van Soldt 2001; for the Lamaštu archive, see van Soldt 2012. For the use of Hurrian in Ugarit, see Vita 2009. For the House of Urtenu, see for now Malbran-Labat 1995. For Emar, see Beyer 2001, 1982; Fleming 2000: 13–21; Di Filippo 2004; Cohen 2009; Pedersén 1998: 61–68.

1.5

The Curricular Context: The Place and Role of Wisdom Literature within the Scribal-School Curriculum

In order to understand and properly assess the place and role of wisdom compositions within the scribal-school curriculum during the Late Bronze Age, a wider perspective must be taken. The place and role of wisdom compositions—proverbs and longer works, mainly in Sumerian but also in Akkadian—in the curriculum of the Old Babylonian school must be examined. This is important because the curriculum of the Old Babylonian period was to provide the basis of Late Bronze Age scribal education. In addition, the Old Babylonian curriculum offers us plentiful data concerned with the use of wisdom literature that can be extrapolated for the subsequent Late Bronze Age period (which is sparser in certain schooling materials, as will be seen). And finally, the examination of the Old Babylonian curricular context of wisdom literature redefines, as suggested in 1.2, this genre for the modern reader. Part of the objective of this chapter is to show how the ancient scribes—composers, students, teachers, and readers—understood in their own terms what wisdom literature is. I will come back to this issue at the close of the chapter.

The Place and Role of Proverbs and Wisdom Literature in the Old Babylonian Curriculum

I will first present a short outline of the Old Babylonian curriculum, then proceed to discuss the place of proverbs in the educational system. I will present the complexities that modern scholarship confronts when trying to define the great Sumerian proverb corpus and on the basis of this discussion consider the educational purpose behind the study of proverbs. To conclude this part, a short appraisal will be given regarding the ways in which proverbs were transmitted from the Old Babylonian period to later periods and continued to be appreciated and studied. Following will come a discussion of the Old Babylonian curriculum and wisdom compositions. Finally, the evidence from Late Bronze Age sites will be examined and assessed.

Since the main purpose of this chapter is to set the background for the book's subject, I will not discuss here the remains of all Old Babylonian wisdom compositions, but deal only with the evidence that can illuminate the place and role of this type of literature in the Old Babylonian curriculum; hence the reader is referred to the full treatment of Sumerian wisdom literature in Alster's studies (1997 and 2005). For Akkadian wisdom compositions of the Old Babylonian period not mentioned here (minor works), see the catalogue provided by Wasserman (2003).

An Outline of the Old Babylonian Curriculum

The curriculum of the Old Babylonian scribal schools is now better understood than ever before. A detailed examination of several thousand school tablets in their archival and archaeological contexts along with a study of literary catalogues, have allowed scholars in recent years to reconstruct to a satisfying degree the structure of the Old Babylonian curriculum and describe the steps of students up the educational ladder. Before I proceed with a description of Old Babylonian schooling it is important to stress that this reconstruction is based overwhelmingly on materials dating to the eighteenth century B.C.E. found at Nippur in Babylonia. As scholars have repeatedly said, in northern Babylonia, the curriculum was probably different—perhaps with more Akkadian than Sumerian compositions, and hence closer to the Late Bronze Age curriculum that I discuss later. Therefore, the description below serves as a plausible model through which one can understand what went on in other scribal schools at this period but no more.

The education of novice scribes involved two phases—elementary and advanced. The elementary stage saw the students learn a basic set of lexical lists (from the easy to the more difficult ones). The lists' main purpose was to acquaint students with writing cuneiform signs and introduce them to the signs' logographic and syllabic values. Toward the end of this phase, students were introduced to a set of four hymns (called in the scholarly literature the Tetrad), which were to be memorized by heart. At the end of the first elementary stage, the students were acquainted with Sumerian proverbs, and perhaps somewhat latter, short wisdom compositions, such as The Ballad of Early Rulers, Enlil and Namzitarra (in their Sumerian-only versions!), and Nothing is of Value, a Sumerian wisdom piece dealing with the vanity theme. Literary letters, which were an important component of Old Babylonian schooling, were perhaps also studied at this intermediary stage.

The second phase of education saw the study of more complex lexical lists and a group of ten literary works (termed in the literature, the Decad). At this stage, however, many other works were studied, perhaps assigned to the more able or talented students. In spite of recent efforts by modern scholarship to delineate more clearly which compositions were studied and in what order in the second stage of education, the picture presently is complex (Robson 2001; Tinney 2011). In fact, its very complexity may speak for an intentionally flexible curriculum open to variations according to the preference of teachers and their students. The great variety of the Late Bronze Age curriculum, as will be seen, may perhaps be considered as a legacy of the open-ended education typical of the second stage.

Progress along this two-stage curriculum involved specific exercises designed to drill the students. At the elementary stage the students were provided with model texts by their teachers which they were to copy on to the same tablet (either on the right-hand column or on the reverse, depending on the size and shape of the tablet).

The second, more advanced stage, saw the employment of extract tablets—tablets containing only a section of a work, and multicolumned tablets or prisms, which contained the whole of the composition. It is assumed that tablets containing entire compositions were the outcome of the memorization of the work after scribes learnt it bit by bit through constant copying of extract tablets. Sometimes several of the shorter compositions were combined on a single tablet. This kind of tablet is called in the scholarly literature a *Sammeltafel* or collective tablet and will be of concern later.

Proverbs in the Old Babylonian Curriculum

It appears that all the textual remains of the great Sumerian proverb corpus or, as it is called in the scholarly literature, the Sumerian Proverb Collection, were the products of students and teachers of the Old Babylonian Edubba. Nonetheless there remains a considerable scholarly debate as to the definition of the Sumerian Proverb Collection and as a consequence of its educational purpose in the Old Babylonian curriculum.

As understood nowadays, calling this body of literature a collection of proverbs is an inaccurate definition. Many of the sayings copied, studied, and assembled in the Sumerian Proverb Collection can hardly fall under the traditional definitions of Mesopotamian wisdom literature. While a large part of the sayings can be defined as proverbial wisdom, others resist an easy classification; some look like quotations from other works, others reported speeches or colloquial expressions. What might this diverse corpus represent? Opinions differ. Some scholars consider the Sumerian Proverb Collection to be a collection of actual popular sayings collated from people's daily speech of a dying language, that is, Sumerian, during the Old Babylonian period. The fact that some of the sayings are even documented in the earliest copies of The Instructions of Šuruppak dated to the Early Dynastic period (ca. the mid-third millennium B.C.E.) may contribute to the view that these were authentic sayings of the people of southern Mesopotamia—at a time when surely Sumerian was still widely spoken (Alster 1997; Volk 2000). Other scholars are less inclined to view these sayings as authentic wisdom articulations that circulated among nonliterary or extrascholarly circles (Veldhuis 2000a; Taylor 2005). A somewhat midway solution to the dispute has advocated the view that the Sumerian proverbs are expressions of scribal wit originating from different sources—the common people, the cultic milieu, and the Edubba classroom (Alster and Oshima 2006). Whichever view is adopted has repercussions on our understanding of the role of the proverbs in scribal education.

Since the purpose of proverbs in education was never stated by the scribes themselves, modern scholars have had to understand their function on the basis of their place in the curriculum and their content. The traditional view regards the purpose of studying proverbs as didactic: these short sayings and maxims—if not all then many—imparted to young scribes values common to Mesopotamian society at large. Another socio-functional approach argues that the study of proverbs was to bestow upon the students a practical knowledge of Sumerian grammar before they moved to more complex compositions (Veldhuis 2000a). This view is not without difficulties and indeed has not gone unchallenged. Their complex grammar and highly abbreviated style hardly make proverbs into fitting materials for imparting language to beginners (Woods 2006; Alster and Oshima 2006). Indeed there are clues that show that some proverbs were not well understood and occasionally as a consequence reinterpreted (leading in turn to create new sayings). Nonetheless, it can be argued (at least from an impressionistic point of view) that proverbs stand at the core education of many cultures (Alster and Oshima 2006). The intrinsic difficulty of the proverb (abbreviated syntax, recherché vocabulary, and so on) in many a language does not prohibit its memorization and study. One may learn a proverb without a proper understanding of its meaning or a correct understanding of its grammatical forms because it is a short sentence.

Word play, similar sounds, onomatopoeia, and other linguistic features help it become as well a *memorable* sentence. After all, much of the Old Babylonian education was about memorization, a technique hardly celebrated, if not frowned upon, nowadays, associated as it is with religious teaching (in Catholic catechism, the Islamic madrassa, the Jewish heder). Perhaps herein lies the durability of the study of proverbs in spite of all the difficulty. Proverbs were studied in the Old Babylonian scribal schools and continued to be in circulation in one form or the other even after the Old Babylonian period, while more serious works vanished from the cuneiform repertoire.

As noted, proverbs remained in circulation well after the demise of the Old Babylonian Edubba. How and why did this happen? By the end of the Old Babylonian period it is obvious that the Sumerian Proverb Collection was no longer studied as previously. However, some of its proverbs were selected (and sometimes provided with an Akkadian translation) to be utilized, so one can assume, in schooling environments in order to educate novice scribes. Other proverbs in circulation were implanted in new works like The Ballad of Early Rulers and *Šimâ Milka*. The fact that proverbs were translated to languages other than Akkadian (i.e., Hurrian and Hittite, for which see here 2.6 and 2.7) once this material started to circulate outside of the Mesopotamian core regions in the Late Bronze Age also speaks in support of the pedagogical value of their study. A bilingual proverb extract tablet, clearly a scribal exercise, dated to circa the first century B.C.E., at the very end of cuneiform civilization, illustrates best the continuity and durability of this genre for a period of over two thousand years (Frahm 2010).

Although of educational value, surely this was not the only reason that proverbs survived after the Old Babylonian period. Once proverbs were considered part of the Old Babylonian curriculum, their status, like other works, became, so to speak, sanctified. Hence they were transmitted along with other works across time to schools either in Babylonia or elsewhere. A parallel case can be provided to serve as an illustration. It can be observed how Sumerian literary letters were still cherished compositions after the Old Babylonian period and even in areas outside of Mesopotamia. These compositions, hardly intelligible to anyone not living in cities of eighteenth-century B.C.E. Mesopotamia, were provided with an Akkadian translation and studied in Ugarit and Ḫattuša (see below). In the same way, in Kassite Babylonia, Sumerian proverbs were still part of the curriculum—perhaps taught as before between the first stage of training and the next level. It is important to remember that although Sumerian was certainly dead by this period it was still cultivated as the language of religion, cult, and scholarship, all interconnected issues in Mesopotamia (Veldhuis 2000b).

Wisdom Literature in the Old Babylonian Curriculum

As with proverbs, most if not all of the Old Babylonian Sumerian manuscripts of wisdom compositions (whose bilingual editions we will meet throughout this book) were the products of students and teachers. The short wisdom compositions were studied at the end of the first stage of the curriculum, before students progressed to longer works. The longer wisdom compositions, such as The Instructions of Šuruppak, The Farmer's Instructions, and the debate poems were studied, like the Decad, in the second stage of the curriculum, although in what sequence remains to be determined.

How were these wisdom compositions studied? The modern reconstruction of the curriculum demonstrates that longer works such as hymns were first learnt piecemeal and copied as extracts on single column tablets. Then they were committed in writing either by memory or by dictation to tablets—each composition in its entirety to a tablet. In this way long wisdom compositions such as The Instructions of Šuruppak or The Farmer's Instructions (e.g., Civil 1994: 12) were studied. Shorter wisdom works were not copied each on its own individual tablet but were compiled with other compositions on a collective tablet or *Sammeltafel*.

Let us look more closely at a few *Sammeltafeln* and see which compositions were grouped with which. I will examine three Sumerian wisdom compositions that are also represented by bilingual Late Bronze Age manuscripts and naturally included in our study—The Ballad of Early Rulers (2.2), Enlil and Namzitarra (2.3), and a small collection of proverbs (2.2; appended to one of the Late Bronze Age versions of The Ballad of Early Rulers). Our summary depends on Kleinerman 2011: 65 and Alster 2005.

The Sumerian Ballad of Early Rulers appears on a compilation tablet that includes a Prayer for Marduk, a Praise to King Abi-ešuḫ (of the first dynasty of Babylon) and the wisdom work Nothing Is of Value (a short vanity-theme wisdom piece). (This compilation is attested on one tablet; it was probably copied on two additional tablets, now broken).

The Sumerian version of Enlil and Namzitarra appears on the same tablet with Nothing Is of Value, a lament-type composition, a literary letter, and a little-known school composition. (This compilation is known from two, if not three, multicolumn tablets. Enlil and Namizitarra occurs again with the school composition on an extract tablet).

The collection of proverbs (later appearing in a bilingual version in Ugarit; 2.2) is included along with Nothing is of Value on the same tablet.

We can see how several wisdom compositions (and some other works) were thematically grouped. Notably all three compositions under the spotlight appeared with Nothing is of Value. Hymns, literary letters or model court records were also arranged by type, grouped each to its own on *Sammeltafeln*. Even if not explicitly stated and with all due care not to impose anachronistic categories on Mesopotamian thinking (cf. Kleinerman 2011:69–74), all this points to a generic organization of the materials. In other words, the curriculum is what establishes genre. This grouping allows us to imagine something of the ancients' conceptualization of wisdom literature. While it lacked an explicit generic definition, wisdom literature was certainly not an empty category in Mesopotamia.

A catalogue from the Old Babylonian period (ETCSL 0.2.11) provides us with additional evidence to support the idea that wisdom compositions, either well-established Sumerian works or relatively newly composed Akkadian compositions, were understood as somehow related. The catalogue names literary works according to their opening lines. Typical Sumerian curricular works, such as hymns to Inanna, are first listed. Then three works with Akkadian titles follow. Only one can be identified—it is [*ši*]*me milkam* "Hear the advice" or, as it is known later and in this study, *Šimâ Milka*. It seems likely that the two unknown Akkadian works mentioned beside it ([*lum*]*un*? *libbi* "*grief* of the heart"; and [...] *mudē šitūlim* "...who knows counsel") were also wisdom compositions. This is supported by what follows in the catalogue. After a ruling line come three more works, the Sumerian wisdom compositions The Instructions of Ur-Ninurta, The Instructions of Šuruppak, and The Farmer's Instructions (note that the latter two compositions are also known from other catalogues). As Sallaberger (2010: 307–9) explains, the relatively new Akkadian compositions, [*ši*]*me milkam* included, were considered as counterparts of the well-known curricular Sumerian wisdom compositions, such as The Instructions of Šuruppak. All were studied at one stage or the other in the Old Babylonian scribal schools. Seeing them listed in one catalogue one after another might suggest that these compositions were considered to hold some relationship to one another.

Once the place and role of wisdom literature in the Old Babylonian curriculum are clarified, one further aspect remains to be emphasized. Let it be understood that proverbs and wisdom compositions were not studied in isolation. Rather, the integration and interplay of this body of literature with other types of literature studied in the scribal school is to be appreciated.

Wisdom literature and in particular proverbs in this formative period of Mesopotamian literature interacted closely with other genres of Mesopotamian literature in circulation in the scribal schools, each influencing the other. A relationship with the lexical lists, which were studied in tandem with proverbs, has been demonstrated time and again. Proverbial knowledge imparted in

Sumerian epic literature is quoted in proverbs (or vice versa: was the wisdom found in Sumerian epics harvested from the Sumerian Proverb Collection?). And close ties between proverbs and laments have recently been nicely exemplified. Later periods did not see such direct ties perhaps because the curriculum became less uniform and more expansive. Nonetheless, as will seen throughout the chapters of this book, links between the various wisdom compositions and other genres did exist and they will be occasionally highlighted.

The discussion of the Old Babylonian curriculum teaches us two things. The first is that wisdom literature was considered as part of scribal education in Old Babylonian scribal schools. At first proverbs were studied towards the end of the elementary stage of education; then came the shorter wisdom compositions, like The Ballad of Early Rulers and Enlil and Namzitarra, followed by, so we can assume, longer wisdom works such as The Instructions of Šuruppak or *Šimâ Milka*. The second thing to be learned is that the ancient understanding of what these compositions were all about was made manifest by their grouping together on *Sammeltafeln* and by their mention one after another in catalogues. It certainly demonstrates that the notion of *wisdom*, although undefined, contained enough weight to see compositions traditionally defined in scholarship as wisdom literature grouped together.

Wisdom Literature and the Scribal Curriculum after the Old Babylonian Period

By the Late Bronze Age our evidence for reconstructing the scribal curriculum seriously diminishes. Textual deposits of thousands of scribal exercises and extract tablets such as found at eighteenth-century B.C.E. Nippur and other sites of southern Mesopotamia are not to be had. Thus the quantity of the finds at our disposal from this period, especially as far as Babylonia is concerned, is much more limited. The dearth of sources ready for study is also the outcome of the lack of publication or proper identification of many finds excavated from Kassite Babylonia. Even sources from Late Bronze Age sites are not fully at our disposal for study. The Ugaritic lexical materials, a crucial source in reconstructing the curriculum, for example, are as yet not fully published. Hence the picture available to scholars today may yet change in the future. With that said, the Late Bronze Age sites provide us with a wealth of new works, among them wisdom compositions, some of which were not previously known. Sources from Middle Assyrian Assur and (mostly unprovenanced) materials from Kassite Babylonia supply additional compositions. All these works provide us with the link between Old Babylonian literature and first-millennium compositions, anticipating in a sense the flood of cuneiform literature that will become available for study in the first millennium (first and foremost from Assurbanipal's library at Nineveh).

In this section I will try to characterize the schooling materials of the Late Bronze Age and assess the role and place of wisdom literature in the curriculum of Ḫattuša, Ugarit, and Emar. I will not however neglect the evidence, sometimes circumstantial, from Mesopotamia. Hence I begin with a general survey of the situation in Kassite Babylonia as a background for understanding better the transmission and reception of wisdom literature in the Late Bronze Age.

Scribal Education and Wisdom Literature in Kassite Babylonia

Kassite Babylonia saw the circulation of wisdom literature composed in the Old Babylonian period (and somewhat later) and also experienced a period of literary creativity. The following wisdom compositions were in circulation during this period: The Instructions of Ur-Ninurta, The Three Ox Drivers from Adab and The Instructions of Šuruppak. The first two are Sumerian compositions; the last an Akkadian translation of the originally Sumerian work. The Councils of Wisdom, The Ox and the Horse (a debate-like composition), The Fable of the Fox, and Bilingual Proverbs (called the Assyrian Collection in *BWL*) are bilingual or Akkadian compositions known almost exclusively from first-millennium Neo-Assyrian copies. The Sumerian tale The Fowler and His Wife appears on a Kassite extract tablet and on some Late Babylonian sources (this composition is known also from a tablet in a very poor state from Emar, but it is not included in this volume; see further below). It is assumed that these works are based one way or the other on Old Babylonian literary prototypes (Sassmannshausen 2008).

As said, Kassite Babylonia is regarded as a place of great creativity and innovation. It is not to be denied that some of the most famous wisdom compositions from Mesopotamia were composed at this period and a bit later, during the time of the Second Dynasty of Isin (twelfth to eleventh centuries B.C.E.). Mention can be made of *Ludlul Bēl Nēmeqi* (and see its "forerunner" from Ugarit; no. 4) and The Babylonian Theodicy. These works although surviving in first millennium copies are generally considered to have been composed by Kassite scribes, who, no doubt relying on literary antecedents, broke new stylistic and conceptual grounds (see recently Beaulieu 2007).

We have seen that wisdom literature was in circulation in Babylonia during the Kassite period. However it is difficult to piece these rather isolated examples (some manuscripts without provenance, others later copies) into a coherent picture that comfortably fits wisdom literature within the scribal curriculum. Indeed a proper understanding of Kassite scribal education is far from our grasp.

The actual remains of student products among the Kassite textual materials are very difficult to come by and to identify properly. This means that a reconstruction of the various stages in education is hard to achieve. The typical tablet formats designed to drill students in the Old Babylonian schools were not frequently produced as before, hence the possibility of establishing the sequence in which wisdom compositions were learnt is diminished. With that said, the existence of Kassite exercise tablets is not to be denied.

A typical Kassite exercise tablet is the so-called pillow-shaped tablet format, its obverse usually consisting of a literary extract, sometimes a proverb in Sumerian or Akkadian, and its reverse including an extract of a lexical text. For example, one pillow-shaped tablet carries two(?) proverbs in Akkadian and on the reverse an extract of the lexical list ḪAR-ra=*ḫubullu*. Sometimes, one of the sides is left uninscribed or erased, showing signs of previous exercises (Veldhuis 2000b; van Soldt 2011). Such tablets are not securely identified in the Late Bronze sites outside Babylonia, although there are a few tablets from Emar and Ugarit that contain lexical-list extracts; some, as will be discussed below, display a tablet format similar to the Kassite pillow-shaped tablet.

It is assumed that these practice tablets were studied at the elementary stage of schooling, as in the Old Babylonian period, and it is here that the student first encountered proverbs and other simple literary works. However, with the lack of a wide distribution of *Sammeltafeln* and only a small number of pillow-shaped tablets studied so far, the role and place in the curriculum of wisdom compositions that are more complex than proverbs, such as *Ludlul Bēl Nēmeqi*, remain speculative. Since we know that *Ludlul Bēl Nēmeqi* was studied during the second, more-advanced stage of education in first-millennium Babylonian scribal schools (Gesche 2001), it is possible that the same place in the curriculum was reserved for it (and works of a similar complexity) during the Kassite and post-Kassite periods. A somewhat clearer image than that achieved for education in Kassite Babylonia emerges when examining the curriculum of the Late Bronze Age sites.

The Late Bronze Age Curriculum and Wisdom Literature

The modern reconstruction of the Late Bronze Age curriculum relies mainly on the textual remains from Ḫattuša, Ugarit, and Emar, which among contemporary sites are the richest in finds. The textual remains of these sites are, however, far from uniform. Once the sources are listed, it can immediately be seen that a single curriculum cannot be reconstructed out of them. There is a great variety between the sites in the type of texts represented; even when the same texts are encountered, they display recensions that are very different from each other. The circumstances of the transmission and the reception of schooling materials in Late Bronze Age sites are the cause of this situation. Although many if not all of the materials of the curriculum can be ultimately traced to the Old Babylonian Edubba, Late Bronze Age sources were not directly transmitted from the Old Babylonian scribal centers. No doubt Babylonia was the point of departure of most compositions, but certainly many works show various traits (in their writing style or their grammatical features) that indicate the byroads through which they were transmitted. The Middle Euphrates region, Assur or areas under Hurrian influence, are good candidates through which Babylonian scholarly literature reached Ḫattuša, Ugarit, or Emar.

Neither is the time of the transmission of the schooling materials consistent throughout all sites and even within each site. It is clear that in Emar, for example, we have two waves of scribal transmission—an earlier one associated with a particular scribal tradition (the Syrian tradition) in the city, followed by another transmission of scholarly materials bringing to Emar more contemporary or updated schooling materials (the Syro-Hittite tradition). Take the great lexical list ḪAR-ra=*ḫubullu*, one of the building blocks in scribal education. At Emar a Sumerian version and a bilingual Sumerian-Akkadian version were recovered. The Sumerian version is representative of an old tradition (when the list was transmitted only in Sumerian, and the Akkadian translation was probably delivered orally, a situation typical of the Old Babylonian period). The bilingual version is an updated recension of the list; it will eventually become—after more modifications—the standard list used in the education of scribes during the first millennium. The same holds true of the curriculum at Ḫattuša: There is an influx of materials brought to the Hittite capital at different times from various sources.

To this complex state of affairs another problem is to be added. Since we possess few extract or exercise tablets (unlike the wealth of such tablets from the Old Babylonian period) it is very difficult to reconstruct faithfully the sequence in which works were studied in the Late Bronze Age curriculum. The situation however is not entirely hopeless. As will be seen on the basis of a few extract tablets and compilation-like tablets, the sequence of at least one important schooling genre—the lexical lists—can be understood, even if partially.

To summarize, the reconstruction of the Late Bronze Age curriculum depends on textual remains that 1) although recovered from (mainly) three sites, originate from a wide geographical horizon; 2) represent the product of a long development going back to the Old Babylonian period; and 3) are, comparatively speaking, poorly represented by extract tablets and student exercises. The character of the Late Bronze Age materials, exciting as it is, renders the reconstruction of the curriculum a challenging task. These basic considerations will all be reconsidered as I proceed to offer a synthetic view of the curriculum with an eye on the place and role of wisdom compositions. Many of the suppositions that will be put forward here are the result of our fairly good understanding of the Old Babylonian curriculum—it helps us fill in the gaps when information is fragmentary.

We can assume that Late Bronze Age education proceeded in two stages, as in the Old Babylonian schooling system. The first elementary stage of scribal education in Late Bronze Age sites began with the study of a series of lexical lists meant to acquaint the novice scribes with the cuneiform script. The sequence in which these lists were studied can be partly reconstructed on account of a few sources that combine more than one list on a single tablet. Hence we know that first came the basic signs lists like *tu-ta-ti* and the *Silbenvokabular* and then the S^a Vocabulary followed by a list-like text called the Weidner god-list. The sequence of lexical lists that is reconstructed here for the first stage of the curriculum is, however, ideal because not all lists were represented in each of the sites. For example, the basic *tu-ta-ti* lexical list meant to drill students in their first steps in writing cuneiform is found in Ugarit but not at Ḫattuša and Emar. And on the other hand, *Silbenvokabular* is well-represented in Ugarit and Emar but hardly known at Ḫattuša; the same goes for the Weidner god-list—likewise not represented in the Hittite capital but found in the Ugarit and Emar. This may speak for a situation where scribes in each site were educated according to different traditions, some schools utilizing more conservative materials than others. To make use of our previous example, the *tu-ta-ti* list was staple material in the Old Babylonian Edubba but later it disappears from the curricular repertoire in Babylonia. Contemporary Late Bronze Age sites, where this list had long gone out of circulation, made use of other, more-modern lists. Hence the use of the *tu-ta-ti* list in Ugarit, a leftover from earlier times, may be considered conservative. Alternatively this uneven situation may demonstrate that basic learning blocks of scribal education—represented by the lists mentioned above—were simply recycled or thrown away (and there is more to commend for this view for which see below) leaving us with little evidence to reconstruct faithfully the first steps in scribal training. The inconsistency of the extant finds, in other words, prohibits us from determining the finer details of the Late Bronze Age curriculum.

Further complexities arise in reconstructing the first stage (as well as the more advanced stage) of the Late Bronze Age curriculum when we realize that its sources were made up of a variety of traditions that were the result of a complicated transmission process, as mentioned above. An example below from one of the basic lexical lists (the S^a Vocabulary) illustrates the problems. Parallel entries from three different recensions of the list found in Ḫattuša, Ugarit, and Emar are provided here.

ḪATTUŠA

Sumerian	**Akkadian**	**Hittite**	
[BAL]	*[i-t]a-aq-qú*	*i-im-mi-ya-[an-za]*	"mixed"
[BAL]	*[pu]-ú-tu*$_4$	*ḫa-an-za*	"forehead"
[BAL]	*[b]u-ul-lu-u*	*ar-pu*$^!$*-[wa-an-za]*	"unlucky"
[BAL]	*[r]e-e-bu*	*kat-[kat-im-ma]*	"trembling"
[BAL]	*[pí]-la-ak-ku*	[...]	"spindle"

(S^a Boğazköy, KUB 3.95, 12′–16′; MSL 3, 79)

UGARIT

Sumerian	**Akkadian**	**Hurrian**	**Ugaritic**	
BAL	*pí-la-ak-ku*	*te-a-ri*	*pí-lak-ku*	"spindle"
BAL	*na-bal-ku-tu*$_4$	*tap-šu-ḫu-um-me*	*tu-a-pí-[ku]*$^?$	"to revolt"
ŠUL	*eṭ-lu*	*uš-ta-an-ni*	*ba-aḫ-ḫu-rù*	"young man"

(S^a Ugarit, Ug. 5.137 ii 22′–24′; Huehnergard 1987: 38–39)

EMAR

Sumerian	**Akkadian**	
BAL	*pí-la-ku*	"spindle"
BAL	*na-bal-ku-tu*$_4$	"to revolt"
ŠUL	*eṭ-lu*$_4$	"young man"

(S^a Emar, *Emar* 537, 629′–631′; Arnaud 1985–1987: 25)

Notice how the Ḫattuša version of the S^a Vocabulary introduces entries not encountered in the Ugarit and Emar recensions. Different recensions from our sites will demand our attention later on as we look at the corpus of wisdom literature in this study, when, say, a manuscript from Emar will be compared to another at Ugarit. Indeed, the fact that Late Bronze Age scholarly materials consisted of and transmitted different traditions from various places and different periods is not to be ignored as we attempt to understand the literary history of wisdom literature.

I take the opportunity to introduce with this example another typical feature of schooling materials from Late Bronze Age sites, namely, their interaction with the local languages. Observe how the version of the vocabulary from Ḫattuša provides a column in Hittite, while in Ugarit the list is given two additional columns: in Hurrian and Ugaritic (written in the cuneiform script). (For the place of Hurrian in Ugarit, see 1.3). Since some entries in local languages in this and other lists do not faithfully render the original Sumerian and Akkadian entries (especially in lexical lists from Ḫattuša), the question arises of the local scribes' comprehension of what they were copying. This is a complicated issue not directly relevant to our discussion, but it is something to bear in mind when considering the interaction of Mesopotamian wisdom literature with languages other than Akkadian or Sumerian.

The more advanced, second stage of schooling saw the introduction of more complicated lists. Probably studied first was the ḪAR-ra=*hubullu* lexical list (of which are attested unilingual and bilingual versions, as well as a Sumerian-Hurrian version from Ugarit and a Sumerian-Hittite version from Ḫattuša). Interestingly enough on the same tablet as an Emar recension of ḪAR-ra=*ḫubullu* we find a popular incantation known from Mesopotamia and elsewhere. Presumably, the incantation was studied after the scribe learned his lexical assignment. This demonstrates for us that, as in the Old Babylonian schools, by the end of the first stage or at the beginning of the second stage, more complex literary works, such as incantations, were introduced to the students' workload.

To the best of our understanding schooling then proceeded with the lexical lists lú=*ša*, izi=*išātu* and diri=(*w*)*atru*. We may note that in Ḫattuša the more advanced lists are in fact better represented than those typical of the first, elementary stage. The reason for this may be that the more advanced and sophisticated lists—the products of students certainly—once faithfully copied, were treated as archival materials. Hence they were retained in storage, perhaps as master copies intended for future instruction. Lesser, more elementary, materials were simply thrown away.

It can be assumed that scholarly or professional literature was studied after, or with, this more advanced second stage: omen literature, incantations, and magic-medical compositions are all well-represented in the Late Bronze Age sites. Epic literature (common at the more advanced stage of the Old Babylonian curriculum) was probably also studied at this stage. This is where students met Gilgameš (at Ugarit, Emar, Ḫattuša, and also at Megiddo) and Atraḫasis (at Ugarit and Ḫattuša).

Compositions popular in the Old Babylonian period died hard. A small corpus of literary or fictitious letters continued to be studied in Late Bronze Age schools just as they were in Babylonia (although by this period provided with an Akkadian translation). A remarkable piece of this genre was found in Ugarit (a fragment of the work was also recovered in Ḫattuša). The literary letter The Message of Lú-dingir-ra to His Mother is attested in Ugarit as an incomplete four-column manuscript: the first column is in Sumerian and the second in what scholars call Syllabic Sumerian, a fully syllabic writing of the Sumerian to assist students in learning the pronunciation of the signs (to clarify—as we would spell out a certain number rather than write it with a cipher; e.g., "four" vs. "4"). The third column gives the Akkadian translation and finally the fourth column supplies a Hittite translation. A short passage of this composition is to be found below. The speaker here is Lú-dingir-ra, requesting that his mother, who is away, be brought to him. By using highly poetic imagery, Lú-dingir-ra provides a description of his mother according to five characteristic signs so that she be correctly recognized. Here is part of the third sign (the Sumerian column, here broken, is reconstructed from the Old Babylonian version(s), hence its correspondence is not exact):

Sumerian	**Syllabic Sumerian**	**Akkadian**	**Hittite**
[giskim ama-mu 3-kam-ma ga-mu-ra-ab-sum]	[na-aš-ki-ma-am-ma-an-ku eše-qa-ma ga-mu-ra-an-sum]	[gis]kim ama-*mi-ia ša-lu-ul-ta lu-ud-din-ku*	[3-*an-na-za nam-ma am-me-e*]*l a*[*n-na-a*]*n* [GISK]IM-*az me-m*[*a-aḫ-ḫi*]
[ama-mu šeg$_{14}$ ud-á-ba a-numun-sag-ĝá-ke$_4$]	[am-m]a-an-ku e-m[u...] a-ni-ma-za-an-qa-ak-k[i]	ama-*mi ša-mu-tù ši-ma-an me-e* numun *maḫ-ru-ú*	*nu-mu an-na-aš-mi-iš ḫé-uš* [...] NUMUN-*aš me-ḫu-ni ḫa-an-te-ez-*[*zi* A.MEŠ-*ar*]

Sumerian	Syllabic Sumerian	Akkadian	Hittite
[buru$_{14}$ ḫé-nun še$^{!}$ ba-til-la gu-nu si-a]	e-bu-ur za-ar-tap-pa še-a-ag-na ús-sa-a	buru$_{14}$ *nu-uḫ-šu ḫu-un-ṭù sal-tù*	BURU$_{14}$-*an-za-ma-aš dam-me-tar-wa-a*[*n-za*] *še-ep-pí-it-ta-aš-ma-aš mar-ra*-[…]
[^{giš}kiri$_6$ la-la asil-lá si-a]	ki-ri la-li-me a-ši-la [š]a-a	^{giš}kiri$_6$ *la-le-e ša ri-ša-ti ma-lu-u*	^{GIŠ}KIRI$_6$-*aš-ma-aš* GIM-*an i-la-li-ya-an*-[*za*] *dam-me-tar-wa-an-ti-it šu-u-wa-an-za*
[^{giš}ù-suḫ$_5$ a dé-a ^{giš}še ù-suḫ$_5$ šu tag-ga]	a-šu-uḫ ši-da-a še-nu a-šu-uḫ ši-táq-qa	giš ù-suḫ$_5$ *ši-iq-qa-ti ša te-re-en-na-a-ti zu-ʿ-na-at*	^{GIŠ}*šu-i-ni-la-aš-ma-aš* GIM-*an še-eš-šu-ra-aš na-aš a-aš-šu-i-it šu-u-wa-an-za*

'Let me give you a third characteristic sign of my mother:
My mother is rain at the right season, water for the finest seeds (Sumerian) // the first water for seeds (Akkadian) // the first [water] for seed-time (Hittite),
(She is) a bountiful harvest of ripe exceedingly fine barley (Sumerian) // a type of … barley (Akkadian) // *a coo*[*ked*] barley (?) (Hittite).
(She is) a garden of delight, filled with joy,
(She is) a fir-tree from an irrigated plot, adorned with fir-cones (Sumerian, Akkadian) // filled with bounty (Hittite).'

(RS 25.421, ll. 30′–40′ = Ug 5.169 + Laroche 1968: 773–79; Arnaud 2007, no. 50; Klinger 2010: 325–26; ETCSL 5.5.1)

The few lines quoted here perhaps illustrate best the cultural interaction typical of this period (as discussed above in 1.3). We meet on a single tablet the traditional language of learning, Sumerian, translated into Akkadian, the vernacular tongue of Mesopotamia and the *lingua franca* of the Late Bronze Age and then further translated into Hittite. The tablet was most probably copied in Ḫattuša and then sent to Ugarit, whence it was recovered. To remind the reader, in Ugarit, West Semitic Ugaritic, was spoken as well, probably, as Hurrian. Truly a multilingual situation! How The Message of Lú-dingir-ra and other similar compositions fitted in the curriculum at Ugarit or elsewhere at Late Bronze Age sites is far from clear. It certainly is questionable what the Hittite scribes made of a work so full of imagery and symbolism associated closely with Babylonian culture. Nonetheless, this literary letter is not a chance find (because there are others), hence it demonstrates the longevity of Old Babylonian schooling traditions in the Late Bronze Age curriculum. This will be an important factor to consider as we now come to discuss the place of wisdom literature in the curriculum.

Having provided a basic reconstruction of the two-stage Late Bronze Age scribal curriculum, I now examine how proverbs and longer wisdom works fitted in the scheme of things. As noted repeatedly, a confident reconstruction of the place of wisdom literature in the curriculum at this period is hindered by the lack of scribal exercises or literary catalogues (although see below). Nonetheless there are two cases in this study that can provide sufficient evidence and allow me to argue persuasively for a definite role for proverbs in Late Bronze Age education (cf. above, Proverbs in the Old Babylonian Curriculum).

The first example to consider is from Ugarit. An Akkadian-Hurrian proverb extract (2.7) is found written on an atypically small tablet. The entire text contains only two Akkadian proverbs, which were provided with a Hurrian translation. The very fact that the proverbs were translated is a good enough reason to assign to the tablet a pedagogical role. But the shape and format of the tablet also speak in favor of this. This rectangular-shaped tablet with the script running along its longer axis recalls the format of pillow-shaped tablets used by Kassite scribes in their exercises (although these usually combine two different textual genres on a single extract tablet). Its shape, although not identical, is also reminiscent of rectangular lexical lists extract tablets from Ugarit (van Soldt 1991: 751–52; and cf. the photos found in *Ugaritica* 7, pls. LXV and LXVI, etc.). There is no conclusion except that these proverbs played a role in scribal education.

The second example comes from Ḫattuša. KBo 12.128 (2.6 Text A) is a collection of Akkadian proverbs in very poor condition. What is important for the current discussion is that the proverbs were written on a four-sided prism. Although almost totally destroyed, the Ḫattuša prism is reminiscent of a particular educational stage in the Old Babylonian school. After the students learned long compositions by copying blocks of twenty to thirty lines on extract tablets, they proceeded to reproduce the entire composition either on multicolumned tablets or, more rarely, on prisms (these educational prisms are to be differentiated from later-day Neo-Assyrian prisms used in foundation deposits and usually carrying historical inscriptions). This learning process is associated with the second, more-advanced level of Old Babylonian scribal instruction. In Ḫattuša this might not be enough to associate this prism with a particular educational level but there is no doubt that the Akkadian proverbs can be safely considered school exercises. Indeed, other school compositions were also recovered on prisms at Ḫattuša: the "giš" section of the lexical list ḪAR-ra=*ḫubullu* and a literary letter (similar to The Message of Lú-dingir-ra and also known at Ugarit; Civil 2000 and Arnaud 2007, nos. 54–55; see also the discussion about the scribe Ḫanikkuli in 1.3).

As for the longer wisdom works in our collection, *Šimâ Milka*, The Ballad of Early Rulers, Enlil and Namzitarra, and The Date Palm and the Tamarisk, we have no exact idea how they fitted into the curriculum and can only speculate that they belonged to the more advanced stage, like the other more complex works for which we have some evidence. Hence, in order to shed fuller light on the curriculum, I bring into the equation another set of factors. Not only the texts and their sequence, their place of origin and language(s), and their archaeological and archival context are to be studied but also the human factor—the people who produced them are to be afforded space in the discussion. I proceed to a consideration of the scribes of Emar and see if their scribal activities can reveal something of the role of wisdom literature in the Late Bronze Age curriculum.

Wisdom Literature and the Emar Curriculum

Old Babylonian textual evidence permits us to study the exercise copies of individual students. It also enables us to establish their relationships with their classmates, and occasionally, teachers and instructors. In fact Old Babylonian student social networking has proven to be quite instructive with respect to understanding how the curriculum was structured. Late Bronze Age data however are much more limited and are of no immediate help in this respect except in one case. The finds from Temple M_1 at Emar afford us a picture of a scribal school inhabited by students—novice and advanced—and their teachers. These are members of the Zū-Baʿla family, whom we have met before. Letters or legal documents from Temple M_1 help us understand the relationship between the family members; and the colophons inscribed at the end of the family's school texts show us who copied which composition under the supervision of whom. In the table provided below (works given in the left column, authors on the right) pay particular attention to Šaggar-abu and his younger brother, Baʿal-mālik. Both were active scribes, the latter probably also busy in instructing his own sons in the scribal school. Another important figure associated with the family is Kidin-Gula, the foreign teacher who instructed younger members of the family in copying lexical lists.

THE FIRST STAGE OF EDUCATION: BASIC LEXICAL LISTS

The *Silbenvokabular*	Member of the Zū-Baʿla family (?)
The S^a Palaeographic Sign List	Šaggar-abu
The S^a Vocabulary	Šaggar-abu
The Weidner god-list	Unidentified

THE FIRST STAGE OF EDUCATION: EDUBBA LITERARY LETTERS

The Sin-iddinam Literary Petition	Unidentified

THE SECOND STAGE OF EDUCATION: COMPLEX LEXICAL LISTS

The ḪAR-ra=*ḫubullu* list	Šaggar-abu (V^b–VII and XIII) Baʿal-mālik (Tablets I, III–V^a, V^b–VII, and XVIII) Zū-Baʿla (Baʿal-mālik's son?) (V^b–VII and XI–XII) Unidentified students (VIII–IX and XVIII; teacher Kidin-Gula)
The lú=*ša* list	Šaggar-abu Unidentified student (teacher Baʿal-mālik?)
The izi=*išātu* list	Unidentified student (teacher Kidin-Gula)
The diri=(*w*)*atru* list	Unidentified
The níg-ga=*makkūru* list	Unidentified

THE SECOND STAGE OF EDUCATION: PROFESSIONAL AND SCHOLARLY LITERATURE

The *iqqur-īpuš* omens	Baʿal-mālik
The *šumma immeru* omens	Baʿal-mālik Unidentified family member

The *šumma izbu* omens	Unidentified
Celestial omens	Šaggar-abu
	Unidentified family member
Medical omens	Unidentified
Incantations	Unidentified

THE SECOND STAGE OF EDUCATION: EPIC AND WISDOM LITERATURE

The Epic of Gilgameš	Unidentified
The Ballad of Early Rulers	Šaggar-abu
Enlil and Namzitarra	Unidentified
The Date Palm and the Tamarisk	Unidentified
The Fowler and His Wife	Šaggar-abu

Although his colophons are not dated (as sometimes the Old Babylonian colophons are) let us try to trace Šaggar-abu's progress in the school. We can assume that he begins his training by copying the elementary S^{a} Vocabulary proceeding from there to the more complex lists—ḪAR-ra=*ḫubullu* followed by lú=*ša*. He then moves (still as a junior scribe, so his colophon informs us) to copy an advanced piece of scholarly literature—the celestial omens. He presumably ends his training by copying two literary compositions. The first is The Fowler and His Wife, a Sumerian wisdom-like tale (known also from Old Babylonian, Kassite, and Late Babylonian sources); the second is The Ballad of Early Rulers. It is very likely that he was the copyist of other works, perhaps Enlil and Namzitarra or The Date Palm and the Tamarisk, but the colophon is broken away from these manuscripts therefore the identity of their scribe remains unknown.

The training of Šaggar-abu through all stages of scribal education can stand as additional testimony to the place wisdom literature had in the Late Bronze Age curriculum. Even if we are very far off from reconstructing in such detail the stages that scribes in Ugarit or Ḫattuša passed through in their training, it stands to reason that their education was not all that different from what we encountered at Emar.

Seeing schooling materials about which I have talked throughout this introduction directly associated with actual students of one family who copied these texts as part of their tutelage clarifies for us the context in which wisdom literature was used. By observing this family, their relationships, and their products we can see in a concrete way that Late Bronze Age wisdom literature compositions are not simply a jumble of random texts but rather part of a corpus that was copied and studied within a specific social context for the specific purpose of learning the cuneiform script and Akkadian language, and later, controlling the technical applications of Babylonian science (i.e., omens and medicine).

By Way of a Conclusion and Towards a Definition: Wisdom Literature in the Babylonian Stream of Tradition

A literary catalogue from Nineveh (Finkel 1986) provides us with important clues regarding the Mesopotamian view of wisdom literature. The catalogue lists the contents of a series—thus the Mesopotamian designation (és.gàr in Sumerian, *iškaru* in Akkadian)—called "Sidu," after the name of its ancient compiler. It presents us with a list of thirty-five tablets or "works," each work titled after its incipit. The works are wisdom or wisdom-like compositions and proverb collections. For example, one entry names The Farmer's Instructions as the fourteenth tablet of the series. The last tablet of the series, number thirty-five, names The Ballad of Early Rulers, while tablet eleven of Sidu is the Sumerian tale The Fowler and His Wife (also known from a very fragmentary manuscript at Emar; see above).

As Frahm (2010) points out, the catalogue indicates that wisdom compositions and proverbs were not treated as two differentiated genres as we tend of think of them, but rather could have been gathered together under one heading. Indeed, like the Old Babylonian catalogue (see above), this catalogue demonstrates that wisdom texts were thought of as a group. To sharpen this a bit further, the catalogue views all these works as consisting of a single series, an indigenous definition, as seen above. The organization of individual compositions into distinct series is associated with the "canonization" or "standardization" processes, as they are often termed, that Mesopotamian compositions underwent in the Kassite period and later. To name one famous example, the medical omens sa.gig were reportedly organized into a series at the times of Adad-apla-iddina (the mid-eleventh century B.C.E.) by the scholar Esagil-kīn-apli (Finkel 1988). This may imply, although it is not pertinent to our argument, that although the manuscript of the literary catalogue of the series of Sidu is dated to the first millennium it was probably put into writing earlier because it reflects the editorial tendencies thought to have begun in all seriousness in the Kassite period.

It is the scholar Sidu, so Mesopotamian sources wish us to believe, that was responsible for the series. The Catalogue of Texts and Authors (Lambert 1962) is a text that links learned compositions to (probably spurious) authors. In this source, Sidu is identified as a lamentation priest, an ancient wise man probably from Nippur, who put together the series (Frahm 2010). In the famous Uruk List of Kings and Sages (Lenzi 2008), which links illustrious *apkallu* (antediluvian sages) and *ummânu* (wise men and councilors) to Mesopotamian rulers, Ahiqar is named as the *ummânu* of King Esarhaddon; and Sidu is considered to be the *ummânu* of Išbi-Erra, an historical figure, the first king of Isin, in the early Old Babylonian period. The association however between King Išbi-Erra and Sidu (if ever there was such an historical figure) is probably not historical in any sense, and neither is the information that Sidu was responsible for writing or compiling the series necessarily true. What is of consequence in the present discussion is the place wisdom literature earned in Mesopotamian learned traditions. Wisdom literature was collected in a series, considered as a singular corpus, behind which stood an illustrious person, Sidu from the city of learning Nippur, the *ummânu* of the first significant king of Mesopotamia after the fall of the Ur III dynasty. Note in this regard Saggil-kīnam-ubbib, the author of The Babylonian Theodicy, who, like Sidu, is also mentioned in the Catalogue of Texts and Authors (under the name of Esagil-kīn-ubba; see Heeßel 2011: 194).

Wisdom literature did not stand alone in the Mesopotamian world of learning but rather closely communicated with other learned textual genres, and as such may be considered as part of the Babylonian stream of tradition. Words or sentences from wisdom compositions such as The Fable of the Fox (a work also mentioned in the Catalogue of Texts and Authors; see also 1.1), the famous *Ludlul Bēl Nēmeqi,* and yet again the series of Sidu, were explicitly quoted in textual commentaries—a genre meant to explicate difficult words or passages in other learned texts, such as omens or medical texts (Frahm 2011: 102–3). The textual commentary was a place where genres meet in order to explicate texts and produce in this process new meanings. Finding the use of wisdom literature in such exegetical works may highlight for us its role in Mesopotamian thinking. Perhaps rather than maintaining an image of wisdom solely learned for the sake of morally improving oneself, we should also think of wisdom as a means of achieving scribal education and erudition, and on a higher level, as a source of exegesis, just as the book of Proverbs was used in Talmud tractates to explicate select passages from the Bible.

Mesopotamian wisdom compositions were studied in schooling contexts along side and in close interaction with other textual genres. They played a significant part in the Old Babylonian school curriculum and continued to be studied in Kassite Babylonia and the Late Bronze Age sites into first-millennium Assyria and Babylonia almost to the very end of cuneiform culture. They achieved their "canonical" or "standard" versions by virtue of continuous copying and study, and reached eventual serialization, as far as the evidence allows us to judge, like other learned genres such as omens or lexical lists that stand at the core of Mesopotamian learning. At some point in this long process, wisdom literature, once collected as a solidified work, came to be considered as the work of Sidu, a famous scholar, just as other compositions were attributed to illustrious scholars.

The purpose of chapters 3, 4, and 5 of part 1 was to set the historical, social, archaeological, archival, and curricular settings of wisdom literature in the Late Bronze Age. The goal was to afford the reader a better appreciation of wisdom compositions in their ancient Near Eastern context, as a background to the Late Bronze Age wisdom literature compositions presented in part 2.

Further Reading

For general introductions on schooling and education in Mesopotamia, see Civil, 1992, 1995; Waetzoldt and Cavigneaux 2009. For the Old Babylonian curriculum, see Delnero 2010a; Robson 2001; Veldhuis 2011; Tinney 2011; George 2005. For the purpose of the Old Babylonian catalogues and their assistance of reconstructing the Old Babylonian curriculum, see the criticism of Delnero 2010b. For wisdom literature and its interaction with other genres, see Veldhuis 2000a; Taylor 2005; Krebernik 2004; Hallo 2010a(=1990); Gabbay 2011.

For wisdom literature in Kassite Babylonia, see Sassmannshausen 2008 and Veldhuis 2000b. For scribal activity in Middle Assyrian Assur, see Wagensonner 2011; Pedersén 1998: 80–88. A detailed study of schooling at Emar is Cohen 2009; also worthy to consult is Cohen and D'Alfonso 2008. Van Soldt 1995, 2011, 2012 deal with many aspects of Babylonian literary culture in Ugarit; see also the studies in Watson and Wyatt 1999. For Ḫattuša, see Klinger 2010, 2012; Weeden 2011a. Canonization in Mesopotamian literature is dealt by (selected studies) Hallo 2010b(=1991); Hurowitz 1999; Lieberman 1990. For the question of genre and wisdom literature, see George 2007a; Vanstiphout 1999a, 2003; and the studies cited in 1.2.

Part 2
Late Bronze Age Wisdom Compositions

2.1

Šimâ Milka, or The Instructions of Šūpê-amēli

The wisdom composition *Šimâ Milka* ("Hear the Advice"), also commonly named The Instructions of Šūpê-amēli, delivers a string of proverbs framed by the narrative device of a debate between a father and his son. After a brief introduction, the first and major part of the composition provides a set of instructions and admonitions spoken by a father, perhaps on his deathbed, named, or possibly titled, Šūpê-amēli ("most famous of men"), to his unnamed, presumably eldest, son. Hence, as previous scholarship has suggested, the father's instructions or admonitions may be characterized as his will. The sayings are mostly concerned with the mundane world of travel, trade, marriage, agriculture, legal disputes, and general conduct, but there is also some concern for religious piety, as far as can be understood from the broken passages. As in the Sumerian composition The Instructions of Šuruppak (about which more will be said below), the instructions of *Šimâ Milka* were not aimed at a particular social class such as the ruling elite or related in any immediate sense to the world of learning and the scribal school—rather they apply to "everyman." In this respect, it can be argued that *Šimâ Milka*, like The Instructions of Šuruppak, no longer reflected a genuine concern for the realities of life but simply collected fossilized proverbs or sapiential sayings that were of little practical use to those who studied them (Alster 2005: 35, n. 19; see also Civil 1994: 3–4). Some of the father's instructions or admonitions include no more than a line, others stretch over several lines that form short prose passages. It is difficult to estimate exactly how many instructions were delivered to the son, since some parts of the composition are broken away.

The second part of the composition, which is much shorter, includes the son's reply to his father. He rebuts his father's advice, rejecting his instructions by offering a string of sayings that reflect his own attitude to life. The son's nihilistic reply follows a sapiential vanity theme, which I have introduced already in 1.2 and which we will meet elsewhere in this book. The son expresses the opinion that nothing is of value and that life is short in comparison to death. After the son's speech, the composition closes with the line "the father (and) his son debated this debate," as far as its last line can be understood.

Šimâ Milka is only known from manuscripts that come from outside of Mesopotamia. The composition was recovered from the Late Bronze Age archives of Ugarit, Emar, and Ḫattuša. Unlike The Ballad of Early Rulers, or Enlil and Namzitarra, to date neither Sumerian forerunners nor Akkadian copies of later or earlier versions of this composition have been found in Mesopotamian scribal centers. Nonetheless, in spite of this state of affairs, there is no doubt that the composition was known in Babylonia in some form or another prior to its transmission to the western sites. We know this because it is named in an Old Babylonian catalogue of literary works. The mention of the composition provides us the evidence that it was in existence already at this early period. We will deal with this issue more thoroughly in the discussion below.

Šimâ Milka is also the longest wisdom literature composition ever to have been found in sites outside of Mesopotamia. When complete it would have stretched out to over 150 lines running on four columns, two on each side of a single tablet. Since its discovery it has undergone several annotated editions and benefited from a few translations, some quite recent. In spite of this state of affairs, there is no call for optimism. Our understanding of this important composition is still partial and it reveals much less than we would like it to for several reasons. First, the condition of all manuscripts is rather poor. Not only are whole parts of the composition lacking, but some of the better-preserved sections are also quite broken and their sense can be arrived at only by the juxtaposition of lines from various manuscripts. Even then, many lines remain incomplete, leaving their reading very insecure. Secondly, poetic units were not properly arranged on the tablet line by line, in contrast to Mesopotamian manuscripts, where this principle was usually adhered to (especially in first-millennium manuscripts). This makes it difficult to gain a clear idea where one unit ends and another begins. Hence, it necessarily affects our understanding of the piece: how are we to know when a new instruction begins or ends? There is also the likelihood that the composition was not fully understood everywhere it was copied, with the result that there are mistakes interspersed in the work. Any misunderstanding of the work was not necessarily solely the fault of the scribes from Ugarit, Ḫattuša, or Emar. The mistakes in the copies could have occurred during the long transmission process, even in Babylonian scribal centers, many years prior to the composition's reception in the Late Bronze Age sites. Lastly, we must acknowledge that many of the instructions are truncated or abbreviated, as we will see in greater detail below. This surely presented a difficulty for scribes who were not intimate with the wisdom of Babylonia and obviously nowadays hinders our interpretation of individual sayings.

Before proceeding to provide our text edition and translation, textual commentary, and discussion, it is important to offer a brief description of the sources of the composition as well as the history of its modern reconstruction, so that the reader will be in a position to appreciate how far we are from a proper grasp of many of the details found in this major composition.

The Sources of *Šimâ Milka*

Three sources of *Šimâ Milka* derive from Ugarit. The first substantial manuscript of the composition to be published—a two-column Akkadian text, not wholly preserved—was edited and supplied with a commentary by Nougayrol (1968) in *Ugaritica* 5 as no. 163 (= RS 22.439). To this single manuscript, Arnaud (2007) added two fragmentary, previously unpublished two-column tablets from Ugarit (RS 94.2544+ and RS 94.5028). The two new Ugarit manuscripts are crucial, for in spite of their poor condition, they help us restore previously missing parts and supply some hitherto unknown lines that further our understanding of the piece as a whole.

Multiple fragments derive from Emar. These in all likelihood originally belonged to a single two-column manuscript, written in the so-called Syro-Hittite script. There is no colophon, but the tablet was probably copied by a member of the Zū-Baʿla family. The Emar materials were first edited by Arnaud (1985–1987, nos. 778–780). The Emar recension is of course a welcome addition that improves our understanding of the piece.

A single incomplete manuscript made up of two large pieces was recovered from the excavations at Ḫattuša. The first piece, KUB 4.3, was published as an autograph by Weidner in 1922; it was recognized to join another fragment, KBo 12.70, published also as an autograph by Otten in 1963. The Ḫattuša manuscript is a bilingual two-column tablet. The Akkadian is found on the left column but it is rather badly preserved; the Hittite translation, in a somewhat better condition, is given in the right column. The Ḫattuša tablet contains the second half of the composition. Its first half probably was copied onto another tablet, now lost. Laroche (1968) edited and translated the Hittite of the Ḫattuša manuscript as an appendix to Nougayrol's (1968) edition of the Akkadian recension from Ugarit.

In the wake of the publication of the Emar recension by Arnaud, there were renewed attempts by Dietrich (1991), Keydana (1991; only the Hittite version), Kämmerer (1998), and Seminara (2000) to edit and translate this difficult composition. Two recent translations have relied on these editions, namely, Foster 2005 and Hurowitz 2007. However, with the recent edition of Arnaud (2007), who supplied us with two new Ugarit manuscripts, former editions and subsequent translations have now proven wanting. Improvements can be made to Arnaud's own edition and these inform our present rendering of the text (and see already Sallaberger 2010).

With all this said, my attempt can be considered as provisional and tentative as the others, for any future treatment of this text may undermine the

---

Text

Prologue

1 *šimâ milka š[a] Šūpê-amēli*
2 *ša uzna iptû Enlilbanda*
3 *emqa milka Šūpê-amēli*
4 *ša uzna išrukuš(u) Enlilbanda*

5 *ina pîšu uṣû paraṣ ūmī aḫirâti*
6 *ana nišī dalāl[a uš]birra*
7 *ana! bukri ittaṣi milikšu*
8 *izzakkara kabtat[a] taslīta*

Šūpê-amēli's Instructions

9 *mārī ēdukkama i-na-mu-ú araḫka*
10 *ālik urḫi ēzib [me]kītišu!*
11 *ēdukkama tekteṣer tallak*
12 *mekīti! ṣēri tartaši ta[...] ṭēmānnû*
13 *qadu šārī parganiš* du-*ka šaknū*
14 *u atta itti ti[lla]ti šipirka tutīr*
15 *ālik itti ibri [...] rēšu*
16 *ālik itti ummāni tukultu ittišu illak*

present interpretation. In this rather precarious situation, I have taken the precaution of including only the (relatively) more secure lines, even at the risk of an incomplete presentation. Note that the line numeration of this eclectic edition does not represent the actual line division on individual tablets (except for the Hittite translation); fragmentary or broken lines are counted here only to give the reader a sense of how much is lost of this composition, but again these are only approximate estimates. I believe that these compromises have to be made for the sake of a comprehensible and accessible text and fluent translation of this major work.

Translation

Prologue

1 Listen to the advice of Šūpê-amēli,
    2 Whose ear Enlilbanda opened,
3 (listen to) the profound advice (of) Šūpê-amēli,
    4 to whom Enlilbanda granted wisdom,

5 and from whose mouth came forth guidance for days to come,
    6 Among the people *he made his praise live long*,
7 *To* (his) son, his counsel came forth,
    8 as he speaks a weighty petition.

Šūpê-amēli's Instructions

9 "My son—for you alone, your moon stops shining,
10 The traveler leaves his [*ha*]*bits*[!].
11 Alone, after you have made ready, you will leave,
12 You will have acquired the *habits* of the steppe, *but will you … wisely*?
13 With the winds to pasturelands your *ways* are established,
14 And with *help* you will have *accomplished* your task.
15 The one who goes with a friend will *succeed*,
16 The one who goes with a crowd, help goes with him.

17 *e te[rd]i māru ina bīt qerīti*
18 [...] ... *kâta mušamriṣ(i) libba*
19 *ul [talī]ak māru itti ṣābē dabābi*
20 *taḫarri bubūtka taḫaddi šikra*

21 *ina sūqi mēteqi rebbāti aya ubla pâka*
22 *ṭupul nišī e taqbi*
23 *tappa la tappašu e tappulšu*
24 *ul ittaṣi*[!] *mê pîka* (var. *pîšu*)

25 *tarašši bilta biltu ḫarruptu*
26 *šuttatu ekeltu* (var. *eṭêtu*) *nukurtu ša la napšāri ibissû niṭil īnī*

27 *e tešši īnīka ana aššat amēli*

28 *ana šupšuqti ša āl Uruk parikti dīni*

29 *kīma ša bā'irimma parikta šēt*

30 *ša urḫu qīššu šalimma la ibšû mūti*

31 *šumma iṣṣa[btū]šu immati umaššarūšu ittēltašu*

32 *itti ili tarašši arna*

33 *šuttatī mala ikšud kibsa*
34 *nēmela mala ša šanīti* (var. diri [...*š*]*anûtu*)
35 *ana nammalti qaqqari tiša arḫī* (var. *teš*(*e*) *ūmī*)

36 (*zuqaqīpu*) *izqut ana ziqtišu mīna ilqe*

37 *iḫḫaz* (*ḫarimta*) *ul ibâr* (*āḫissa*) (*ana bīt irrubu*) *iša*[*ppuḫ*...]

17 Do not proceed, (my) son, into a tavern,
18 … over you, will cause your heart to be sick,
19 (For otherwise,) O son, are you not joining a band of slanderers?
20 You will *satiate* your hunger, enjoy (your) beer.

21 In the street, the passageway, the city quarter, your mouth will not speak (in vain).
22 Don't speak the disgrace of (other) people.
23 Don't *disgrace* a friend in front of somebody who is his enemy.
24 *Do not speak in vain.*

25 You will acquire a yield—but it will be an immature yield,
26 a dark pit, an irreconcilable enmity, sudden losses.

27 Don't covet another man's wife.

28 Upon difficulties (in birth) in Uruk—'Injustice' in the course of justice.

29 Avoid an obstacle as (you would avoid) a hunter's (snare).

30 The one who has been granted a journey is safe, (*he is the one who*) *does not have* (*anything of*) *death's.*

31 *If somebody's caught, he always will be released the first time.*

32 You will suffer the punishment (delivered) from (your) god.

33 My trap—as much as it traps the footstep (of an approaching animal)—
34 (did it achieve) additional profit as is (possible) in other ways,
35 when (it entrapped) the beasts of the land for nine months (var. nine days)?

36 (A scorpion) stings—but what will it gain by stinging?

37 If he marries (a prostitute), he (as her partner) will not last long (because) she will squand[er (the wealth of the household into which she enters)].

38 *addar ul aṣṣub* (*dama*) *ul aššuk šīra*
39 *ul umalli pî*[*yama…*] *ākil karṣi mīna ilqe*

(about six fragmentary lines)

47 [*…*] *iriqqā*! *šinnā*

48 *akul šīra* [*…*] *eṣemta ana kalbi tīr*

49 [*…*]*…ana ili elû*

50 *gišimmaru šukî ili*

51 *gašīša aya imḫaṣ šumēlû alapka*

(One fragmentary line)

53 *māru la ašru murru*[*q…*]
54 *aplu uppulu ibissû da*[*nnātu*]

(Two fragmentary lines)

57 *mārī itti ša iṭe‹nnū›*! *ṭêna e tamlula*

58 *luppun eṭūli itti šībūtī e tēpuša*

59 *namūt*(*i*) *ili ša la tal-ta-ka-áš*! *e taqbi*

60 *mala malki lu emūqāka itti bēl emūqi la taktappil*

61 *palga rapša* (var. *īka* ⸢*rapalta*⸣) *la tašaḫḫiṭ*
62 *tukassas ramānkama tarašši simma immarkama asû emqu uḫaṭṭâ*

63 *aššum laḫri u puḫādi ana mê šatê šamma akāla*! *innaddā ina šul*[*mi*]

64 *ana muḫḫi simti isimmāna* [*e*]*siḫma la tapallaḫma*! *nēbeḫa teddeq*

38 I am reverent—I did not suck (the blood), I did not bite into the meat,
39 I did not fill [my] mouth [with…]. A slanderer—what did he gain?

…

47 […] … the teeth will be idle (after dying).

48 Eat the meat,[…] throw the bone to the dog.

49 …to the god…go up…

50 The date-palm is the door-post of the god.

51 Your left-hand ox should not crush the stake.

…

53 A *dishonest* son is *free from* …
54 A late heir—losses!, har[dship]!

…

57 My son do not plunder *from those who grind flour (for food rations)*,

58 Impoverish neither young nor old.

59 Do not mock a god whom you have not *provided with provisions*.

60 As much as your strength is of a king, do not grapple with a strong(er) man.

61 Do not jump over a wide canal!
62 You will hurt yourself and you will have a wound. A wise doctor will inspect you but *misdiagnose* (you)!

63 *Because sheep and lamb have to drink water and eat fodder, they must be put to pasture in peace.*

64 Assign food-provisions (for travelling) up and above what is necessary, so that you will not have to worry and fasten the belt.

65 *ana aššati* (var. *ana amti*) *ra'īmtika e taptâšši libbaka*
66 *kunuš* (*iqabbi*) *lu šabsat lu tīšu nāmušta ina bīt kunukkika*
67 *qereb kīsika aššatka aya ilmad*

68 *ultu panama iškunū panûtuni*
69 *abbūni* [...]... *izuzzū milka*
70 *irtû te*[*mmen ab*]*ni*$^{?}$ *ukinnū qulla*$^{?}$ *ṭiṭṭa ipḫû kunuk qulli*

71 *ritima sikkūra limi qulla bītka uṣur*
72 *lu kunukka lu pīt qaqqad k*[*aspika*]
73 *mimma ša tammaru ezib ina libbi*[*šu*] *ibašši ḫišiḫtakama ta*-x[o]-
˹*qi*˺-*ši*
74 *immatima nišū kî ištammâ*

75 *murrurta ša pî ezib e tāḫuz*
76 *murrur*[*ta*] *ša pî taḫḫaz e takkud kapdā*[*ti*]
77 *inazzaq libbu tušša* [...] *mārī*

78 *itti abi u ummi lil*[*lik*$^{?}$ ...]

(There is a gap of an unknown numbers of lines in our textual reconstruction here; only very poorly preserved lines are available in the Emar and Ugarit manuscripts).

79′ ... *lu šēṭūtu*

80′ *iṭṭapil kigallu mēš rubu izzabbal amtu* (*iqabbi*)

81′ *ša arrēšēti šūtur* igi *ša agri murtappidi*
82′ *idūšu gamrū quṭṭûma ašrū*...

(The next five lines are very fragmentary hence they are supplemented by the Hittite text)

65 Do not open your heart to your beloved woman (var. girl):
66 'Submit!' (she will say). Even if she will be angry, hold (your) gift in your sealed store-house.
67 Your wife shouldn't discover what's inside your pocket.

68 Since days of old, (thus) our ancestors established,
69 Our fathers *shared counsel…*,
70 They set up a *fou*[*ndation of sto*]*ne*, they set up the *lock*. They sealed the seal of the lock with clay.

71 Drive (the lock) into the bolt, surround (with clay) the lock, protect your house!
72 May your seal be the only access to [your silv]er capital.
73 Leave inside (your house) whatever you see fit. There will be (enough) for your needs, you will … for her.
74 People have always thus *constantly obeyed.*

75 Ignore bitter words—do not heed (them).
76 Should you heed bitter words—do not worry about *evil plots*,
77 (For your) heart will grieve … slander … my son.

78 *May he go* with (his) father and mother …

…

79′ … May (these things) be scorned.

80′ The pedestal (of the god's statue) was shamed, the prince—despised. The slave-girl (will say): 'It will be performed' (when it is not).

81′ (The wages) of an *errēšu*-tenant are higher than (those) of an itinerant hireling—
82′ his wages are gone, finished or *rationed…*

…

Hittite Parallel Text A (KBo 12.70 obv.! ii 6′–11′= ll. 83′–87′)

attit=ten=ta peran le [*kuiški*] / *ḫurdai annaš=ma=ta* x x [...]
nu=šši=kan lē šulliyaši /
nu=tta=kkan addaš=daš [*ḫurd*]*aiš* / *lē ari šuppayašš=a=ta=kkan* DINGIR.MEŠ.MUNUS-*aš* / *ḫurdaiš lē ar*[*i*]

88′ [*nidni ḫar*]*imti tanad*[*dinšu*...]
89′ *nid*[*na la tanaddinšu ana ḫarr*]*āni ša la* [*tīdû*] *iša*[*ppar*]*ka*

90′ *ākul akla u*?
91′ [...*la mitḫā*]*riš am*[*ēla*...] *ina āli ša la tīdû lāpit qēmi ubbalka*

Hittite Parallel Text B (KBo 12.70 obv. ii 12′–16′ + KUB 4.3 ii 3′–5′= ll. 88′–91′)

nu=tta tarrun šašdan wekzi / ⸢^{MUNUS}KAR.KID⸣-*dann=a=ta wekzi* / *nu=šši ḫappir pe*[*ški maḫḫan*] /
ḫappir=ma natta pešk⸢*iwar*⸣ / *natta šekkantan=*[*ta*] *palšan uiya*[*zi*]

azzikši=ma=za kuwapi nu antuḫšan lē / ⸢*šar*⸣*ganiyaši natta šekkanti=tta* / *ḫappiri wagāiš arnuzi*

92′ *ina rēš* [*eqli*]*ka būrta la teḫerri*!
93′ *ina rēš* [*eqli*]*ka būrta teḫerri*!*ma* (var.: *ibaššima*) *tūta*⸢*ššar*⸣ *šēpīka* [*n*]*akrāti ina eqlika*
94′ *kâta īṣ*[*ūt*]*u šūrubtu*! *ša muṭêti* (var.: [*š*]*ulpika ḫummuṭāti*)
95′ *u ak-kâša ušeṣṣû ina māmīti* (var. [*iš*]*addadūka ana māmīti*)

Hittite Parallel Text A (= ll. 83′–87′)

Let [no one] curse your father in front of you; (your) mother for you […].
Do not behave disrespectfully *to her*.
May the curse of your father not reach you and also may a curse of the pure goddesses not reach you.

88′ You will pay for him the [wages of a *who*]*re*.
89′ [(If) you will not pay for him] the wages, he will send you upon a road with which [you are unfamiliar].

90′ Eat the food,
91′ *but if you do not share with the person* (*your food*)…, the flour weevil will send you to a city with which you are not familiar.

Hittite Parallel Text B (= ll. 88′–91′)

If he seeks out a spread-out bed(roll) from you and he also seeks a ⸢prostitute⸣ from you, give him the price.
But [*when*] the price is not *given*, he will send you on an unfamiliar road/journey.

Do not *tear* a person *apart* (from food?), while you are eating.
(Otherwise), the flour weevil will transport you to an unfamiliar city.

92′ Do not dig a well at the head of your [field].
93′ (If) you dig a well at the head of your [field], (var.: or there is one there already) you will be letting your hostile feet (i.e., strangers) roam free through your field.
94′ Losses, deficient yields will be upon you (var.: your area under cultivation will be burnt)—
95′ Then you'll be brought under the oath (to stand trail).

Hittite Parallel Text C (KUB 4.3 obv. ii 6′–10′= ll. 92′–95′)

A.ŠÀ-*ni=ma=za=kan anda* TÚL-*tar lē iyaši* /
mān=ma=za=kan A.ŠÀ-*ni=ma anda* TÚL *iyaši* / *nu=za=kan*
LÚ.KÚR-*aš* GÌR-*ŠÚ anda tarnatti* /
nu A.ŠÀ-*aš=tiš ḫallanniyattari* / *ištalkiyattari*
tuk=ma lingai / *šallanniyanzi*

96′ *e tašām* [*al*]*pa ša dišāti*? *e tāḫuz batulta ina isinni*
97′ [*alpu marṣumma*] *idammiq ina kašād*? *simāni*

(ll. 98′–100′ are very fragmentary but the content of the passage is not lost due to the Hittite translation given below)

Hittite Parallel Text D (KUB 4.3 obv. ii 12′–17′ = ll. 96′–100′)

ḫamešḫi=za GU_4-*un lē wašti karšaten=ma=za* / *galšitarwanili*
lē! *datti*! *maršanza* / GU_4-*uš ḫamešḫi=pat lazziyattari*
idaluš=ma=za / *karšanza galšitarwanili unuwatar*[*i*] /
nu=za uekantan wašpan waššiya[*zi*] / *kuššanian=ma=za šagan*
iškiya[*zi*]

101′ *e tašām ketṣura*? *amēla*
102′ *šīmšu* ½ (var. ma.na) *kaspi šīm idīšu* ⅔ (var. 4 gín) *kaspi*

Hittite Parallel Text E (KUB 4.3 obv. ii 18′; only a partial translation of ll. 101′–102′)

mešriwandan=za antuḫšan

(Two very fragmentary lines)

Hittite Parallel Text F (KUB 4.3 obv. ii 19′; only a partial translation of ll. 103′–104′)

aran=za ḫaddandan

Hittite Parallel Text C (= ll. 92′–95′)

Do not dig for yourself a well in (your) field.
But if you dig for yourself a well in (your) field and you let the foot of an enemy in,
your field will be trampled down and leveled.
They will drag you away to the 'oath' (to stand trial).

96′ Don't buy an ox during *springtime*. Don't marry a young girl during festival time.
97′ [Even a sick ox] will appear healthy upon the arrival of the proper season.

...

Hittite Parallel Text D (= ll. 96′–100′)

Do not buy an ox in springtime. Do not marry a *karšanza* girl (made up) for a festival.
Even a sick ox will look good in springtime.
An unworthy *karšanza* girl will dress up for a festival. She will dress up in a loaned garment and she will anoint herself with oil that has been borrowed.

101′ Don't buy a professional such-and-such man.
102′ His price is ½ (a mina) (var. one mina) of silver; the cost of his wages ⅔ (var.: four shekels) of silver.

Hittite Parallel Text E (= l. 101′)

A *splendid* person (accusative).

...

Hittite Parallel Text F (only a partial translation of ll. 103′–104′)

A wise companion (accusative).

(About twelve to thirteen very fragmentary lines)

The Akkadian version from Ḫattuša supplies these lines (KUB 4.3 rev. iv):

4 [...] *anāku ištarīti*! *lūpulka*
5 [...]x *u kabtūtka*
6 [...*in*]*a bīt abika nabû šūmka*

(ll. 7–13 in this section from the Ḫattuša version are very fragmentary)

14 [...*ina*] *bīti terrub*
15 [...] *meṭrāta*

Hittite Parallel Text G (KUB 4.3 rev. iii 4 = l. 4 above)

MUNUS*šatuḫen=za* MUNUS-*an*! *lē datt*[*i*...]

(The Emar and Ugarit manuscripts, here more fully preserved, now resume)

116′ [...] *tarān* sag.gìr [*tar*]*tâ tarān* sag.gìr
117′ *mārī aššu šumšî tēpuš bīta*

THE SON'S REPLY

118′ [*mā*]*ru pâšu īpuša iqabbi*
119′ *izzakkara ana abišu malki*
120′ *amāt abiya malki anāku ašme*
121′ *abu* ⸢*ina*⸣ *qūlimma amāta ana kâša luqbakku*

122′ *anenna summatu dāmimtu*! *iṣṣuru murtappittu*
123′ *ša alpi danni alê bīssu*
124′ [*ša dam*]*dammatu anenna mārūšu*

125′ [...]... *Šamaš rēṣ sabsê*
126′ *rēṣu Ištar išātu multāṣê‹t› bilat sab*[*sâti*]
127′ ... (not clear)
128′ [*e*]*rrāša ina kirî mušarû inaṣṣar*(*u*)!
129′ *danna šipir šammi ul ikkal*

…

(Translation of Akkadian from the Ḫattuša tablet)

4 [...] *Would I procure for you an ištarītu-woman* (as a wife)?
5 [...] ... and your honor ...
6 [...i]n the house of your father your name is called.

…

14 ...You will enter the house...
15 ...The irrigation canals...

Hittite Parallel Text G (cf. above l. 4)

Don't take a *šatuḫe*-woman as wife.

(The main sources resume)

116′ [...] a canopy *of*... [You will in]stall a canopy *of*...
117′ My son, you will have built (your) house so you can rest at night."

THE SON'S REPLY

118′ [The s]on made ready to speak:
119′ He speaks forth to his father, the advisor.
120′ "The speech of my father, the advisor I have heard,
121′ Father with great respect, my speech to you I will say.

122′ Where is the moaning dove—the bird that is always on the move?
123′ As for the strong ox—where is its household?
124′ [As for] the mare mule—where are its children?

125′ ... Šamaš is the helper of the obstetricians,
126′ Ištar is the helper, *the fire*? *helping to bring out* the yield of the mid[wives].
127′ ... (not clear)
128′ In the date-grove does a garden watch over (its) cultivator?
129′ It wins no benefit from the hard work of weeding.

130′ [...] *miṭirtumma*! *ul išatti mêša*
131′ [...]... *ṣūmišu šamê idaggal ul inagga*[*š*]
132′ [*Ada*]*d iraḫḫiṣ u ša kabtāti* [*bilt*]*i* (var. [*kabi*]*tta bilta*) *ul ubbal*

133′ *abī tēpuš* ⌜*bīta*⌝
134′ *dalta tulli ṣuppā rupuška*
135′ *mīna talqe*
136′ *rugub bīti*[*ka*] *ēma mali u ganīnšu*! *mali* ^{d}*Nisaba*
137′ *ana ūmi ša šīmtika* 9 *kurummāti imannûma i*[*šakk*]*anū ina rēšukka*
138′ *ina makkurika* (var. *bīti*(*ka*)) ‹‹*ana*›› *līm ṣēnū enzu kusītu* [*zit*]*taka ina libbika*
139′ *ina kaspika ša taršû u qīš‹tu› u bilat šarri* (var.: *kasapkama*! *aṣima*)

Hittite Parallel Text H (KBo 12.70 rev. iv 10′–18′ = ll. 133′–136′)

atti=me pēr=za uetet
n=at marnan / parqanut palḫašti=ma=at 9-*an ḫaštai iyat /*
arḫa=ma=kan kuit datti /
ḫarištaniuš :tarpiušš=a kuieš / ḫalkit šunneššer!
maḫḫan=ma=ta / ^{d}*Gulšaš* U_4.KAM-*uš tianzi / nu* 9-*an aralien kappuwanzi / n=an=ta kitkarza zikkanzi / kartiyaš=taš tarnaz(a)*

140′ *mīṣū ūmētu ša nikkalu akla mā'dū* [*ūmē*]*tu ša iriqqā šinnāni*
141′ *mīṣū* [*ūmē*]*tu ša nidaggalu Šamaš mā'dū ūmētu ša nuššab*(*u*) *ina ṣilli*
142′ *rapšat* ki *erṣētumma nišū inīlū*
143′ *Ereškigal umminima nīnu mārūši*
144′ *iššaknūma ina bābi* ki *erṣēti ṣalūlū*

130′ When the irrigation canal [is empty] and it (the garden) cannot drink its water,
131′ [To (*quench*)] its thirst, it looks up to the sky and does not move.
132′ [If a stor]m devastates it, it does not need to bring in a heavy yield.

133′ My father, you built a house,
134′ You elevated high the door; sixty cubits is the width of your (house).
135′ But what have you achieved?
136′ Just as much as [your] house's loft is full so too its storage room is full of grain.
137′ (But) upon the day of your death (only) nine bread portions of offerings will be counted and placed at your head.
138′ From your capital (var. [your] household) (consisting of) a thousand sheep, (only) a goat, a fine garment—that will be your own [sha]re.
139′ From the money which you acquired either bribes or taxes (will be left); (var.: (so what will become of) your[!] money? It will be lost!').

Hittite Parallel Text H (= ll. 133′–137′)

O my father, you have built for yourself a house
and raised it (as) high as a *marna*-; in width you made it nine (cubit) 'bones.'
But what will you gain?
(You have) storehouses and storerooms which were filled with grain.
But when the fate-goddesses determine for you the days (of death), (only) nine *arali*- (bread portions) will be counted and placed at your head.
This is your lot (lit. "the lot of your heart").

140′ Few are the days in which we eat (our) bread, but many will be the days in which our teeth will be idle,
141′ Few are the days in which we look at the Sun, but many will be the days in which we will sit in the shadows.
142′ The Netherworld is teeming, but its inhabitants lie sleeping.
143′ Ereškigal is our mother and we her children.
144′ At the gate of the netherworld, blinds have been placed,

145′ *aššum balṭūtu la idaggalū mītūti*

146′ [...] *annâ dabāba abu mārušu mitḫāriš* DI-KU

Notes to Individual Lines

1: The prologue (ll. 1–8) and the beginning of the son's reply (ll. 118′–121′) can be recognized as poetic units although, we remind the reader, the Late Bronze Age manuscripts (as some sources from Mesopotamia in this period) do not break up lines according to poetic considerations. This continuous writing without marking syntactical or poetic units is a great hindrance for a secure textual reconstruction.

The verb *šimâ* is taken as singular, although others have suggested understanding it as a plural form; see Seminara 2000: 488 and the remarks of Sallaberger (2010: 307, n. 9). Following Sallaberger 2010, the reconstruction of the first line is secure; see the discussion below.

6: The line is difficult; reading here RS_1 i 6: [*uš*]-*bi-ra* as a Š stem (admittedly unattested) of *bâru* "to make last, endure" (ARG). See also Sallaberger 2010: 305.

8: Following here Dietrich 1991: 38–39 and see also the discussion in Sallaberger 2010: 305–6.

9: The reading and analysis of the verb are difficult; we follow Lambert 2003.

10 and 12: The reading *mekītišu* and *mekīti* follow Arnaud 2007: 162, 10; see also *CAD* M/2, 7 where the rare lemma *mekītu* is equaled in the lexical tradition to *alkakātum* "way, behavior." Dietrich (1991: 40–41) understands this differently.

13: For a different interpretation of this line, see Arnaud 2007: 162, 13.

20: Following *CAD* Š/2, 421.

24: Literally, "The water of your mouth had not gone out."

27: *e teššī* for the expected *e taššī*, lit. "do not lift (your eyes)…."

28: Possibly the meaning of this abbreviated saying is something like "to a woman giving birth in Uruk there was an obstacle in the way of justice," i.e., the stuck baby was preventing a successful outcome, like an opponent in a law case (ARG).

145′ So that the living will not be able to see the dead."

146′ [...] this dispute the father (and) his son *disputed* together.

29: Read here: RS$_1$ i 28: gim *šá* šu-ḫa; RS$_2$ i 13′: *ki-i-ma ša ba-i-ri-ma*; *Emar* 778 21′: [*ki-i*]-*ma šá ba-i-ri-im-ma* "like that of the hunter"; translation after ARG.

31: Following ARG; the Ugarit recension is probably corrupt here.

32: ARG suggests: "(All) you get from a god is guilt."

37: ARG compares the meaning of the verb *ul ibâr* "he will not endure" to Gilgameš's words to Ištar: *ayyu ḫāmiraki ibūr ana dāriš* "What bridegroom of yours endured for ever?" (The Epic of Gilgameš, VI 42; George 2003: 620–21).

47: For the verbal form see below under 140′.

51: RS$_3$ i 14′ reads *ga-ši-ša* (ARG).

53: The interpretation and meaning of the form *ašru* is not certain; see Dietrich 1991: 45, n. 58. For suggestions regarding the form *murru*[*q*], see Arnaud 2007: 167, 54.

57: The reading and translation are very tentative. Reading (with a slight emendation) RS$_1$ ii 6: *šá i-ṭe$_4$-‹nu› ṭì-⸢e⸣-na* … (lit. "who grind a grinding"). Is *itti* (wr. ki) confused here with *ištu*? For other suggestions, see Seminara 2000: 500–501.

59: The verbal form is problematic here. ARG suggests an attempt to write *tultakkalšu* (> *taltakkašš*(*u*)) resulting in the following sense: "Do not mock a god whom you do not feed." For other suggestions see Seminara 2000: 501, n. 72 and Arnaud 2007: 167, 60.

62: The verbal form is from *kasāsu*, "to hurt" (found many times in medical texts; see *CAD* K, 242) with the object expressed in the reflexive *ramānka*, "yourself." This fits the following sentence about the doctor's visit. The verbal form *ú-ḫa-da-a* is found only in RS$_2$; it is missing in RS$_1$, where the proverb is evidently truncated. We take it from *ḫaṭû* in the D Stem, with the meaning "to damage, to injure" but possibly an ambiguous sense is intended here, punning with the verb *ḫâṭu* "to examine, investigate (in the medical sense)." Arnaud (2007: 156, l. 64) translates "le médecin le plus savant t'examinera, sans comprendre."

64: After ARG's reading and translation. The verbal form is difficult. RS_1 obv. ii 15 has *la ta-ta-pal-la-aḫ-ma* and RS_2 obv. ii 10′ *la ta-ta-pal-láḫ-ma*.

66. RS_1 obv. 17 (*ku-nu-uk* "seal!") is perhaps corrupt here.

71: The reading and interpretation of this line is far from secure. We follow here *CAD* Q, 298.

72: With *CAD* P, 446.

73: The final verb is read by Dietrich (1991: 48) as *ta-na-din-ši* for *tanaddišši* "you will give her," but this does not fit the traces; see Arnaud 2007: 151, l. 79 for a different suggestion altogether.

74: We read here with Nougayrol 1968: 279, ii 28 and Huehnergard 1989: 57 *iš-tam-ma* as a pl. fem. Gtn stem of *šemû*, "to hear, to obey."

75: Understand *murrurta ša pî*, literally, "bitter things from the mouth," as "bitter words."

81′: Read RS_3 rev. iii 4′: *šá ar-ri-še-ti*; *arrēšētu* is a different vocalization for *errēšūtu* "tenancy of a field" (*CAD* E, 306–7). It is not clear how igi is to be normalized (a scribal mistake for ugu = *eli*?; ARG) but it serves as a comparative after *šūtur* "higher, exceeding"; Arnaud 2007: 151, l. 88′ takes this line differently.

88′: Perhaps read RS_1 rev. iii 1′: [*nidni ḫar*]-⸢*im*?-*ti*⸣ "[Wages *of a wh*]*ore*"; see discussion below.

Hittite Parallel Text B: see *HW*² Ḫ, 216.

93′: The reading of the verb is not certain. We read here with Seminara (2000: 508) and Dietrich (1991: 50) *tu-ta-*⸢*šar*⸣ > *tūtaššar* but in an active sense. Cf. *šēp nakri ana mātika ūtaššar* "the enemy will run free in your land" (ARG; and see *CAD* U–W, 324).

94′: For the Akkadian of the Ḫattuša recension, we follow here Arnaud 2007: 172, 103′. See Sallaberger 2010: 311 for a different reading.

Hittite Parallel Text D: wr. TÚG-*an* as *wašpan* "clothes" (Acc.).

Hittite Parallel Text G: Reading with *CHD* Š/2, 314–15.

121′: *ina qūlimma* lit. "in silence" but here used figuratively, "with great respect" (ARG).

122′–124′: Reading and translation after ARG. Note *anenna* = *anīna* interrogative "where."

123′: The end of the line confirms the Ḫattuša manuscript (KUB 4.3 rev. iv 23; read previously incorrectly): [*e-ki*]-⸢*a*⸣-*am* é!-*sú* "[whe]re is its home?"

124′: Lack of gender agreement can sometimes be seen in Late Bronze Age compositions; otherwise read *Emar* 778: 90′ [anš]e.nun.na-«tu_4».

128′–132′: Reading and translation after ARG.

130′: The writing *me-eṭ-ri-tu-um-ma* (*Emar* 778: 96′) stands for *miṭirtum* "canal or ditch"; the form is singular.

134′: This verse is made up of the Ḫattuša and Emar manuscripts but the reconstruction here is not secure.

135′: *talqe* for Babylonian *telqe* "you took."

138′: With Sallaberger (2010: 314).

139′: Reading here *Emar* 778: 106′ as níg.‹ba› (for *qīštu*), "bribe, gratuity." Taking the logogram as ninda (= níg), "bread, food," does not yield sense here. Abbreviated logograms are a phenomenon known from this period and area. The Ḫattuša Akkadian version has kù.babbar-*šu-ma* (*kasapšuma*), "his silver" probably by force of attraction, but the sense requires "your$^{!}$."

Hittite Parallel Text H: possibly read ^{GIŠ}*me-na-an* "its face"; see *CHD* L–N, 192; written HA.LA-*za* for possibly *tarnaz*(*a*), "portion" (Kloekhorst 2008: 846).

140′: The verbal form written *ir-ri-qa* (RS_1 rev. iv 4′) or (x-)*ri-qa* (*Emar* 778: 106′) probably stands for *iriqqā* or *rīqā* < *râqu* "to be empty (of food)" or "to be idle (from chewing)" (ARG).

141′–142′: Translation after ARG.

144′: Seminara's (2005: 520) reading of RS_1 rev. iv 9′ as *k*[*ir*$^{?}$ (in order to justify a syllabic writing of the putative word **kerṣētu* in this text) is to be read as ⸢*i*⸣-[*na* (ká) *ir*]-⸢*ṣi*⸣-*ti*. The writing ki *erṣētu* (rather than **kerṣētu*) for "underworld" finds support in the S^{a} Vocabulary from Emar, reading idim = ki *ir-ṣi-tu*$_{4}$; see further on this issue Huehnergard 1991; Seminara 1995; and the following section.

Text Exposition

ll. 1–8

These lines constitute the prologue of the composition. They briefly introduce the father, Šūpê-amēli, and his unnamed son. The opening line, spoken by the father to his son is reminiscent of Prov 23:19, שמע־אתה בני וחכם "Listen my son and grow wise." See below for a wider discussion regarding the identity of the protagonists and the opening scene of the prologue.

ll. 9–16

In this short, loosely connected passage the ways of the traveler are described. The theme of travelling alone (l. 11) is also encountered in The Instructions of Šuruppak.

dumu-mu ki ^{d}utu-è-a-aš
dili-zu-ne kaskal na-an-ni-du-un
My son—to the east—
Don't travel alone.

(The Instructions of Šuruppak, ll. 165–166; Alster 2005: 85 and 152)

The treatment reserved for travelers coming to visit one's town is treated later on in this composition (ll. 88′–91′ and the Hittite Parallel Text B).

Success on a business trip is assured when relying on friends (l. 15); the theme of friendship is also brought up in other compositions, most famously in The Epic of Gilgameš, although not absent from Mesopotamian wisdom literature; cf. in this study, 2.6.

ll. 17–20

Behaving in public—whether in the tavern or in the street—is a matter of concern. The theme is common to wisdom literature because in these situations the individual may have felt somewhat free from restraints once outside the confines of home, hence no doubt in need of fatherly advice. Compare l. 17 to the following saying where a warning is issued against the dangers of excessive drinking that the tavern offers:

ana qerīt aštamme la taḫâšma
šummanna la tenne'il
(If) you do not hasten to a banquet in a tavern—
You will not be bound by a tethering rope.

(Bilingual Proverbs, ll. 9–12; *BWL* 256)

Line 20 seems to say that one should enjoy oneself to one's fill but no more. Note that the word *bubūtu* "hunger" can also be understood as "food."

ll. 21–24

These admonitions prohibit disgracing friends. The proverb of line 24 is not entirely clear; water is used here a metaphor for words, possibly of vanity.

ll. 25–26

The theme of this saying is business losses. A warning is issued against hurrying into business propositions that may initially look promising but then turn out to be loss-making.

l. 27
A typical theme of wisdom literature is encountered in this line. Compare the following proverbs from The Instructions of Šuruppak:

> ki-sikil dam tuku-da e-ne nam-mu-um-KA-e inim-sig-bi ma[ḫ-àm]
> *itti ardati ša muti aḫz[u la t]eṣêḫ karṣ[u ...]*
> Don't "laugh" with a maid who is married—slander will [*spread*].
>
> dumu-[mu] daggan-na lú dam tu[ku-d]a dúr nam-bí-e-gá-gá
> *ina takkanni itti ašti amēli la tu[ššab]*
> (My son), don't stay (alone) with a man's wife in a chamber.
> (The Instructions of Šuruppak, ll. 33–34; Alster 2005: 63)

l. 28
The city of Uruk is the setting but the context of the saying eludes us although there must have been some story behind it. Note that the fact that the city of Uruk is mentioned here does not require that we understand it as the place from which the composition or its key characters originated; see further on this issue below.

ll. 30–31
The meaning of these sayings is not clear.

ll. 33–36
These sayings are concerned with gain by deceitfulness. Lines 33–35 speak of a devious trap that will not provide one with more profit than is obtained in proper ways. As Arnaud (2007: 164) recognized, this proverb alludes to an episode in The Epic of Etana, when the eagle, because it betrayed its friend the snake, was caught in a trap for a period of eight months, until released by Etana. For the episode, preserved in the Old Babylonian version of the myth, see Haul 2000: 112–13.

Line 36 is an example of a truncated proverb. It reads as follows, *izqut ana ziqtišu mīna ilqe* "It stung—but what did it gain by stinging?" The sense of this truncated proverb can retrieved by comparing it to the following saying:

> *[z]uqaqīpu amīlam izqut [m]īna ilqe*
> A scorpion stung a man; what did it gain (by it)?
> (Bilingual Proverbs, ll. 22–23; *BWL*, 240)

As will be seen, some single-line proverbs in *Šimâ Milka* remain senseless until we understand that they are truncated versions of longer and fully expressed sayings. When recognized as such, a recourse to the fuller proverb can provide us with the missing sense, provided of course it is in our possession. Truncated sayings are not unique to this composition but typical of other proverb collections (Alster 2007: 5–6).

l. 37
This is a seriously truncated proverb; only the verbs have been retained. It reads *iḫḫaz ul ibâr iša[ppuḫ...]*, "He will marry; he will not survive; she will des[troy...]." The fuller version from Counsels of Wisdom provides the key to its understanding:

> *e tāḫuz ḫarimtu ... ana bīt irrubu isappuḫ ul ibâr āḫissa*
> Do not marry a prostitute ... she will squander the household into which she will enter; her partner will not last.
> (Counsels of Wisdom, ll. 72–80; *BWL*, 102–3)

The theme of warning against marrying a prostitute for the destruction she will wreak upon one's household is perhaps revisited later in the composition (The Akkadian version from Ḫattuša, ll. 4–6, p. 96).

ll. 38–39
These partly preserved lines are probably truncated quotations from the poorly-known disputation or mock-heroic composition The Fable of the Fox. It involves a disputation between the fox, the wolf, and the dog into which jumps the lion. Following the thread of the narrative of the fable, echoed in *Šimâ Milka*, it seems that either the fox or the wolf was accused by the dog of having eaten the flesh of cattle or sheep. However, the fox or wolf denies this, calling the dog a slanderer (cf. *BWL*, 187 and 202–3, F). All figures remain unspecified in *Šimâ Milka* probably because these lines would have been immediately identified by their hearers or readers.

l. 48
Compare with this proverb from the Sumerian Proverb Collection:

> ur-gi$_7$-re gìr-pad-du nam-ba-an-sì-ge-dè-en
> Don't throw bones to a dog.
> (Sumerian Proverb Collection 5.75; cf. 5.115–116; Alster 1997: 135, 142–43; 405 and 408)

Both proverbs may imply that the dog will become even greedier after feeding than before (Alster 1997: 405).

l. 50
A date palm is heaven's door post (ARG). Compare the saying with this entry from an Emar lexical list (ḪAR-ra=*ḫubullu*): giš gišimmar an-na "the date palm of heaven" (cited in Weeden 2011a: 119). For additional uses of the date-palm in Mesopotamian society and economy, see The Date Palm and the Tamarisk (2.5).

l. 51
The owner is warned against his left-hand ox hitting a stake, probably upon making a turn in plowing. The meaning of the saying is probably "don't take shortcuts" (ARG).

ll. 53–54
These lines (the last two very poorly preserved) seem to discuss wayward or unsuccessful sons. A late heir, born probably after the birth of daughters, will lead to the loss of the heirloom. Is it because everything has already been wasted on the daughters' dowries and the sons' inheritance?

ll. 57–58
The two proverbs are thematically related. The first advises against greediness—plundering possibly food provisions; the second against impoverishing young as old.

l. 60
The advice given to Šūpê-amēli's son is to recognize one's limit of power over greater forces. This theme is also known from The Sayings of Ahiqar:

> With one who is more exalted than yourself, do not pick a *quar*[*rel*].
> (The Sayings of Ahiqar, no. 54; cf. nos. 55–56; Lindenberger 1983: 142; Porten and Yardeni 1993: 44–45, l. 142)

The theme is found also in the Sumerian Proverb Collection but it is developed further and given a twist. Physical strength, although valued, cannot compare to wisdom.

á-tuku lugal ki-in-du-ka
The strong one is king of the world.

á.kal ka lú-ta-àm àm-ku_4-ku_4
Strength comes from a man's mouth.

á.kal igi-gál-tuku nu-mu-e-da-sá
Strength cannot equal wisdom.
(Sumerian Proverb Collection 10.5–7; Alster 1997: 188)

A somewhat similar proverb is also found in The Instructions of Šuruppak, ll. 63–64 (Alster 2005: 69).

In *Šimâ Milka*, the theme of wisdom versus physical strength is not explicitly stated like the second and third Sumerian proverbs above although it is perhaps also alluded to. The collocation *mala malki* "as much (strength) as of a king's" can also be understood as "as much counsel (you may have)." This may turn the meaning of the proverb into something like "as great as your strength is in counsel, do not grapple with a strong(er) man." Indeed note that later on in the composition, when it is the son's turn to speak, the father is called a counselor (*malku*; l. 120′).

ll. 61–62

The warning of not jumping over a canal is given a farcical turn. Hurting oneself will bring a visitation from the wise doctor. And calling the doctor *emqu*, "wise" or "able," is of course ironic for the doctor is obviously not that. The doctor will arrive to inspect the patient only to misdiagnose him. The motif of the foolish or incompetent doctor (which features in fables and proverbs worldwide) implicitly teaches the reader where the origin of real wisdom lies. The doctor's wisdom is contrasted to the profound wisdom (*emqa milka*) of Šūpê-amēli.

Note that the last two proverbs, concerned with the limits of physical strength, are also attested in the collection of Bilingual Proverbs. Compare *palga ul tašaḫḫiṭ* "Do not jump over a canal" (Bilingual Proverbs, ll. 8–9; *BWL* 253; the Sumerian is lost). In the same source, *tuštegger* "you are grappling" (with *CAD* E, 42) is the abbreviated version whose full version is found this time in our composition (l. 60): *itti bēl emūqi la taktappil* "do not grapple with a stronger man."

l. 63

The saying is apparently concerned, as far as can be understood, with taking care of one's herds when putting them to pasture. Note that the reading and understanding of the line are very conjectural.

l. 64

The saying is probably related to the theme of leaving for travel, which we have met at the beginning of the composition (ll. 9–16). Here the son is advised to prepare more travel provisions than is required so that he will feel secure. The *isimmānu*, "a malt preparation," was a base ingredient required for producing a kind of replacement beer when on the road; see Durand 1998: 399 and *CAD* I–J, 193–95.

ll. 65–67

A set of misogynistic proverbs, typical of male schooling environments whether in Mesopotamia or elsewhere; see, e.g., Klein 2003. The son is warned against opening his purse to his wife, regardless of how much he loves her.

ll. 68–74

This rather long and difficult passage speaks about securing one's belongings under lock and key. The method described here is typical of ancient Near Eastern locking practices. The door is sealed with a clay lump, which is stamped with the owner's seal; see Radner 2010 and Otto 2010.

The counsel itself is framed by a narrative that speaks for following the custom of the ancestors, when they established their dwelling (ll. 68–69) and so conforming, if l. 74 is correctly understood, with the way people have always behaved.

ll. 75–77

Earlier in the composition, the son was advised not to speak ill of others (ll. 21–24). Here, should he be on the receiving end, he should ignore bitter words.

ll. 79′–80′

These lines seems to contain a string of truncated proverbs. For one proverb (l. 80′) a fuller parallel proverb could be found:

> ⌜gi$_4$⌝-in al$^?$-⌜tum$_4$⌝$^?$-me na-ab-bé-e
> This is how the maid speaks: "It has been performed (lit. carried away)."
> (Sumerian Proverb Collection, 11.24; Alster 1997: 192 and 423)

Apparently the maid promised to perform a service but had not actually performed it. The rest of the proverbs here remain unclear, but seem to be concerned with the notion, occasionally found in wisdom literature, of the maintenance of proper respect to religion and the authorities. Compare *Ludlul Bēl Nēmeqi*, ll. 12–22 (*BWL*, 38–39) and The Babylonian Theodicy, ll. 212–220 (*BWL*, 82–83).

ll. 81′–82′

These lines comment on the wages of a tenant farmer compared to those of an itinerant worker. Lines 82′ff. remain however partly obscure.

ll. 83′–87′

These lines are very poorly preserved in the Akkadian versions, but the Hittite translation provides what is missing. As best as can be understood, the son is instructed not to allow others to curse his parents. What the Hittite translation means by the "curse of the pure goddesses" is unclear. It is possible that these proverbs are echoing a set of somewhat similar instructions found in other wisdom compositions. Compare the following injunctions from The Instructions of Šuruppak:

> ama-zu-úr inim-diri nam-ba-na-ab-bé-en ḫul ša-ba-ra-gig-ga-àm
> inim ama-za inim dingir-za ka-šè nam-bí-ib-díb-bé-en
>
> Don't speak an arrogant word to your mother; there will be hatred against you.
> Don't take to the mouth the word of your mother and the word of your god (i.e., do not curse?).
>
> (The Instructions of Šuruppak, ll. 265–266; Alster 2005: 98; cf. Sumerian Counsels of Wisdom, ll. 76–77; Alster 2005: 245)

Since the exact meaning of the Sumerian proverb is also not established (see the discussion in Alster 2005: 171), we are yet some way away from a full understanding of the intention of this passage in *Šimâ Milka*.

ll. 88′–91′

The theme with which these proverbs are concerned is the care to be bestowed upon a traveler reaching a strange city. The theme recurs in other wisdom collections. Compare the following proverb from the Sumerian Counsels of Wisdom:

> gir$_5$-tur lú-ra giskim mu-un-èd-dè ninda gu$_7$-ni-ib
> tukum-bi ki-ná nu-tuku ki-ná gar-ì
>
> (Even if it is only) an insignificant stranger who makes himself known to somebody—feed him bread.
> If he has no bed, provide him with a bed.
> (Sumerian Counsels of Wisdom, ll. 174–175, cf. 179; Alster 2005: 252)

The Akkadian of all the *Šimâ Milka* manuscripts is not well preserved. In order to understand properly the proverbs in these lines, recourse is made to the Hittite translation (Hittite Parallel Text B), which, although not in perfect shape itself, is in better condition. I suggest understanding these two proverbs as follows.

In the first proverb of *Šimâ Milka*, apparently one is advised to provide the stranger with a bed and, if requested, to pay the wages of a prostitute for him. The key word for undertaking this proverb is *nid*[*nu*] "wages," or in Hittite version, *ḫappir* "price, payment." The wages probably are those of the *ḫarimtu* or ^{mí}KAR.KID, "prostitute" (the word can be very tentatively restored in the Akkadian manuscript from Ugarit; in the Hittite text, the word is written logographically; its Hittite equivalent remains unknown).

The second proverb is concerned with the feeding of a stranger in town; one is advised not to keep all the food to oneself. The saying is very fragmentary in all Akkadian sources so the translation is *ad sensum* on the basis of the Hittite translation.

In both proverbs, should these injunctions be transgressed the fate of the transgressor will be that of a stranger himself—he will be chased out of town to an unfamiliar road or unfamiliar city. The fate of the unknown traveler or foreigner is well expressed in the following sayings from the collection of Bilingual Proverbs.

gir$_5$ uru-kúr-ra-àm	*ubāru ina āli šanîmma*
sag-gá-àm	*rēšu*

A foreigner in a strange city is but a slave.
(Bilingual Proverbs, ll. 16–17; *BWL*, 259)

ll. 92′–95′

This is an injunction against digging a well at the head of one's field. It is not immediately clear why such an act is prohibited but its consequences are obviously negative and may incur a legal proceeding against the owner of the field. The saying is also found in The Instructions of Šuruppak (preserved here also in its Akkadian version).

> gán-zu-àm pú na-an-ni-dù-e-en un-e ša-re-eb-ḫul-ḫul
> *ina mērešika* [*būrta*] *la teḫerri* [*nišū un*]*akkarka*
>
> Do not dig a well in your irrigated field; (otherwise) people will be hostile to you.
>
> (The Instructions of Šuruppak, l. 17; Alster 2005: 59)

In *Šimâ Milka* the phrase *tūtaššar šēpīka nakrāti* "you will be letting your hostile feet (i.e., strangers) roam free…" is to be understood as synonymous in sense to [*nišū un*]*akkarka* "[people] will be hostile to you."

Although the saying in The Instructions of Šuruppak is not as developed as in *Šimâ Milka*, being limited to one sentence, we can try and reach a better understanding of the sense of this proverb by investigating how it is set with other sayings within the same composition. It is encountered with other proverbs (not found in *Šimâ Milka*) that are concerned with various agricultural and building activities: the cultivating of fields, the plowing of fields, and the building of private dwellings—when, however, undertaken respectively in the vicinity of a road, a pathway, or the city quarter—will lead to conflict and possibly litigation. Understood within its wider context, we see that the proverb describes a situation whereby digging a well in one's field may render the field a property that incurs losses and gives rise to a legal dispute over its ownership.

ll. 96′–97′

Buying an ox at springtime is comparable to taking a young girl as a wife during a festival. In springtime the ox may look healthier than it actually is and the young girl may look to hold more than she actually possesses because of the festive occasion (see Hittite Parallel Text D). This admonition is preserved as a single line also in the Sumerian Proverb Collection (11.150; Alster 1997: 196) and echoed in The Instructions of Šuruppak:

ezen-ma-ka dam na-an-du$_{12}$-du$_{12}$-e
šà-ga ḫug-gá-àm bar-ra ḫug-gá-àm
kù ḫug-gá-àm za-gìn ḫug-gá-àm
túg$^{?}$ ḫug-gá-àm gada$^{?}$ ḫug-gá-àm

Don't choose a wife during a festival.
Inside it is (all) borrowed, outside it is (all) borrowed:
The silver is borrowed, the lapis-lazuli (jewelry) is borrowed,
The *dress* is borrowed, the *linen* is borrowed.
(The Instructions of Šuruppak, ll. 208–212; Alster 2005: 92 and 162–63)

ll. 101′–102′

The state of preservation of line 101′ leaves it uncertain who the person not to be bought is, although it is said that his wages are less than his price. Hittite Parallel Text E, although not broken, is not of much help because its defines this person as a *mešriwanza*, a term whose meaning is opaque to us. Moreover, the Hittite offers only one sentence as the translation of the Akkadian passage, leaving us in the dark as to the exact meaning of this saying.

Various suggestions have been put forward in regards to the identification of the persona behind the Akkadian and the Hittite terms. Some have suggested that this person was a third gender figure in the service of the goddess Ištar but there is no compelling reason to accept this explanation over others. There is no doubt, however, that he was some kind of professional as his title is expressed as an *amēlu* compound (see *CAD* A/2, 52); it is also likely that he was employed in a religious or cultic context, if one investigates the meaning of the Hittite term (see *CHD* L–N, 298–99).

At this point the Emar and Ugarit manuscripts are very fragmentary. The parallel Akkadian version from Ḫattuša includes a saying describing in negative terms the procurement of an *ištarītu* woman as a wife because she may harm one's honor. The *ištarītu* woman was somehow related to the goddess Ištar. She is mentioned in Counsels of Wisdom with other disreputable women that one should stay away from:

e tāḫuz… ištarītu ša ana ili zakrat
Do not marry…an *ištarītu* woman who is dedicated to a god.
(Counsels of Wisdom, ll. 72–73; *BWL*, 102–3)

This idea is possibly paraphrased by Hittite Parallel Text G, where we find the prohibition of marrying a *šatuḫe*-woman. Nothing is known about a *šatuḫe*-woman, because this is the only time she is ever mentioned in Hittite documentation—in other words, this term is a hapax.

ll. 116′–117′

This is where the father's sayings end. The last injunctions forwarded to the son, as far as we can understand, recommend the building of a solid house.

ll. 118′–121′

These are the opening lines of the son's speech, which continue to the penultimate line of the composition. In the Ugarit and Ḫattuša manuscripts (but not in Emar) the speech is separated from the father's instructions by a dividing line.

ll. 122′–124′

The son questions the recommendations of his father in building a household. What is its advantage? The moaning dove roams about from one place to the other, the ox lives alone without a family, and the mule is childless (ARG).

ll. 125′–127′

The mention of Šamaš and Ištar as assistants of male and female midwives is a reflection of the well-known role assigned to these two gods in Mesopotamian belief in producing or helping to produce offspring. Because these lines are however not well understood their intent and connection to the rest of the son's speech remain unclear.

ll. 128′–132′

These lines continue the vanity theme introduced in the son's description of the living condition of various animals in order to question the usefulness of having a household. Here the subject is the garden—unlike the farmer, its existence is passive, it does not have to work for its living: it cares not if there are weeds growing about it, if it receives no water, or a storm devastates it. After all, it does not have to pay rent! (ARG)

ll. 133′–139′

The son now comes to address the father. In a series of pithy sayings he demonstrates how material wealth is actually worthless. By doing so he rejects many of his father's sayings. Building a house (cf. ll. 116′–117′), amassing a fortune in storerooms locked tight (cf. ll. 65–67 and 71–74), and having a thousand sheep (cf. l. 63)—all of these are of no use at the hour of death. Only a burial garment and a single goat (for the funerary sacrificial rites) will be of use—this is what will remain of one's wealth. Even capital saved for future purposes will serve for taxes and bribes and go to waste.

ll. 140′–145′
The son closes his speech by contrasting the shortness of life with the eternity of death, a theme we will reencounter in The Ballad of Early Rulers (2.2). Few are the days we look at the sun in comparison to sitting in the netherworld and few are the days we spend eating in comparison to the days our teeth will be idle.

Finally, the son places emphasis on the strict separation between the dead and the living, a topos found in other Mesopotamian compositions. The underworld where the dead dwell is called here ki *erṣētu*—a Sumerian-Akkadian double name. Compare the opening line of The Descent of Ištar where the Sumerian literary name for the underworld, kur-nu-gi$_4$, is glossed over by the Akkadian *qaqqari* [*la târi*] "A land of no-return." See also the remarks of a similar phenomenon by Michalowski (2011: 29).

l. 146′
The closing line of the composition sums up the debate between father and son.

Discussion

The Origin and Curricular Setting of *Šimâ Milka*

Although the composition was copied in Late Bronze Age sites outside of Babylonia *Šimâ Milka* has a longer history. As Civil (1989: 7) recognized, the composition is mentioned in an Old Babylonian catalogue listing a variety literary works (see ETCSL 0.2.11). The catalogue includes the entry [*ši-me*]-*e mi-il-kam*, a title of a work that is no doubt to be identified with the composition under study because it opens with the same words (in spite of the reservations expressed by Seminara 2000: 488, n. 10). It is very probable that it is by this title that the work was known in antiquity.

Apart from mentioning *Šimâ Milka*, the Old Babylonian catalogue names other compositions that formed part of the Old Babylonian scribal-school curriculum. Some royal hymns are mentioned, but, more pertinent to our discussion, also wisdom compositions. These are the Sumerian compositions The Instructions of Šuruppak, The Instructions of Ur-Ninurta, and The Farmer's Instructions. In the same paragraph which mentions [*šim*]*e milkam*, three incomplete titles of Akkadian compositions appear. They seem to belong to the genre of wisdom literature, although a secure identification with known compositions is so far lacking (Sallaberger 2010: 307–9). Nonetheless, it is a further demonstration that Akkadian wisdom compositions were written as early as the Old Babylonian period. Indeed, although until recently it was assumed that independent Akkadian wisdom compositions only appeared in the Late or post-Old Babylonian period, a recently published bilingual Old Babylonian Sumerian-Akkadian proverb collection dated to the early Old Babylonian period challenges this view (Alster 2007, no. 4). It shows us that the process of translating Sumerian wisdom compositions and, probably a bit later, of composing independent works had already begun prior to the Kassite period.

To conclude, the catalogue demonstrates two things: first that the composition existed prior to the Late Bronze Age and secondly that it originated in Babylonia. It also affords us a view of the curricular setting of *Šimâ Milka*. The composition was considered as part of the scribal curriculum and studied in conjunction, so we can cautiously assume, with other wisdom literature compositions, Sumerian and Akkadian alike. It is therefore of no surprise, as already seen above, that *Šimâ Milka* bears a close relationship to other Babylonian wisdom compositions and other works.

The Chief Characters of *Šimâ Milka*: Šūpê-amēli, His Son, and the God Ea

The composition opens with the line *šimâ milka š*[*a*] *Šūpē-amēli*, "Listen to the advice of Šūpê-amēli." Who is Šūpê-amēli and what does this name mean?

Former opinion was divided as to whether the name Šūpê-amēli refers to the speaker delivering the admonitions or to his son (e.g., Dietrich 1993: 52). However, recent collations of the manuscripts by Sallaberger (2010) seem to have settled this issue. Because the reading of the sign *ša* ("of") in the poem's opening line is now securely established, we are to translate the first sentence as "Listen to the advice *of* Šūpê-amēli." It is therefore obvious that the name Šūpê-amēli must refer to the speaker of the admonitions or the giver of advice, that is, the father rather than his son. It is he who receives wisdom from the god Ea, as the second line reveals. The addressee of the composition, the father's "son," on the other hand, remains nameless throughout the composition.

The name Šūpê-amēli (wr. *šu*-(*ú*)-*be*-*e*-lú-*lì*) is without parallel in other sources, be they literary or documentary. Most commentators translate the name as "most glorious, most famous of men." The thematic similarity between *Šimâ Milka* and The Instructions of Šuruppak (as we will demonstrate below) has suggested to some that Šūpê-amēli was a garbled rendering or an interpretative writing of the name of Šuruppak, or perhaps of that of his son, Ziusudra, "He of long-lived days," otherwise known as Atra(m)-ḫasīs, "Super-sage," the hero of the Flood Myth (Nougayrol 1968: 275–76; Seminara 2000: 490). Substantive proof for this hypothesis, suggestive as it may be, however, cannot be found.

Another suggestion is that *Šūpê-amēli* is not the personal name of the protagonist but his honorific epithet ("*homme exceptionnel,*" so Arnaud in his editions). In this regard, it is worth considering Alster's (2005: 32) recent understanding of the identity of the speaker in The Instructions of Šuruppak, a composition with much affinity to *Šimâ Milka*.

In The Instructions of Šuruppak, so Alster argues, the father who delivers the admonitions remains unnamed, receiving only the title "the man of Šuruppak" (lú Šuruppak), along with a string of other epithets. Hence, properly speaking, Šuruppak is not the speaker's name, but only his title—"the Šuruppakean." As Alster notes, the son also remains unnamed in the older versions of the text, although in the Old Babylonian recensions he is called Ziusudra. One may be inclined to think therefore that if the characterization of the protagonists of *Šimâ Milka* depends on the earlier *Šuruppak* blueprint, Šūpê-amēli is the father's honorific title or epithet. However, some complexity remains. Although "the man of Šuruppak' may have been initially only the epithet of the speaker in The Instructions of Šuruppak, other traditions (as manifest for example in the Sumerian King List) suggest that Šuruppak was understood as the name of the father of Ziusudra. Hence, in Babylonian literary traditions, Šuruppak may also have been a proper name, and not only an epithet. Indeed in the Akkadian translation of the Instructions of Šuruppak, Šuruppak appears to be the name of the speaker, while his son is called Utnapištim, the Akkadian rendering of Sumerian Ziusudra.

If that is the case for Šuruppak in the Akkadian translation of The Instructions of Šuruppak, there is no good reason to suppose, given the relationship between the protagonists of both compositions, that *Šūpê-amēli* was necessarily the epithet of the speaker; it could equally be his name. The son in *Šimâ Milka*, as in the earlier versions of The Instructions of Šuruppak, remains unnamed: his role is merely generic—he is the son of a famous sage from whom he receives counsels of wisdom.

Having discussed Šūpê-amēli and his son, we turn to examine the third character mentioned in the poem—Enlilbanda, the craftsman god, a nickname of the more familiar Ea, the Mesopotamian god of wisdom. The choice of the name Enlilbanda as Ea's nickname is not accidental here. Although Enlilbanda is usually translated as "junior-Enlil," surely that is not the meaning of the name here. The Sumerian word banda means wisdom (equated with Akkadian *tašimtu* "wisdom, sagacity"), hence Enlil-banda is to be understood as "The Enlil (i.e., the chief god) of Wisdom," a suitable choice for the god who bestows wisdom upon Šūpê-amēli.

Ea features in other Babylonian sources as the deity responsible for passing wisdom on to humankind—most famously in Atraḫasis but not solely. In the wisdom composition The Instructions of Ur-Ninurta we find king Ur-Ninurta of the Isin dynasty of the early Old Babylonian period receiving wisdom from Ea in order to govern justly and piously throughout the land (Alster 2005: 227). Most explicitly, in the recently published Old Babylonian work The Scholars of Uruk (about which more will be said below; George 2009, no. 14) the god Ea himself is considered to be the source of all wisdom. He is called an *apkallum*—an epithet usually reserved for the antediluvian sages—and described as *ḫassu*(*m*), "wise."

Mesopotamian Wisdom Compositions and *Šimâ Milka*: Genre, Structure, Key Themes, and Content

As far as we can judge on the basis of the materials at hand, although the structure of *Šimâ Milka* as a debate-like wisdom composition between father and son remains without a parallel, the general structure of admonitions delivered by father to son is not unique, but encountered in other wisdom literature compositions from Mesopotamia.

The Instructions of Šuruppak is the most obvious candidate to have served as a template for *Šimâ Milka* (even if not directly) by the virtue of the fact that it is the oldest Mesopotamian wisdom composition known to us. Manuscripts of the composition, in Sumerian, have been found at the sites of Abu-Salabih and Adab, dating to the early- to mid-third millennium; it is also known from more recent manuscripts, dating to the Old Babylonian period, closer to the time when *Šimâ Milka* was probably composed. In addition, there are two Akkadian fragmentary manuscripts as well as a barely preserved Akkadian-Hurrian version of composition (Alster 2005: 48; Lambert 1960: 92–94). Although these Akkadian manuscripts date to the post-Old Babylonian period, they can safely be considered copies or recensions of older versions from a time when The Instructions of Šuruppak was first translated into Akkadian, probably sometime in the Old Babylonian period. This was the period, as discussed in 1.5, in which such wisdom compositions, as well as the corpus of Sumerian proverbs, were translated into Akkadian (Alster 2007: 96–122).

The Instructions of Šuruppak contains admonitions or sayings (some very similar to those found in *Šimâ Milka*) placed within the frame of a "father to son" discourse (Alster 2005: 47–48; Sallaberger 2010). The introduction to the work, setting the scene in which the admonitions of the father will be delivered, is highly reminiscent of the opening lines of *Šimâ Milka*, as will be demonstrated below. However, in spite of the apparent closeness of the two compositions, we need not assume a direct link between the two. The structure and content of Šuruppak could have reached *Šimâ Milka* through a variety of intermediaries, first and foremost, Akkadian translations or adaptations of the Sumerian composition, for which we have some evidence in hand, and possibly other models, now lost to us.

A remarkable Old Babylonian bilingual composition recently published under the title The Scholars of Uruk is not a wisdom composition (George 2009, no. 14). Nonetheless it shares with *Šimâ Milka* a tone of reproach that the father adopts towards his son, expanding for us the social and literary background of our composition. The composition consists of an address of a father to his son, both apparently learned scholars. In response to a quarrel between the two, the father, while apparently acknowledging the son's scribal abilities, takes measures to remind him not to overstep the line and remember his place in their relationship. The background of the quarrel is not explicitly given but stated in very metaphorical language by which we learn of the son's poor scribal abilities. At the end of composition, which closes remarkably similarly to *Šimâ Milka*, the two reconcile. The Scholars of Uruk, in conclusion, although not a wisdom composition, offers a framework by which we can appreciate better the setting of *Šimâ Milka*: it is a debate between two scholars or sages—an older, more experienced father and a representative of the younger generation, his son.

Consideration of this work also raises the next question. If The Scholars of Uruk introduces a father–son debate and the city of Uruk is also mentioned in *Šimâ Milka* (l. 28), are we to identify that famous Mesopotamian city as the setting of our work? Indeed, it seems to be a fitting location for the piece. However, because the sayings in *Šimâ Milka* are culled from different sources and strung together rather artificially, the city's mention does not necessarily indicate a connection between Uruk and our protagonists. Perhaps if the figures of Atram-ḫasīs or Šuruppak served as their model, the city of Šuruppak may be thought of as a suitable setting for Šūpê-amēli and his son. However, traditions about the locality of the flood and its heroes have shifted with time, relocating to different Babylonian cities (Sippar for example), as these vied for prestige as ancient seats of wisdom. Hence, there is not much in the work to commend assigning it to one Babylonian city over the next. With that said, it should not be forgotten that in Mesopotamian literary traditions Uruk was regarded as the traditional city of learning, the seat of scribal activities during the Ur III dynasty, although by the Old Babylonian period, its role of course was no more than a distant memory, the stuff that myths are made out of (George 2009: 78).

There are other wisdom compositions that, like *Šimâ Milka*, include a string of sayings, one following the other without particular reason. The Counsels of Wisdom, an Akkadian composition of the post-Old Babylonian period, whose beginning is unfortunately lost, contains a selection of proverbs very much like those found in our composition. The work may even have been structured like *Šimâ Milka*, because of the evocation of the speaker's son in one of its passages. Whether it was framed around a father–son debate is not known because its opening and closing lines are missing.

The so-called Assyrian Proverb Collection and collections of proverbs from elsewhere likewise consist of proverbs (either in a bilingual or an Akkadian-only format) that deal with similar themes, but we are not in position to know anything of their narrative structure, if ever it existed (*BWL*, 225–80).

The interrelationship of all these works demands a far more detailed study than can be offered here, so only a few issues are considered in order to illustrate the interconnectedness of the various compositions we have been talking about, as we now turn to discuss the structure, key themes, and content of *Šimâ Milka*.

Šimâ Milka opens with a passage announcing that the father will deliver his admonitions. As suggested above, the opening lines of The Instructions of Šuruppak may have served as inspiration for this passage, even if not directly. The latter work opens as follows:

> In those days, in those far remote days,
> In those nights, in those far-away nights,
> In those years, in those far remote years,
> In those days, the intelligent one, the one of elaborate words, the wise one, who lived in the country,
> Šuruppak, the intelligent one, the one of elaborate words, the wise one, who lived in the country,
> Šuruppak gave instructions to his son,
> Šuruppak, the son of Ubartutu,
> Gave instructions to his son Ziusudra (Akkadian version: Utnapištim).
> "My son, let me give instructions, let my instructions be taken!

Ziusudra, let me speak a word to you, let attention be paid to them!
Don't neglect my instructions!
Don't transgress the words I speak!
The instructions of an old man are precious, you should comply with them!"

(The Instructions of Šuruppak, ll. 1–13; following Alster 2005: 56–58 with slight revisions)

In *Šimâ Milka* the introduction is much shorter. And after eight introductory lines, the father proceeds to deliver his admonitions. In and of themselves, they instruct the son on how to live a good and righteous life by offering advice on what to do when, warning against pitfalls that can occur in various situations. There is no connecting thread between one theme and the next. The instructions however gain coherence when ingeniously juxtaposed with the reply of son. Taken as a whole, they advocate "positive wisdom": by following the father's advice, the son will lead a fulfilled life. The son's reply, in contrast, is a prime example of nihilistic or negative wisdom, which, following Alster's definition, was called here the vanity theme; see the discussion in 1.2 (Key Themes).

After receiving the advice of the father, the son counters with a series of sayings that expose the uselessness of the father's instructions. The father's instructions are in fact pointless because death is fast approaching. Although one may possess wealth, as the son concludes, it will not hinder death's arrival (Hurowitz 2007: 42–43; Seminara 2000: 525–27). His words engage with similar ideas expressed in The Ballad of Early Rulers (2.2) and more poignantly in Enlil and Namzitarra (2.3). Such a discourse can be recognized also in The Epic of Gilgameš, when Utnapištim speaks to Gilgameš about the condition of man. Utnapištim characterizes death as a distant realm from which there is no return; man is destined to die and stay eternally in the netherworld, cut off from the living (Seminara 2000: 526). Compare Utnapištim's speech with ll. 140′–145′ of *Šimâ Milka*:

Man is one whose progeny is snapped off like a reed in the canebrake:
The comely young man, the pretty young woman,
all [*too soon in*] their very [*prime*] death abducts (them).
No one sees death,
No one sees the face of [death],
No one [hears] the voice of death,
(yet) savage death is the one who hacks man down.
At some time we build a household,

At some time we start a family,
At some time the brothers divide (the inheritance),
At some time feuds arise in *the land*....
The abducted and the dead, how alike they are!
They cannot draw the picture of death.
The dead do not greet man in the land.

(The Epic of Gilgameš, X, ll. 301–318; translation following George 2003: 697; see also, 504–8)

In Hurowitz's (2007) analysis of *Šimâ Milka*, the father's admonitions are to be compared to the sayings found in Proverbs, while the son's reply echoes sentiments expressed by Qohelet. One is positive whereas the other is pessimistic. Whether the son represents a newer or more modern approach that stands in opposition to the traditional approach of wisdom is a possible hypothesis. However, it is less clear whether the son's reply is indicative that the work in front of us is a sophisticated parody of the "Instructions" genre, as Seminara (2000) argues. On the face of it, there is nothing in the work itself, apart from one's own interpretative inclinations, to view the work as a parody. The content of *Šimâ Milka*, according to our understanding, does not contain any narratological or other ploy that indicates satire. Even works that may have been written in a humorous vein, such as The Poor Man of Nippur or The Dialogue of Pessimism, resist easy classification in terms of their genre and literary objectives. At any rate, it is important to remember that both wisdom themes—the vanity theme on the one hand and the positive wisdom theme on how to lead a proper life on the other—had a long literary history in Mesopotamia, as Alster (2005) demonstrated. The expression of critical views of traditional (positive) wisdom may have gained a growing popularity in the Kassite period (as Seminara 2000: 526 argues and see below), but there is no doubt that it originated much earlier because it already appears in major Old Babylonian Sumerian wisdom compositions. This new type of wisdom offered a critique of traditional wisdom, but it hardly looks to have parodied the genre of instructions.

Having discussed the structure and key themes of *Šimâ Milka*, there is one further issue that demands our attention, namely, the content of the sayings or instructions that make up most of the composition. As already demonstrated above, it is clear that although many of the instructions or sayings are original to *Šimâ Milka* or at least not known so far from elsewhere, quite a few sayings find parallels in other wisdom compositions. This should not come as a surprise now that we have discussed how *Šimâ Milka* and other compositions share a structural similarity that opened the door for the exchange of individual proverbs between works. From this it can be assumed that some sayings were in circulation among scribal or learned circles, and were fitted randomly into wisdom collection of proverbs, without particular concern for the proverbs preceding or following them. The findings of the same proverbs, for example, in The Instructions of Šuruppak or Counsels of Wisdom need not speak of direct borrowing into *Šimâ Milka*.

The Hittite Translation of *Šimâ Milka*

The Hittite translation of *Šimâ Milka* appears on the right-hand column of a single tablet. As we have seen in our edition and exposition, the Hittite translation can help clarify damaged Akkadian parts whether on the opposite column of the Ḫattuša tablet or in the Emar or Ugarit manuscripts. Although it is sometimes more of a paraphrase than a precise rendering, the Hittite translation remains invaluable in several cases.

Regardless of the precision of the Hittite translation, unexplained is the fact that some parts of the Akkadian composition were either left wholly un-translated or otherwise translated by a single Hittite phrase. A look at the Ḫattuša tablet shows that while the left-hand Akkadian side is fully inscribed, some sections of the Hittite part on the right-hand side remain blank or else inscribed with a single sentence. It is not certain, as is generally assumed, that this was due to a serious inability of the Hittite scribe to understand the Akkadian. It is equally possible that only parts of the instructions were translated in writing, sometimes in summary forms, whereas most of the Hittite translation was provided orally, perhaps as part of the scribes' education in the process of copying the piece. Evidence in support of this claim, with all due reservations of course, comes from a rare exemplar of an Old Babylonian bilingual Sumerian-Akkadian proverb collection tablet. Interestingly enough, like the Hittite translation, the Akkadian translation of the Sumerian was selective. Some of the proverbs were left untranslated, as indicated by the blank spaces of the Akkadian right-hand column (and compare also a Late Babylonian first-millennium Sumerian-Akkadian bilingual proverb with a partial Akkadian translation; Frahm 2010). Alster (2007: 96–122), who published this collection of proverbs, has suggested that the Sumerian column was written by the teacher whereas the Akkadian column was provided only with a selective translation by the student. Hence, some kind of pedagogical purpose may underlie the Hittite selective translation, although note that the two columns of the Ḫattuša manuscript were written by the same hand.

Whatever the reasons for the Hittite partial translation of *Šimâ Milka*, this attempt at providing a Hittite translation of a learned Mesopotamian composition is not an isolated example. Hittite translations of Mesopotamian scholarly materials can be found in various genres: omens were translated and adapted; Sumerian religious literature and Sumerian and Akkadian bilinguals (such as The Message of Lú-dingir-ra to His Mother, a school composition, for which see 1.5) were also provided with Hittite translations. Lexical lists, the building blocks of scribal education, were provided with a Hittite column. And literary compositions of the same level of complexity and difficulty as *Šimâ Milka*, like The Epic of Gilgameš, were also translated and/or adapted into Hittite. (Klinger 2005, 2010 and 2012; Weeden 2011a).

Is *Šimâ Milka* a Syrian or a Mesopotamian Composition?

One of the chief concerns of this book is the origin of wisdom compositions found in Late Bronze Age sites outside of Mesopotamia: Are the works Mesopotamian compositions or local Syrian creations? In this section I will try to answer this question in regards to *Šimâ Milka.*

As argued above, there is no doubt that although copies of the composition were not found in Mesopotamia, *Šimâ Milka* can be considered a Babylonian work. This is because its opening line is mentioned in an Old Babylonian catalogue of literary works. The question however is whether this piece, once transmitted to the Late Bronze Age sites, underwent serious modifications so as to render it almost completely a new literary product of Syrian scribes active in Emar or Ugarit. At the close of an edition and detailed study of *Šimâ Milka*, an affirmative answer to this question was advocated by Seminara (2000). He rested his opinion that the composition is a native Syrian work on two intertwined arguments: on the one hand the internal structure and content of the work and on the other its socio-historical dimension. Let us take a closer look at Seminara's opinion of the work's origin. The discussion we offer here serves as an introduction to an issue with which we will have to contend throughout this book.

Seminara argues that because *Šimâ Milka* is found only in the Late Bronze Age sites outside of Mesopotamia and because the father–son debate is unique to this composition, this work is to be considered a product of Syrian scribal circles, whether at Ugarit or Emar. Seminara finds support for the dating of the work in the reply of the son to his father. He argues that the son's sarcastic answer displays a nihilistic attitude that is typical of wisdom compositions of the Kassite period. Even more so, it is a specific reflection of the social and political situation in Late Bronze Age sites, specifically, Ḫattuša, Ugarit, and Emar. On the basis of these assertions, Seminara sets the date of the composition of *Šimâ Milka* as we have it to around the second-half of the second millennium B.C.E. (although admitting that it might have depended on a simpler version from Babylonia, which did not contain the reply of the son).

It can indeed be argued that the manuscripts of *Šimâ Milka* recovered from Ḫattuša, Ugarit, and Emar represent an expanded and more refined version of an Old Babylonian period recension, now lost to us. It is certainly likely that some themes in *Šimâ Milka* were more fully articulated than the initial stage of the composition. Arguably, the pessimistic tone introduced by the son may be taken as an indication of the changes wisdom literature underwent on the whole. For example, as we will see, the vanity theme was expanded in the later version of The Ballad of Early Rulers from Ugarit and Emar. Likewise, the same theme became more elaborate in Enlil and Namzitarra where Namzitarra's reply to Enlil was expanded beyond what was found in the work's Old Babylonian version. The same conclusion may hold for *Šimâ Milka* as well. With that said, it remains very difficult to date these changes to the work. All that can be said, on the basis of an internal textual analysis (which examines, e.g., spelling conventions or linguistic features of the various manuscripts), is that the recension of *Šimâ Milka* and those of other works we will study in this book were inscribed in clay after the Old Babylonian period.

In order to provide additional support for dating the composition to the Kassite period, Seminara turns to historicize the work. The social or historical background of the Kassite period acts, in his words, as a great catalyst for a change in social attitudes that are in turn reflected in the literary works of the period. Seminara characterizes Kassite Babylonia as a state where power struggles changed forever the relationship between the elite and royalty, for the worse for the former. As a result, a pessimist or nihilist tone was embedded within wisdom compositions (such as The Dialogue of Pessimism) dating to that period.

The irony or sense of disenchantment in *Šimâ Milka* was probably influenced by these sociopolitical developments, but it was, so Seminara argues further, the political situation of the vassal states in Syria under the rule of the great powers of the day, Ḫatti, Egypt, and Mitanni (and later Assyria), that gave rise to the composition as we have it. In the Late Bronze Age, the royal courts of the vassal states had lost their real power. Vassal kings, once in control over their own state, became no more than administrators in an imperial system governing vast territories.

Further changes to the traditional economic structure of the family household throughout Syria, whereby the sons were in a position to lose their father's estates, contributed to the formulation of the debate between the father and son in *Šimâ Milka*. Just as the wisdom composition The Instructions of Šuruppak serves as a mirror of an ideology current in third-millennium Mesopotamia,

Seminara goes on to claim, so *Šimâ Milka* reflects political and social trends of Late Bronze Age Syria.

As we have already said, we may concede the idea that *Šimâ Milka* is endowed with an innovative look at the role of wisdom. However, it is difficult to assign the composition to a particular political period or social scene. To think that the political or social situation typical of Kassite rule in Babylonia (as described by Seminara 2000: 527) finds a reflection in wisdom compositions like *Šimâ Milka* or others we will study here is a somewhat naïve conclusion. In the past, historicizing literary works has found some favor (perhaps a prime example although engaging with this trend in a subtler way is Thorkild Jacobsen's *Treasure of Darkness*, 1976). However, nowadays, one is less inclined to forge an explicit connection between pieces of literature that contain no overt political or ideological agenda and contemporary socio- or geopolitics. In this regard, *Enūma Eliš* and The Epic of Erra are exceptional pieces of literature that can be located, albeit not without controversy, more comfortably in historical periods and can be said to reflect religious, social, and historical tendencies. For the most part, Mesopotamian literary compositions cannot be linked to specific historical events and whether or not they sprang out of such situations is a moot question.

The political situation in Syria as described by Seminara, wherein weak local dynasties felt the power of stronger empires, such as that of the Hittites, in and of itself is not a fully reliable characterization of the dynamic relationship between the vassal states (such as Ugarit and Emar) and the imperial powers. Describing vassal kings as local administrators running their estate-like city-states while politics were being conducted elsewhere oversimplifies the whole historical complexity of the period.

In addition, Seminara's understanding of the economic and social situation of the Syrian private household is far from precise: there is no evidence that traditional inheritance patterns underwent any change. At any rate, does a critique of relations between father and son expressed in a literary form such as *Šimâ Milka* require a definite historical event? The generation gap existing since time immemorial found its voice on countless occasions in numerous stories and myths all through the ancient Near East.

Finally, in support of his thesis, Seminara (2000: 529) wishes to claim that this work arose independently of the scribal school. It was neither composed by novice scribes nor had it any role in their education. Although Seminara claims an out-of-school existence for the work, and in doing so implicitly divorces it from its Babylonian background (because most of the scribal school curriculum was transmitted to the Late Bronze Age sites from Babylonian scribal centers), he does not provide us with evidence of a milieu where *Šimâ Milka* may have flourished. He mentions the few sapiential sayings interspersed throughout the letters of Rib-Adda of Byblos as proof of the dissemination of local or Syrian wisdom outside the scribal milieu. Nobody would deny that proverbs circulated in nonscribal environments as a popular form of expression (see 2.8), but the fact that many of the proverbs in *Šimâ Milka* can be found in other Babylonian sources speaks against identifying them as particular to Syria. Indeed, there is not a single obvious line in the work that can be identified as written in Syria (for the discussion of ^{KI}*erṣētu* or **kirṣētu*, see pp. 103 and 115). On the contrary, the mention of the city of Uruk (l. 28) speaks for the Babylonian origin of the composition. The allusion to the Epic of Etana (ll. 33–35), the quotations from the Fable of the Fox (ll. 38–39), and the mention of the underworld goddess Ereškigal (ll. 143′) likewise betray the Mesopotamian origin of the work. And the overall structure of the composition as well as its themes, such as the vanity theme, are highly dependent, as was demonstrated in our discussion, on other models or blueprints of Mesopotamian wisdom literature, which, we argue throughout this book, was studied in, and disseminated by, scribal schools in Mesopotamia, and later, in the sites of the Late Bronze Age.

To conclude our discussion, *Šimâ Milka* is a Babylonian creation, transmitted in almost parallel versions to Emar, Ugarit, and Ḫattuša. Steeped in Babylonian literary traditions, it was part of the school curriculum of scribes in Mesopotamia and in sites all across the western regions of the ancient Near East. As we move to discuss additional compositions, we will be able to offer additional support for this claim.

The Relationship of *Šimâ Milka* to Non-Mesopotamian Wisdom Compositions

Since the first publication of the work by Nougayrol in *Ugaritica* 5 (in 1968), parallels have been drawn between the general tone as well as the individual admonitions of *Šimâ Milka* and the biblical wisdom books. A few sayings have been compared with the proverbs of The Sayings of Ahiqar. Mention can be made of the more extensive discussions: Hurowitz 2007; Khanjian 1975; and Alster 2005: 42–44. However, it is crucial to note that since Arnaud's edition (2007) was not yet available when these studies were published, caution is to be used. The overall content of the work and structure merit a comparison with biblical wisdom precepts such as found in Proverbs or Qohelet, but it will be for a serious new edition of *Šimâ Milka* to suggest with confidence additional parallels and discuss its relationship to biblical wisdom.

Sources

Ugarit: RS_1 = RS 22.439 (Nougayrol 1968, no. 163); RS_2 = RS 94.2544+ (Arnaud 2007, no. 49); RS_3 = RS 94.5028 (Arnaud 2007, no. 49).
Emar: Arnaud 1985–1987, nos. 778–780.
Ḫattuša: KUB 4.3 + KBo 12.70 (Keydana 1991).

Editions and Translations

Nougayrol 1968, no. 163; Laroche 1968; Arnaud 2007, no. 49; Dietrich 1991, 1992; Keydana 1991; Seminara 2000; Foster 2005: 416–20; Hurowitz 2007; Kämmerer 1998.

Additional Discussions

Alster 1991, 2005: 42–45; Gianto 1998; Khanjian 1975; Sallaberger 2010.

2.2

The Ballad of Early Rulers

The second wisdom composition chosen for this collection is nowadays named The Ballad of Early Rulers, although in antiquity it was titled after its opening line. The work is known from manuscripts found at Emar and Ugarit. It is written in Sumerian, syllabic Sumerian, and Akkadian. Although the Emar and Ugarit recensions are not identical in their arrangement of individual lines, it is obvious that we are facing a single composition, which in and of itself relies on a Sumerian forerunner, called here, following Alster 2005, the Standard Sumerian Version. The Standard Sumerian Version is represented by a few Old Babylonian manuscripts probably originating from Sippar in Babylonia. Apart from a very fragmentary manuscript dated to the Neo-Assyrian period from the library of Ashurbanipal, no Akkadian version of the composition is as yet known from Mesopotamia. However, the Neo-Assyrian recension, albeit its poor condition, demonstrates that the composition continued to be copied through the centuries into the first millennium. The composition is also mentioned in a catalogue listing wisdom compositions compiled or written by Sidu (see below and 1.5). All this suggests very strongly that a Babylonian recension, written in Akkadian, was at one time present and circulating during the Kassite period in Babylonia.

The manuscripts from Ugarit were published already in 1968, but it was only in the 1980s with the publication of the Emar version and the study of the Sumerian manuscripts from Sippar that the structure and meaning of The Ballad of Early Rulers were properly understood. It was demonstrated that the Late Bronze Age versions of the composition had already departed from their Sumerian forerunner. First of all the work was offered in Akkadian translation and secondly, it was expanded beyond its earlier version. Furthermore, it was claimed that the new passages of the reworked composition were first composed in Akkadian and only later translated to Sumerian. That is to say that because Sumerian was poorly understood after the Old Babylonian period, the new lines of the composition were first put into Akkadian, which then was translated into Sumerian in order to convey the impression that they were originally composed in that language of prestige.

Much of the discussion regarding The Ballad of Early Rulers has focused on defining the literary genre of the poem. The composition has been generally considered to belong to the genre of wisdom literature, but more specific definitions have also been aimed at. The first editor of the Emar Ballad of Early Rulers, Arnaud (1982), saw it as an intellectual reflection on life, a piece of ancient philosophy, while Wilcke (1988), for example, because of the mention of Siraš, the goddess of beer, and the overall *carpe diem* sentiment of the poem, viewed The Ballad of Early Rulers as a "drinking song, cheeky and cynical," reminiscent of the famous student drinking song *Gaudeamus Igitur* and celebrating the now-and-here of life in face of impending death.

Considerable debate was also devoted to the origin of The Ballad of Early Rulers. While all acknowledged the Babylonian origin of The Ballad of Early Rulers, some scholars have argued (like Seminara in regards to *Šimâ Milka*) that the Late Bronze Age versions we have are the outcome of the efforts of Syrian scribes. Whether at Ugarit or Emar, it was the local scribes who effectively rendered the poem a Syrian composition. A more conservative view held that The Ballad of Early Rulers was thoroughly Babylonian, Syrian input being virtually nil. The apparent differences between the Standard Sumerian Version of the Old Babylonian period and the Late Bronze Age versions, so the argument went, were the result of the poem's transmission by continuous copying, study and eventual reworking through the ages in Babylonia, hence not the result of local editing or rewriting of the work at Ugarit or Emar. We will return to this crucial question in the discussion section.

Previous editions of The Ballad of Early Rulers have tried to reconcile all versions, presenting a so-called *partitur* or score edition in order to demonstrate the unity of the composition and the relationship of the later Ugarit and Emar versions to the Standard Sumerian Version. Thus each version was presented below the other with the Standard Sumerian Version regarded as the *Vorlage* (the original text) on which the later versions were based. At this stage of research, when the relationship between the versions has been more fully explored, we are at liberty to present full and separate editions of the Late Bronze Age versions from Emar and Ugarit in order to reveal their differences, rather than attempt to provide a composite edition of all versions (as we did for the edition and translation of *Šimâ Milka*). A separate treatment of each version will allow the reader to discern how blocks of lines were manipulated and inserted at different points of the composition, once the opening and closing lines of The Ballad of Early Rulers framed the entire poem. This is especially apparent in Version I from Ugarit, where the first two lines are repeated in order to frame the end of The Ballad of Early Rulers on the obverse of the tablet, and then repeated again on its reverse in order to bring to a close a series of proverbs. Such an arrangement of the lines is apparent also in the Neo-Assyrian version: lines 1–3 appear at the beginning and the end of the fragment in order to frame several proverbs which form the main bulk of what we have of the composition. The insertion of proverbs, which are only indirectly related to the main theme of the composition, and the fluidity of the order of the lines among the different versions demonstrate the flexibility of The Ballad of Early Rulers to incorporate new materials on the one hand and to suffer internal changes to the line order on the other, while still retaining its general structure and tone.

The Manuscripts

The Emar Version is the most complete of all Late Bronze Age versions. It contains the entire composition, although some of its twenty-four lines are totally broken away and many are in a fragmentary state (they can be mostly completed, however, from the Ugarit manuscripts). The manuscript is arranged in a "trilingual" format. The tablet has three parallel columns: Sumerian (col. i); Sumerian written syllabically (col. ii; in order to assist the scribes in the reading of the logographic script of the first column, although these two columns interchange); and an Akkadian translation (col. iii). The cryptographic colophon at the end of the composition identifies the diviner Šaggar-abu of the Zū-Ba'la family as the copyist of the composition (see 1.3 and 1.5). Since it is known when Šaggar-abu lived, we can surmise that the manuscript was probably copied in the second-half of the thirteenth century in Emar.

Three manuscripts were found at Ugarit. Version I is an interlinear text—a Sumerian line followed by its Akkadian translation. Although it is the best preserved of the Ugarit manuscripts it is still quite fragmentary. The obverse is missing at least ten lines of its beginning; the reverse of the tablet includes a series of proverbs, which are then followed by the opening lines of the composition (lines 1–3 according to the Emar version). The Ugaritic proverbs were recognized by Alster (2005: 323–26) also in an Old Babylonian Sumerian source, which is in very poor condition.

Versions II and III from Ugarit, now heavily damaged, were originally probably arranged as a three-column tablet (Sumerian, syllabic Sumerian, and Akkadian) like the format of the Emar manuscript. In spite of their poor condition, Versions II and III can help us restore the Emar manuscript where broken. Version II includes a fragmentary colophon but the name of the scribe is missing.

The Akkadian versions presented here rely on previous studies, among which Arnaud's (2007) edition is chiefly utilized, based on recent collations of the Ugarit tablets. We have also included here a reconstruction of the Sumerian

---

Akkadian Text

The Emar Version

(For the Sumerian Text see below)

Obverse

1 [*i*]*tti Ea uṣ*[*ṣurāma uṣurātu*]
2 *ana ṭēm ilim*[*ma ussuqā usqētu*]
3 [*i*]*štu ūmi pana ibb*[*aššâ anniātu*]
4 *immatimê ina pî āl*[*ik panî*] *ul* [*itta*]*šme*
5 [*eli*]*šina šinam*[*a elišunu*] *šanût*[*uma*]
6 [*elēnu bīt*] *ašā*[*bi*(*šunu šaplānu bīt dārītišunu*)]
7 [*kīma šamû rūqūma qātu mimma la i*]*kaššud*
8 [*kīma šupul erṣēti mamma la idû*]
9 [*balāṭa kalāšu tūrti īnimma*]
10 [*balāṭ amīl*]*utti* [*dāriš ūmī*] *ul ibb*[*ašši*]
11 [*a*]*lê Alulu* [*ša* 36,000 *šanāti*...]
12 *alê* [*Enten*]*a ša* [*ana šamê ilû*]
13 *alê Gil*[*gameš š*]*a k*[*īma Zius*]*udra napu*[*ltaš*]*u i*[*šte"û*]
14 [*al*]*ê Hu*[*wawa ša*...] *ina* [...]

Reverse

15 [*a*]*lê Enkidu ša dannūti ina māti u*[*šāpû*]
16 *alê Bazi alê Zi*[*zi*]
17 *alê šarrānu rabbū*[*tu*] *ša ištu ūmi pana adi inan*[*na*]
18 *ul innerrûma ul imma*[*lladū*]

version on the basis of the Sumerian and syllabic Sumerian of the Emar and Ugarit manuscripts. Where missing, this reconstruction is supplemented by Old Babylonian fragmentary manuscripts which represent the Sumerian Standard Version. We base our Sumerian text on the reconstruction and translation of Alster (2005), Arnaud (2007), and Klein (1999). Note that this Sumerian text serves as no more than a basis for comparison with the Akkadian versions.

Translation

Obverse

1 [The fates are] de[termined] by Ea,
2 [The lots are drawn] according to the will of the god,
3 Since days of yore there are [(only) *these things*],
4 Has it never been heard before from the mouth of (our) predecessor(s)?
5 Those (came) after those, and others (came) after others,
6 [Above—the house] where [they] lived, [in the netherworld—the house where they stayed for eternity],
7 [Like the heaven is distant, no one at all can] reach (them),
8 [Like the depths of the netherworld, nobody can know (them)],
9 [All life is but a swivel of an eye],
10 [Life of man]kind cannot [last forever],
11 Where is Alulu [who reigned for 36,000 years]?
12 Where is [Enten]a who [went up to heaven]?
13 Where is Gil[gameš w]ho [sought] (eternal) li[fe] like (that of) [Zius]udra?
14 Where is Hu[wawa who…]?

Reverse

15 Where is Enkidu who [*proclaimed*] (his) strength throughout the land?
16 Where is Bazi? Where is Zizi?
17 Where are the great kings of which (the like) from then to now
18 are not (anymore) engendered, are not bo[rn]?

19 *[bal]āṭu ša la namāri [ana m]ūti mīna utter*
20 *[eṭl]u ša ilka kīniš … [...]*
21 *sikip kuššid nissā[ti m]īš qūl[āti]*
22 *dīnānu [ūm ḫ]ūd libbi ištēn ūmu [(ša) qūli] ešerēt šār[u (šanātu) lillikā]*
23 *kīma māri [^{d}Siraš] lirīška*
24 *annûm uṣ[urtu] ša amīlutti*

(double dividing line and colophon)

UGARIT VERSION I

(Sumerian not included; the numbers in brackets follow the numeration of the Emar version)

Obverse

2′ (15) *[alê] ^{d}Enkidu š[a...]*
4′ (17) *alê šunūti šarrānu [rabbūtu ša ištu ūmi pana adi inanna]*
6′ (18) *ul innerrû[ma] ul [imma(lladū)]*
8′ (7) *kīma šamû rūqūma qāta mamma$^{?}$ la ik[aššad]*
10′ (8) *kīma šupul erṣēti mamma la idû*
12′ (9) *balāṭa kalāšu tūrti īnimma*
14′ (19) *balāṭa ša la namāri ana mīti mīna utter*
16′ (22) *ana dīnan ḫūd libbi ūmakkal ūm qūli*
17′ (22) *ešerēt šāru šanātu lillikā*

(double dividing line with BE sign)

19′ (1) *itti ^{d}Ea uṣṣurām[a u]ṣurātu*
21′ (2) *ina ṭēm ilimma us‹su›qā usqētu*
23′ (3) *[ištu ūmi pana]… ibaššâ anni[ā]tu*

Break

19 Life without light—how can it be better than death?
20 Young man let me [*teach you*] truly what is your god's (nature; i.e., his eternity).
21 Repel, drive away sorrow, scorn silence!
22 In exchange for this single [day of h]appiness, let pass a time [of silence] lasting 36,000 [(years)].
23 May [Siraš] rejoice over you as if over (her) son!
24 This is the fate of humanity.

(double dividing line and colophon)

TRANSLATION

Obverse

2′ (15) [Where] is Enkidu w[ho…]
4′ (17) Where are these ones? The [great] kings [of which (the like) from then to now]
6′ (18) Are not (anymore) engendered, are not [born]?
8′ (7) Like the heaven is distant no one at all can [reach (them)],
10′ (8) Like the depths of the netherworld, nobody can know (them),
12′ (9) All life is but a swivel of the eye,
14′ (19) Life without light—how can it be better than death?
16′ (22) Instead of happiness for one single day, let pass a time of silence
17′ (22) Lasting 36,000 years!

19′ (1) The fates are determined by Ea,
21′ (2) The lots are drawn according to the will of the god,
23′ (3) [Since days of yore] there are (only) these things,

Break

Reverse

24′ [… n]i nu-zu-a
25′ *awīlūtu* x[o-o-o]x *ša ramāniša la idû*

26′ u$_4$-da$^!$ šu-dù-bi ge$_6$-[m]e-a-bi-[da ki] dingir ì-in-gál
27′ *ṭēm urriša u mūšiša itti ili ibašši*

28′ a-dù nam-lú-u$_{18}$-lu-ke$_4$ na-me na-na-zu$^!$
29′ *adê*$^!$ *awīlūti mamma la u'adda*

30′ šu-kúr nam-lú-u$_{18}$-lu-ke$_4$ na-me na-an-dug$_4$-ga
31′ *ṭapilti awīlūti mamma* ‹*la*› *iqabbi*

32′ igi-tur sig-ga na-me ‹šu na›-gíd-i
33′ *šēṭūt enši mamma la ileqqe*

34′ dumu lú ad$_4$-ad$_4$-ke$_4$ dumu lú kaš$_4$-e dab-ba
35′ *mār ḫummuri mār lāsimi iba'a*

36′ dumu lú-níg-tuku-tuku dumu lú-kur-ra-šè šu nu-ba-[?]
37′ *mār šarî ana mār lapni qāssu itarra*[*ṣ*]

38′ e-‹ne› giš-šub-ba lú-silim-ma-k[e$_4$]
39′ *annû isiq šalmi*

(double dividing line)

41′ (1) *itti* ^{d}*Ea uṣṣurā* [*uṣurātu*]
43′ (2) *ina ṭēm ilimma u*[*ssuqā usqētu*]

Break (after fragmentary Sumerian line, 44′ = (3))

Reverse

25′ Mankind does not recognize its own [life-span],

27′ Decisions over its day (i.e., life) and its night (i.e., death) are with the god,

29′ None can reveal mankind's workload (i.e., life-span).

31′ One should ‹not› speak in disrespect of others,

33′ One should not treat the weak contemptuously,

35′ The cripple may overtake the runner,

37′ The rich may beg the poor.

39′ This is the fate of the sound person.

41′ (1) [The fates] are determined by Ea,
43′ (2) [The lots are drawn] according to the will of the god.
44′ (3) From days of old…[…] (Sumerian only)

Break

UGARIT VERSION II

Obverse (*Face B*)

1′ (1) [*itti*] ^{d}*E*[*a uṣṣurā uṣ*]*urē*[*tu*]
2′ (2) [*ina ṭ*]*ē*[*m ilimma ussuqā usqētu*]

(Break of Akkadian column)

Reverse (*Face A*)

1′ (18) *ul in*[*nerrûma*] *ul imma*[*lladū*]
2′ (10) *balāṭ a*[*mīlutti ul dāriš ūmī ibbašši*]
3′ (20) *eṭlu ša ilka* [...]
4′ (21) *sikip kuššid nissāti mīš qūlāti*
5′ (22) *ana dīnāni ūmi ḫūd* [*libbi*] *ištēn ūm qūli ešerēt šār*[*u* (*šanātu*) *lillikā*]
6′ (19) *balāṭu ša la namā*[*ri*] *eli mūti mīna u*[*tter*]
7′ (23) ^{d}*Siraš kī*[*ma māri*] *lirīš*[*ka*]
8′ (24) [*an*]*nûmma iṣu*[*rtu*] *ša amīlutti*

TRANSLATION

Obverse (*Face B*)

1′ (1) The fates [are determined by] Ea,
2′ (2) [The lots are drawn according to the] will of [the god],

Reverse (*Face A*)

1′ (18) Are (they) not en[gendered] (anymore), are not bo[rn]?
2′ (10) Life of m[ankind can not *last forever*],
3′ (20) Young man [let me *teach you* truly] what is your god's.
4′ (21) Repel, drive away sorrow, scorn silence!
5′ (22) In exchange of a single day of happi[ness, let pass] a time of silence lasting 36,000 [(years)].
6′ (19) Life without light—how can it be b[etter] than death?
7′ (23) May Siraš rejoice over [you] as [if over (her) son]!
8′ (24) This is the fate of humanity.

UGARIT VERSION III

Obverse

1′ (2)	*[ana ṭēm ilimma uss]uqā usqē[tu]*
2′ (3)	*[ištu] ūmi panānu ibba[ššâ anniātu*[?]]
3′–4′ (4)	*[immatim]ê ina pî ālik pani [ul it]tešme*
5′–6′ (5)	*[eli]šunu šunuma [eli]šunu šanûtuma*
7′–8′ (6)	*elēnu bīt ašābi[(šunu)…]*
8′–9′ (7)	*[kīma š]amû rūqūma qāta la mamma ikaššad*

Break

Reverse

1′–2′ (19)	*[balāṭu ša] la na[māri eli mū]ti mīnam utter*
3′–4′ (23)	[[d]*Siraš] kīamma māri [lirī]ška*
5′–6′ (24)	*[annûm]ma iṣurtu [ša amī]lutti*

(double dividing line; end of composition)

TRANSLATION

Obverse

1′ (2)	[The lot]s are dr[awn according to the will of the god],
2′ (3)	[Since days] of yore [there are (only) these things],
3′–4′ (4)	[Hasn't it been he]ard from the mouth of (our) predecessor(s)?
5′–6′ (5)	Those (came) [after] those, and others (came) [after] others,
7–′8′ (6)	Above—the house where (they) lived […],
8′–9′ (7)	[Like] the heaven is distant, no one at all can reach (them),

Break

Reverse

1′–2′ (19)	[Life] without l[ight]—how can it be better [than d]eath?
3′–4′ (23)	[May Siraš re]joice over you as if over (her) son!
5′–6′ (24)	[This] is the fate of humanity.

(double dividing line; end of the composition)

THE LATE BRONZE AGE SUMERIAN VERSION (BASED ON THE EMAR AND UGARIT MANUSCRIPTS AND SUPPLEMENTED BY THE OLD BABYLONIAN MANUSCRIPTS)

1 ki ^{d}En-ki-ke$_4$ giš-ḫur ḫur-ḫur-re

2 dimma dingir-re-e-ne-ke$_4$ ki nam-sur-sur-re

3 u$_4$-da-ta ní$^{?}$ al-gál-la (Ugarit Ver. I.) // u-du i-gi-du-uṭ-ṭu i-ni$_7$$^{?}$ ni-ig-gal-la (Emar; syllabic column)

4 me-na-àm$^{!}$ ka lú-igi-du-ka$^{!}$-né giš la-ba-an-tuku

5 diri e$^{!}$-ne-ne lugal-bi…

6 an-ta é ùr-ra-ke$_4$-e-ne ki-ta é da-rí-ke$_4$$^{!}$-e-ne

7 an-sù-ud-da-gim šu-ti n[am-bi-in-dug$_4$]

8 ki-bùru-da-bi me-na nu-un-zu-a

9 nam-ti-la dù-a-bi igi-nigin-na-kam

10 nam-ti-la$^{!}$ nam-lú-u$_{18}$-lu u$_4$-da-ri-iš nu-níg-gál

11 me-e ^{m}A-lu-lu mu-šár-[10-àm in-ak]

12 me ^{m}En-te-na lú an-šè bí-in-èd$^{!}$-dè

13 me-e ^{md}GIŠ-TUK-m[aš zi-u$_4$-sud-rá-g]im nam-ti-la kin-kin

14 me-e ^{m}Ḫu-wa-wa [ki ba-an-za-za dab$_5$$^{?}$-ba-ta]

15 [me-e] ^{m}En-ki-dù nam-kalag-ga-[a-ni …]-ta mu-un-na-an-te

16 me-e ^{m}Ba-zi me-e ^{m}Zi-zi

17 me-en ì-tí-eš lugal-gal-gal-e […] (Ug. Ver. I) // me-e lugal gal-e-ne u$_4$-sag-gá-ta e-ne-e-še-ta (Emar)

18 nu-peš-peš-e-ne nu-tu-t[u-e-ne] (Ug. Ver. I) // nu-peš-ša-me-en nu-tu-tu-men$_5$ (Emar)

19 nam-ti-la nu zalag-ga ugu-nam-úš-a ta-àm me-diri

20 guruš dingir-zu šu-zi-bi-šè ga-ra-an-zu

21 isiš sí-ki-ib-ta ša-ra lu-ul-bi ù-la mu-un-na-ka-ke$^{!}$

22 níg-sag-íl-la šà-ḫúl-la [u$_4$]-⸢diš⸣-kam u$_4$-ní-ba-kam mu 10 šár ù-in-na-ak (Ug. Ver. I) // sá-an-ke-el-la u$_4$ šà-ḫúl-lal lu-ul-bi ù-šèr-šèr hé-en-du (Emar)

23 ni-in-gim lu-ú tur-ra-bi Sí-ra-aš ḫi-li ma-an-zu

24 e-ne giš-ḫur nam-‹lú›-u$_{18}$-lu gi-na

NOTES TO INDIVIDUAL LINES

1: The text and translation of the Sumerian version are mainly based on Alster 2005: 312–19.

3: Wilcke (1988) tried to reconcile the Akkadian with what he understood from the Sumerian line of the Ugarit Version I manuscript (im al-gál-la). Con-

TRANSLATION

1 The fates are determined by Ea,
2 The lots are drawn according to the will of the gods,
3 *Since always so it was.*
4 Has it never been heard from the mouth of (our) predecessor(s)?
5 Above these were the kings… (the rest is corrupt)
6 Above the houses of their dwelling, below their house of eternity.
7 Like the distant heaven, nobody can reach (them),
8 Like the depths of the Netherworld, nobody can know (them),
9 Life is but a swivel of the eye,
10 Life of mankind cannot [last] forever.
11 Where is Alulu who reigned for 36,000 years?
12 Where is Entena who went up to the sky?
13 Where is Gilgameš who sought (eternal) life like (that of) Ziusudra?
14 Where is Huwawa who was subdued when bowing down (*to Gilgameš*)?
15 Where is Enkidu who was famous in his strength [*throughout the land*]?
16 Where is Bazi? Where is Zizi?
17 Where are they—the great kings (Ugarit Version I) // Where are the great kings from past days up to now (Emar Version)?
18 They are not (anymore) engendered, are not born.
19 Life without light—how can it be better than death?
20 Young man let me teach you truly about (the nature of) your god.
21 Chase away grief *from* depression; have nothing to do with silence.
22 In exchange for a single day of happiness let pass a time of silence of tens of thousands of days. (Ug. and Emar combined)
23 May Siraš rejoice over me as if over her little child!
24 Thus the fates of mankind are established.

---

sequently, he read the Akkadian of this version as *i-ba-áš-ša-a-an-n*[*i ša*]-*ru*, "gibt es Wind!"; the verbal form, however, is problematic and recent collations lead Arnaud (2007: 142) to read the end of the line as *i-ba*(sic)*-áš-ša-a an-ni*-[*a*]-*tù*. The Emar version has Sumerian i-nim, perhaps the syllabic spelling of inim = *awātu*, if one follows Arnaud although Alster (2005: 306) disapproves of this suggestion. Our suggestion is perhaps to read Ugarit Version I as ní (=im), along with the Neo-Assyrian manuscript which reads here ne-e, and understand all these forms (including the Emar i-nim read here as i-ni$_7$) as writings for Sumerian ne(n), "this" (Akkadian *annûm*), corresponding somehow in our text with Akkadian *anni*[*ā*]*tu*.

In the Emar version, following George's recent copy, we can read the signs "i" and "ba," hence we restore the verb as ˹*i-ba*˺-[*aš-ša*]. See Cohen 2012.

6: Compare this line with *Šimâ Milka*, ll. 150′–156′. The restoration of the Akkadian depends on Alster's (2005: 307–308) reconstruction.

7: The restoration of this line is not certain and is possibly corrupt. Ugarit Version I possibly reads šu ˹na-me˺ nu ˹*i*˺-*k*[*a-ša-ad*]; Ugarit Version III reads *qa-ta* ˹*la*˺ [o] / [x-x]˹:˺ (*Glossenkeil*) *ma-am-ma i-kaš-šad*. The Akkadian idiom is *qātu* (*mimma la*) *ikaššad*, lit., "the hand will (never) reach, conquer."

9: The phrase *tūrti īnimma* (Sum.: igi-nigin-na-kam) "the turning of the eye" is difficult; Alster (2005:310) translates "an illusion." ARG suggests "swivel of an eye," which I adopt.

10: The Sumerian of this line (and consequently the restoration of the Akkadian) can be restored on the basis of Ugarit Version II, *Face B*, 14′–15′: [nu]-níg-gál and the Emar Version, 10: nu-ni-i[g-ga-al].

11. The line about king Alulu is preserved in the Emar version, and also very fragmentarily in Ugarit Version II, *Face B*, 16′: [me-e ^{m}A-lu]-lu mu šár-[10-àm in-ak].

12. This line is also found in Ugarit Version II, *Face B*, 17′: [me-e ^{m}En-ta-na lú] an-[šè bí-in-èd-dè].

13: The verb of the Emar version follows the reading of Alster 2005: 314 and others; a trace of its initial sign can be seen in George's new copy (the sign is possibly "iš") in Cohen 2012.

14: Following Alster's (2005: 309) understanding.

22: Translation of the Akkadian after ARG. Ugarit Version I: the Sumerian follows *CAD* U–W, 93.

Ugarit Version I, Proverbs:

24′–39′: The text edition of the Sumerian relies on Alster's (2005: 323–326) interpretation. For a comparable set of proverbs see *BWL*, 119 (Bilingual Hymn to Ninurta).

27′–29′: Following the suggestion ARG, these lines are to be taken together.

39′: Alster (2005: 326) reads *annû isiq šal-m*[*i*] "This is the fate of a healthy man"; Arnaud (2007: 143) has *annû isiq mám-m*[*an*] "tel est la part de [tout] homme" but this does not fit with the Sumerian text.

Discussion

Summary

In the composition examined in the previous chapter, *Šimâ Milka,* Ea bestowed wisdom upon Šūpê-amēli. In The Ballad of Early Rulers we learn that it is Ea who determines fates, allotting them to humankind. Since time immemorial, man's days are numbered as one generation follows the next. Has anybody of our predecessors proved differently? All life is but a swivel of an eye. Even illustrious heroes of the past whose deeds are not surpassed and of whom the like are not born anymore eventually succumbed to death. Hence it is best to enjoy the present while it lasts and reject sorrow, because once death arrives it is eternal. Only your god truly is of everlasting life. This the fate of humanity.

Key Themes of The Ballad of Early Rulers

Arnaud ingeniously titled the composition *La Ballade des héros du temps jadis* (from which the English title) after François Villon's poems *Ballade des dames du temps jadis* and *Ballade des seigneurs du temps jadis*. Even if arguably the aims of the two poems are different, Villon's poems show an uncanny similarity to The Ballad of Early Rulers's list of early rulers (Rubio 2009). Note that although Villon (ca. 1431–1463 C.E.) listed semilegendary heroes and heroines of long-ago such as Charlemagne or Eloise and Abelard, he also referred to his near-contemporaries, such as Pope Callixtus III or King Alfonso V, forging a tie between past and present. The poet of The Ballad of Early Rulers likewise chose for his own purpose past figures who however retained an association with contemporary readers or hearers. They were chosen to represent two often linked issues—immortality and wisdom.

King Alulu of an extreme reign of 36,000 years and Ziusudra, famed for his immortality, were chosen as exempla of well-known figures from antiquity who were noted for their wisdom. Kings Gilgameš and Etana were chosen for their attempt to reach immortality. Dead but not forgotten heroes of their like are not born anymore.

Consider in this respect a gathering of ancient and prominent men in Ezekiel 14. They are brought on in order to illustrate the severity of the prophet's prophecy of doom for it is only they who will be saved. Although serving a different purpose from that of the early rulers of The Ballad of Early Rulers, Noah, Danel, and Job in Ezekiel 14 represent the age of righteous men, not born anymore. They share with the Mesopotamian early rulers longevity, wisdom and the quest of continuity either of life itself or of progeny. Biblical

Noah can be identified with Ziusudra (or Atram-ḫasīs), and Danel is generally identified with Ugaritic Danilu, the father of Aqhat, who shares traits with Etana as both heroes have to contend with infertility, thus with the issue of progeny and the survival of their memory. Our comparison does not wish to claim a relationship between Ezekiel 14 and The Ballad of Early Rulers, or for that matter, Villon's poems, but rather to demonstrate how well-known figures from the past can be brought together in order to illustrate for the present generation the futility of life.

When considered as a whole the list of early rulers is meant to advance two key themes of The Ballad of Early Rulers, the first leading on to the next—the vanity of life and consequently the fulfillment and enjoyment of life while it lasts. This double theme, as explored by Alster (2005), has had a long history in Mesopotamian literary traditions. It finds a pithy expression in short Sumerian wisdom compositions all beginning with the statement "Nothing is of value, but life itself should be sweet-tasting"; they then proceed to expound upon this theme in different directions. That these compositions stood in some relation to The Ballad of Early Rulers is evident by the fact the Sumerian version of our poem is found together with one of these works in what is termed a *Sammeltafel*—a single tablet that collects several diverse works (see 1.5). A fuller expression of this double theme, apart from The Ballad of Early Rulers, as has been pointed out by several scholars, is found in the Siduri's message to Gilgameš near the close of the epic in its Old Babylonian version.

> Gilgameš wither you rove?
> The life you pursue you shall not find!
> When the gods created mankind,
> Death for mankind they set aside,
> Life in their own hands retaining,
> You, Gilgameš, let your belly be full,
> Make you merry by day and by night,
> Of each day make you a feast of rejoicing,
> Day and night, dance and play!
> Let your garments be sparkling fresh,
> Your head be washed; bathe in water!
> Pay heed to the little one who holds on to your hands,
> Let your spouse delight in your bosom;
> For this is the destiny of [mankind]!
>
> (The Epic of Gilgameš, OB Version, iii ll. 1–14;
> Klein 1999: 214; George 2003: 278–79)

In The Ballad of Early Rulers, however, the advice to enjoy life is much circumscribed, limited in fact to a few lines at the end of the poem. Was it enough for the poet to invoke Siraš, the goddess of beer, to bring to the reader's mind a variety of associations (cf. line 21 of the Standard Sumerian Version) such as feasting and merriments explicitly expressed in The Epic of Gilgameš?

Is The Ballad of Early Rulers a Syrian or Mesopotamian Composition?

A question that was of concern in the previous chapter was to what degree, and if at all, the composition *Šimâ Milka* changed upon its transmission to the Late Bronze Age sites outside Mesopotamia? The same question can be asked of the work we have been examining here. Is The Ballad of Early Rulers a Syrian or Mesopotamian composition? This was already the concern of Arnaud, who was the first to publish the Emar manuscripts. Arnaud (1982) viewed the piece as the product of a Syrian intellectual who departed somewhat from Mesopotamian models by developing his particular sentiments of disenchantment and vanity. Dietrich (1996) likewise considered the piece from Emar and Ugarit to be a Syrian creation. Dietrich stated that the Akkadian and Sumerian texts used in scribal education had a meager influence on Ugarit's own literary and religious traditions. Nonetheless, some of these Mesopotamian compositions were rewritten to fit the tastes and religious attitudes of "Ugaritian theologians and poets" to use his own words. Such a thorough reworking was typical of the Emar and Ugarit recensions of The Ballad of Early Rulers. Dietrich (1992: 27 and *passim*) explained that the scribe or scribes at Emar rewrote The Ballad of Early Rulers on the basis of Mesopotamian traditions and that it suffered further modifications at Ugarit. Specifically Dietrich argued that the Ugarit versions were missing the list of the early rulers. It was removed because these were figures that meant nothing to the Ugarit scribes. A closer investigation of the textual remains reveals, however, that the list of early rulers, although very poorly preserved, nonetheless exists in two of the Ugarit versions. Ugarit Version I includes the line mentioning Enkidu (see above l. 15); and Alulu and E(n)tana (ll. 11–12) are also present in Ugarit Version II (as our study reveals now).

Klein (1999), although more cautious than Dietrich, likewise spoke of "Eastern and Western traditions" when writing about The Ballad of Early Rulers in its Babylonian version vis-à-vis its Late Bronze Age recensions. The Ugarit version was in his view "a free selection and reworking of the Sumerian Vorlage...." Klein was less specific in regards to the place where the Emar version underwent editorial changes, clearly recognizing the Mesopotamian forerunners of the work, although he remarked (p. 204) that, "in Emar these texts were sometimes embellished with touches of local color, or greatly expanded…." Indeed, it has been claimed (by Hallo 1992 for example) that the list of long dead heroes, although dependent on the Old Babylonian Standard Sumerian version, suffered modifications in Emar. Two figures, Bazi and Zizi (who are absent from the Old Babylonian Standard Sumerian version) were added to the Late Bronze Age poem as representative of local Syrian heroes. However, as we will show below, the list is thoroughly Mesopotamian, and nothing in its contents hints at a Syrian origin. It was composed in Babylonia, and although the heroes Bazi and Zizi are associated with the regions west of Mesopotamia, their inclusion in the list could not have taken place except in Babylonian scribal centers.

To conclude this argument over the origin of The Ballad of Early Rulers, we bring in Lambert's opinion on the matter. Lambert (1995) stressed that the main idea of The Ballad of Early Rulers concurs with the motif of the futility of life found elsewhere in Mesopotamia. He continued to argue that Dietrich (1992)

> regards the Ugarit and Emar pieces as related but distinct literary compositions [from the Old Babylonian version]. The differences, however, are less than the recensional differences between the variant editions of Akkadian texts from southern Mesopotamia in the Old Babylonian period, e.g., the Gilgamesh Epic, and there is of course no proof that the Ugarit and Emar copies of the texts under discussion offer editions created in the west.

What Lambert claims, in other words, is that the changes between the Old Babylonian recension and the later post-Old Babylonian versions first do not imply a total reworking of The Ballad of Early Rulers and secondly may have not necessarily happened in the Late Bronze Age sites of Emar or Ugarit.

We turn now to examine more closely the list of early rulers—we will investigate who are the figures mentioned, what is their relationship to one another, and where they stand in Mesopotamian literary traditions. Our aim is to place The Ballad of Early Rulers in its proper literary context and to demonstrate, in line with what this section has been discussing, that the work is not a product of local Syrian scribes.

The List of Early Rulers

The Ballad of Early Rulers begins by stating that ever since the fates were determined by Ea life is transient and not meant to last forever. The poem then offers a list of early illustrious rulers. The reader is asked to question what their fate was in spite of their heroic deeds. Did these rulers ever reach immortality? Alulu, Entena, Gilgameš, Bazi, and Zizi, in spite of the fact that none like these past rulers are born anymore, were eventually mortal, so we are to understand.

As has been made evident by several scholars, the list of The Ballad of Early Rulers rests heavily on Mesopotamian scholarly and historiographical traditions, particularly on the Sumerian King List and, as will be seen, The Epic of Gilgameš.

Alulu of The Ballad of Early Rulers can be identified with Alulim from the city of Eridu, the first king of the antediluvian section in the Sumerian King List. Alulim or, in his Akkadian rendering, Ayyalu is also known from the Uruk List of Kings and Sages, where he is mentioned in the company of the famous sage Adapa. Otherwise Alulu is also known as a magic power called upon to ward away pests in several incantations.

Following Alulu in The Ballad of Early Rulers is Entena, or, as he is better known to us, Etana King of Kiš, who also appears in the Sumerian King List. The mention of Etana's ascent to heaven in The Ballad of Early Rulers (l. 12, partly preserved in the Sumerian Standard Version) refers to the mythological story The Epic of Etana. As in The Ballad of Early Rulers, the Sumerian King List speaks of "Etana, the shepherd, who ascended to heaven."

After Kiš, the Sumerian King List informs us that kingship passed on to Uruk, whose most famous king was Gilgameš. As in the Sumerian King List, so in The Ballad of Early Rulers, it is Gilgameš who follows Etana. Both kings failed to reach immortality but were somewhat compensated for their brave but futile attempt when they achieved a place in the Netherworld as venerated figures.

Once Gilgameš is mentioned in The Ballad of Early Rulers, other characters known from his Epic show up. First comes Ziusudra, better known as Atra(m)-ḫasīs or Utnapištim, the only person to have reached immortality in Mesopotamian literary tradition. He is followed by Huwawa, Gilgameš's adversary, and then by Enkidu, the hero's companion.

The next two characters, Bazi and Zizi, are mentioned only in the Emar version. They are missing from Ugarit Version I (which mentions Enkidu and then jumps to line 17) and the Sumerian Standard Version. Nonetheless, in spite of what has repeatedly been claimed in the scholarly literature, both characters were not inserted in the list by scribes from Emar.

Like other early rulers of The Ballad of Early Rulers, Bazi and Zizi are also found in the Sumerian King List. Known from a recension of the Sumerian King List found at Tel Leilan (an ancient site located in the Habur Triangle), they are included in the section of the list dedicated to the kings of Mari. Like many other pre-Sargonic kings of the Sumerian King List, Bazi and Zizi were legendary figures of probably no historical background. The Tel Leilan Sumerian King List section dedicated to listing the kings of Mari reads as follows:

> (In Mari) Anbu [was] king for 90 years,
> Anbu son of Anbu ruled for 7 years,
> ^{d}Bazi the leatherworker ruled for 30 years,
> Zizi the fuller ruled for 20 years,
> [L]imer the gudu-priest ruled for 30 years,
> Šarrum-iter ruled for 7 years,
> 6 kings ruling in total 184 years.
> (Sumerian King List, col. v, ll. 24–33; Vincente 1995; Glassner 2004: 122–23)

Note that in the Sumerian King List Bazi is designated as a god—his name is proceeded with the divine determinative "^{d}" (for Sumerian dingir, "god"). Indeed Bazi was considered a divine figure in Mesopotamia, as can be seen in a recently published hymn dedicated to his honor. The Song of Bazi (George 2009, no. 1) celebrates the god Bazi whose temple is located in Mounts Bašar and Šaršar, double names of the modern typonym—the Jebel Bishri—in the Syrian desert.

Once we realize that Bazi was connected in Mesopotamian tradition with regions west of the alluvium, that is, with the Jebel Bishri and that he and Zizi were considered kings of Mari, it can be argued that these two rulers were chosen by force of association with Gilgameš, Enkidu, and Huwawa because it is to the west that the focus of the narrative of The Epic of Gilgameš moves, when the two heroes proceed to the Cedar Forest to kill Huwawa. It is this connection that brought about the mention of Bazi and Zizi in the Emar version of The Ballad of Early Rulers.

To conclude, it is clear therefore in our opinion that only a scribe learned in Mesopotamian literary traditions could have composed the list in its entirety, taking his inspiration from the Sumerian King List and other scholarly sources (Cohen 2012). The reason that Version I from Ugarit does not include Bazi and Zizi is because it depends on a Mesopotamian recension closer to the Old Babylonian Standard Sumerian Version (which as said does not include the duo) than the Emar version. The latter probably depends on a more contemporary and updated post-Old Babylonian or Middle Babylonian version.

The Ballad of Early Rulers within the Mesopotamian Stream of Tradition

In Mesopotamian learned circles, The Ballad of Early Rulers was considered to belong to a larger collection of wisdom compositions. This collection was recognized as a single series allegedly written or compiled by a sage called Sidu (Finkel 1986; Frahm 2010). The contents of the series are listed in a catalogue found in Nineveh, although dating probably to the end of the second millennium. The Ballad of Early Rulers, like other wisdom texts in this catalogue (not all have been identified), is cited by its opening line, ki [d]En-ki giš-ḫur-ḫur-ra, "With Enki the fates are determined." The mention of The Ballad of Early Rulers together with other wisdom compositions, firmly places the work within the Babylonian stream of tradition. And the attribution of the series to the person Sidu, who was considered as one of the sages of ancient times, shows, as Frahm rightly claims, the importance given to wisdom compositions in Mesopotamian eyes. They were considered part and parcel of the intellectual heritage of learned scholars, who studied lexical lists, god lists, omens, and Sumerian prayers (Frahm 2010: 171; see 1.5).

The Ballad of Early Rulers and Biblical Wisdom

As several scholars have already noted the general tone of The Ballad of Early Rulers and some of its specific lines bring to mind Qohelet. Notable are the following passages (1:4 and 11; 5:17 [NRSV 5:18]) in comparison with ll. 5–17 and 20–22 of The Ballad of Early Rulers.

> דור הלך ודור בא והארץ לעולם עמדת
> A generation comes, a generation goes and the land remains as always.
>
> אין זכרון לראשנים וגם לאחרנים שיהיו לא־יהיה להם זכרון עם שיהיו לאחרנה
> There is no memory of the first or the last who have been; even not those of recent times.
>
> הנה אשר־ראיתי אני טוב אשר־יפה לאכול־ולשתות ולראות טובה בכל־עמלו
> שיעמל תחת־השמש מספר ימי־חיו אשר־נתן־לו האלהים כי־הוא חלקו.
> This is what I have seen to be good: it is fitting to eat and drink and find enjoyment in all the toil with which one toils under the sun the few days of the life God gives us; for this is our lot. (NRSV)

Lines 7–8 in our composition speak about the vastness of the sky and depth of the netherworld as a metaphoric expression of our inability to understand the ways of the world. The same metaphor articulates a similar notion in Job 11:8–9:

גבהי שמים מה־תפעל עמקה משאול מה־תדע:
ארכה מארץ מדה ורחבה מני־ים

It is higher than heaven—what can you do?
Deeper than Sheol—what can you know?
Its measure is longer than the earth,
and broader than the sea (NRSV)

For additional discussions, the reader is referred to Lambert 1995, Klein 1999, and Alster 2005.

Sources

Emar: *Emar* 767 = Arnaud 1985–1987.

Ugarit: Version I = RS 25.130 (*Ugaritica* 5, no. 164; Arnaud 2007: 142–45, no. 48); Version II = RS 23.34+ (*Ugaritica* 5, no. 165; Arnaud 2007: 145–48, no. 48); Version III = RS 25.424 (*Ugaritica* 5, no. 166; Arnaud 2007: 145–48, no. 48).

The Old Babylonian Standard Sumerian Version: Alster 2005: 298, 300–311, with previous literature; Klein 1999.

The Neo-Assyrian Fragment: Alster 2005: 299, 320–22.

The Sumerian King List: Glassner 2004; Marchesi 2010; Vincente 1995; ETCSL 2.2.1 (note that Jacobsen's standard edition [1939] is outdated).

Editions and Discussions

Alster 2005; Arnaud 1982, 2007, no. 48; Dietrich 1992, 1996; Foster 2005: 769–70; Hallo 1992; Klein 1999; Kämmerer 1998: 103–4, 208–13; Lambert 1995; Rubio 2009; Wilcke 1988.

For figures mentioned in the "Early Rulers" list, see Beaulieu 2007; Cohen 2012; George 2003; George and Taniguchi 2010, nos. 24–25; Lenzi 2008.

2.3

Enlil and Namzitarra

The wisdom composition Enlil and Namzitarra expounds on one of the key themes we are concerned with—the shortness of human life and inevitability of death. Both of these themes were encountered in our presentation and discussion of *Šimâ Milka* and The Ballad of Early Rulers.

In Babylonia, the composition Enlil and Namzitarra is represented by seven Old Babylonian Sumerian manuscripts. Sometimes other compositions were copied alongside Enlil and Namzitarra on the same tablet: lexical lists or a notable Sumerian wisdom composition titled Nothing Is of Value (Civil 1974–1977; Alster 2005: 327). It can safely be assumed that these compositions, wisdom and lexical, all formed part of the scribal training in the Old Babylonian period (see 1.5).

The Late Bronze Age manuscripts of the composition derive from Emar and Ugarit. In Emar, several separate fragments, written in the so-called Syro-Hittite script, originally made up one single manuscript. In Ugarit, all that remains of the composition is a fragment. Nonetheless, the Ugarit fragment contributes to the reconstruction of missing lines from the Emar manuscript. Both the Emar and Ugarit manuscripts represent the bilingual stage of the composition when the Old Babylonian Sumerian version was expanded and translated into Akkadian. It can be observed how two strophes of the Old Babylonian Sumerian version dealing with the vanity theme were developed into a longer section that brought the composition to its conclusion. As mentioned above, one Old Babylonian manuscript of Enlil and Namzitarra also included the Sumerian wisdom composition Nothing Is of Value, which explicitly deals with the vanity theme. Hence, the familiarity with this theme already in the Old Babylonian period may have promoted its development and expansion in the bilingual version of Enlil and Namzitarra.

It has been suggested that with the development of the key theme of the composition as we have it preserved in Late Bronze Age bilingual manuscripts, some elements of the original plot were omitted. However, according to my reconstruction of the Emar manuscript (see below) it appears that they were retained. Nonetheless, the ending of the Sumerian version was not transmitted to the bilingual version, so much is clear, because it ends differently (see below).

Another difference between the Old Babylonian composition and its later version is that at the end of the story of Enlil and Namzitarra, the Emar version (the Ugarit version is destroyed at this point) follows with two quite fragmentary Akkadian columns that contain sayings of an unclear nature delivered by a father apparently reporting from the Netherworld to his sons. The manner in which these sayings relate to the main composition is not entirely clear, but as previously demonstrated, proverbs could be incorporated within the framework of a wisdom composition narrative, as in The Ballad of Early Rulers, hence there is good reason to assume that this is the case here as well.

The Plot of Enlil and Namzitarra

The plot of the Old Babylonian Sumerian version combines folkloristic motifs with a favorite literary ploy of the Sumerian Edubba scribes—the learned use of sound- and sign-based puns, upon which the understanding of the whole story hinges. The plot tells of a meeting between the god Enlil and Namzitarra, a priest serving at Enlil's temple and holding a temple prebend. Enlil, disguised as a Raven, asks Namzitarra to identify him. Namzitarra sees through Enlil's disguise and successfully names the god. Recounting a line from an obscure myth (otherwise almost completely lost to us) about Enlil and a god called Enmešarra, Namzitarra by way of a pun discovers Enlil's identity. The Sumerian word for raven is embedded within the myth Namzitarra retells. After Namzitarra identifies Enlil correctly, as a reward, the god decrees a favorable destiny (Sumerian nam) upon him. This again involves a pun since the meaning of the hero's name is Nam-zi-tar-ra—"The one allotted (tar-ra) a good destiny (nam-zi)" (Vanstiphout 1980). Enlil grants Namzitarra material gifts but they however are spurned because they are of fleeting value. In the Old Babylonian Sumerian version, instead of these gifts, Namzitarra receives from Enlil an everlasting favor—Namzitarra's sons and successors are granted the holding of a prebend in Enlil's temple forever (Lambert 1989). The gift of the prebend (Sumerian nam-gudu$_4$), again involves a pun between the hero's name and his destiny (Cooper 2011).

In the Emar and Ugarit Versions, Enlil's gifts are spurned likewise. We learn that material gains hold no substantial value because man's life is limited, as the day of his death approaches. Hence, nothing is of value. Nothing is offered to Namzitarra instead (unlike the prebend offered to his successors in the Sumerian Version) and he walks home. At this point, the Akkadian proverbs commence.

Text and Translation of Enlil and Namzitarra

The beginning of the bilingual version from Emar and Ugarit is broken but we can make up what is missing by relying on the Old Babylonian Sumerian version. It tells of how Namzitarra met Enlil. The Late Bronze Age version follows here.

Section A (Emar 773 (+) Emar 592)

	Sumerian Column	Akkadian Column
1′	(edge + Emar 773)	[...]
2′	Nam-zi-tar-ra ^{d}En-líl	[...]
3′	mu-tál-[le inim in-na-an-dug$_4$]	[...]
4′	[me-ta-àm Nam-zi-tar-ra é]-^{d}En-líl-ta	*ay*[*yānu*...]
5′	[bala-gub-b]a-mu silim-ma-[àm]	*mazza*[*ltī*...]
6′	[ki gu]-du...	*ašar* [*pāšišu*...]
7′	[é-šè gá-e-me-en]	*ina* [*bītiya allak*]
8′	[u$_4$ gìr-mu ub-bi]	*šu*[*ḫmuṭāku*...]

Translation (Section A, ll. 1′–8′)

> Namzitarra walked by Enlil. Enlil said to him, "Where are you coming from?" (and Namzitarra answered) "From Enlil's temple, (where) my duties are done, where I am a *pāšišu*-priest ... I am going home now, I am in a hurry."

At this point the Emar version breaks off but the plot can be picked up again from the Old Babylonian Sumerian version. In the Old Babylonian Sumerian version we read how Enlil disguises himself as a raven but Namzitarra recognizes him. When Enlil asks Namzitarra how he saw through his disguise, Namzitarra recounts a part of a myth (obscure to us now) in which by way of a pun the Sumerian word for raven, Enlil's disguise, was embedded. Hence Namzitarra identifies Enlil and this is where our Emar version resumes. After correctly identifying Enlil, Namzitarra presents himself. He is promised riches by Enlil. However, in line with the vanity theme we have been exploring, Namzitarra rejects material gifts since they are of no lasting value.

SECTION B (EMAR 771 (+) EMAR 774 // RS 22.341 + RS 28.53A)

	Sumerian Column	Akkadian Column
7′	^{d}En-líl-⸢me-en⸣ nam-tar-[ra]	[...] *Enlil att*[*a*...]
8′	Nam-zi-tar-ra ^{d}En-líl [...]	[...] *Namzitarra* [...]
9′	[a-b]a-àm [mu-zu]	[...] *šumka*
10′	[Nam]-zi-tar-ra mu-mu-[um mu-zu-gim]	[...*Na*]*mzitarra* [*šumī* ...]
11′	[nam]-zu ḫi-ib-[tar-re]	[... *namtarri*]*ka* ⸢*liššīmku*⸣
12′	ḫe-ib [...	
13′	en-na kù.babbar ḫé-tuku	[*kaspam l*]*u tīšu*
14′	na$_4$ za.gìn ḫé-tuku	[*uqnî lu*] *tīšu*
15′	gud ḫé-tuku	[*alpī lu tī*]*šu*
16′	[u]du ḫé-tuku	*immerī lu tīšu*
17′	kù.babbar-zu na$_4$ za.gìn-zu gud-zu udu-zu	*kasapka uqnîka alpīka immerīka*
18′	me-šè al-tùm	[*ayyik*]*â* ⸢*alqe*⸣ *anāku*
19′	u$_4$ nam-lú-u$_{18}$-lu al-GAM-na	*ūmū amēlutti* ⸢*lu qerbū*⸣
20′	u$_4$-an-na ḫa-ba-lá	*ūmi ana ūmi limṭi*
21′	iti-an-na ḫa-ba-lá	*arḫi ana arḫi limṭi*
22′	mu mu-an-na ḫa-ba-lá	*šatti ana šatti limṭi*
22a′	[...ḫa-ba-lá]	[...] *limṭi*
23′	mu 2 *šu-ši* mu-meš nam-lú-u$_{18}$-lu	2 *šūši šanātu lū ikkib*
24′	níg-gig-bi ḫi-a	*amēlutti ba-la-ša*$^?$
25′	ki-u$_4$-ta-ta nam-lú-u$_{18}$-lu	*ištu* u$_4$-da *adi inanna*
26′	e$^!$-na ì-in-éš ti-la-e-ni	*amēluttu balṭu*
27′	é-šè gá-e-me-en	*ina bītiya allak*
28′	nu-na-an-gub na-an-gub	u$_4$ gìr-mu ub-bi

TRANSLATION (SECTION B, LL. 7′–28′)

(Namzitarra)

7′ "You are Enlil!,"
8′ Namzitarra (thus says); (to which replies) Enlil,

(Enlil)

9′ "[Wh]at is your name?"

(Namzitarra)

10′ "Namzitarra is my name."

(Enlil)

10′–11′ "Your [fate] will be decreed [in accordance with your name],
12′ … May it be that …
13′ You will have silver,
14′ You will have lapis lazuli gems,
15′ You will have cattle,
16′ You will have sheep."

(Namzitarra)

18′ "[To whe]re will I *take*
17′ Your silver, your lapis lazuli gems, your cattle, your sheep?
19′ The days of mankind are near,
20′ Day after day—so it (life) will diminish,
21′ Month after month—so it will diminish,
22′ Year after year—so it will diminish,
22a′ […]—so it will diminish (Ugarit only),
23′–24′ 120 years—such is the limit of mankind's life…
25–26′ From *that day* till now as long as mankind lived!
27′ I am going home,
28′ One cannot stop me, do not stop me, I am in a hurry!" (Sumerian only)

I quote here the Old Babylonian Sumerian version so that the expansion of the key theme in the Emar bilingual version (ll. 18′–26′) will be properly appreciated.

After Namzitarra recognized Enlil correctly, the god proceeds to say,

19 kù ḫé-tuku za ḫé-tuku gud ḫé-tuku udu ḫe-tuku

19 "You will have silver, you will have precious stones, you will have cattle, you will have sheep."

To which Namzitarra replies,

20 u_4 nam-lú-u_{18}-lu al-ku-nu
21 níg-tuku-zu me-šè e-tùm-ma

20 "The day of mankind is approaching,
21 So where does your wealth lead?"

Indeed, the passage is much shorter than the later Late Bronze Age version where the vanity theme is more developed.

Following Namzitarra's departure to his home, the bilingual part of the Emar tablet ends and a new section begins. The Sumerian column is wholly

---

THE PROVERBS

Left Column

29′ *luna'id abakunu šība*
30′ *ša milka iddina mārīšu*
31′ *iddina*$^!$ *milka mārīšu*

32′ *ṭēma*$^!$ *uterra ana bītišu*
33′ *mārūyama šimâninni ana milkiyama*
34′ [*u*]*znākunu libšâ*$^!$

35′ [*e*]*nūma allika mītūti*
36′ [*ur*]*ḫa allika anāku maḫrû*

37′ x-*ru-ma nišī mītūti*
38′ *tamḫur nuppulta u tamḫara*

39′ *ultēšir urḫa padāna nesûti*
40′ *allik itt*[*i*] *elliti padatti*

dispensed with and two Akkadian columns, arranged side by side, present a speech pronounced by a father to his successors, which he delivers apparently on his way to the Netherworld. The contents of the speech remain very unclear because of the poor preservation of the tablet. Regardless of the exact contents of the father's sayings, given that the vanity theme dealing with the shortness of life was introduced in the main composition of the tablet (that is to say, in the Enlil and Namzitarra part), perhaps it is of no coincidence that the new section deals with the passing away of the father. If this is the case, perhaps we can consider that the father in question was Namzitarra himself, following Alster (2005: 330). He suggested that the final lines of Enlil and Namzitarra, which tell of Namzitarra's departure home (ll. 27–28) are to be understood metaphorically as the protagonist's descent to the Netherworld. Indeed it is possible that the original ending of the Old Babylonian composition, whereby Namzitarra receives his prebend from Enlil was done away with and a pessimistic tone was introduced (the "vanity theme"), in order to allow for the inclusion of the proverbs themselves.

Following are the proverbs that are appended to Enlil and Namzitarra. I present first the left column and then the right.

The Proverbs

Left Column

29′ "Let me praise your (pl.) old father
30′ for the advice he gave to his sons
31′ he gave the advice to his sons.

32′ He imparted *knowledge* to his household":
33′ "My sons! Hear me! To my advice
34′ Pay attention!

35′ [W]hen I went to the dead,
36′ I was first to take the road,

37′ ... and the dead people..."
38′ "Did you meet *annihilation* and strife?"

39′ "I proceeded upon the road, the distant path,
40′ I went with pureness of form,

41′ *[an]a puḫri [šup]šuqti!*

Right Column

29″ *ṭupul mamma (ē taqbi) u liqallila ši'ātiša*
30″ *eṭlūtu ina qinnāzi ir-qú-ma ana qūlte*

31″ *ultu mārī bi-iṣ-ṣí ši-ba iz-za-qa-ra*
32″ *ana maḫrûtišu maḫrûtišu šimâninni! mārū?*

33″ *mārūki ša tanādāti mārātu[ki ša…]*

34″ *adi ṭardāku […ip]allaḫūka*

(A few lines remain but they do not merit to be included here because they very fragmentary)

Lower Edge (end of the composition; the colophon, which would probably have been written in the right lower edge, is now broken away)

pašāḫa […
nē[ḫta…
limad…[

The integration of the proverbs into the story of Enlil and Namzitarra utilizes a technique we have met before. As we saw, a set of proverbs foreign to the main composition was framed within The Ballad of Early Rulers (in one of the Ugarit manuscripts and the later Neo-Assyrian manuscript). In the same fashion, a new section of sapiential sayings with some thematic relationship to the main composition was incorporated in the tablet of Enlil and Namzitarra.

41′ [t]o the assembly of *difficulty*."

Right Column

29″ "(You should not speak) disgracefully against whoever"; and "May she belittle *her secondary wives*."
30″ "The young guys (suffering on the work gang) by the whip *became silently idle*."

31″ After the sons *of* (?), … *it will be said*…
32″ to his predecessors his predecessors (say): "Obey me (*my*) *sons*."

33″ "Your (fem.) sons are worthy of praise; [your] (fem.) daughters are […]."

34″ "Once I am driven away (to the Netherworld)…" … "They will honor you."

(The remaining text does not merit translation because of its very fragmentary state)

Lower Edge (end of the composition)

Peace […]
Qu[iet…]
Learn about…[…]

NOTES TO INDIVIDUAL LINES

17′: The speaker here is Namzitarra and not Enlil; "your" refers back to Enlil's gifts about to be bestowed Namzitarra and not to Namzitarra's future gains. See the discussion below.

19′: Reading here ⸢*lu qè-er-bu*⸣ on the basis of the Old Babylonian Sumerian al-ku-nu; the Sumerian of the Emar version is corrupt (ARG).

22a′: The Ugarit fragment includes an additional line, again ending with *limṭi*, "it will diminish."

23′–24′: The end of the Akkadian line is not clear. The Sumerian ḫi-a is a syllabic Sumerian spelling for ḫé-a "may it be," which may have been misunderstood, hence a corrupt Akkadian translation. Some scholars have understood the Akkadian as *ba-šu*[!]*-ša* > *bašûša* "(this is) its (mankind's) existence." Klein (personal communication) considers reading the Akkadian here as *palâša* "(this is) its (mankind) term." For more suggestions, see Alster 2005: 331.

25′: For this line, see Alster 2005: 331.

27′–28′: The end of the composition is marked by the citation of two lines from its beginning (hardly preserved in *Emar* 592). These two lines may have been the name of the composition by which it was known in antiquity. Their repetition may have thus signaled the end of the poem. Note how Ugarit Version I of The Ballad of Early Rulers closes with the opening lines of the composition in a ring-like fashion.

The Proverbs: Akkadian left column

29′: We follow Klein 1990: 67; Arnaud 1985–1987, no. 771 reads differently: *ši-ma* (i.e., hear!).

34′: The verbal form is written *li-ib-ši*; either take as a contracted form, i.e., *libšê* (typical of Old Babylonian Mari), or assume a mistake for *libšâ*.

41′: We read here [*šu-up*]*-su-uq-ti* > [*šup*]*šuqti* "of difficulty."

Akkadian right column

29″: Arnaud read here the initial signs as *um-mi ma-am-ma* "mother of who-so-ever," but the signs are probably to be read *ṭup-ul ma-am-ma* > *ṭupul mamma* "the disgrace of who-so-ever"; it is also possible that we are facing an abbreviated proverb; cf. *Šimâ Milka*, l. 22.

29″: For the second half of the line see *CAD* Š/2, 363.

30″: Perhaps a corrupt form of *râqu* "to be idle." The meaning of the saying however remains obscure. Compare here *Šimâ Milka* (2.1), l. 140′.

Discussion

Our main concern with the composition Enlil and Namzitarra lies in lines 17′–24′ which expound upon the vanity theme we have met already in The Ballad of Early Rulers. Before dealing with their content, we need to consider by whom they were spoken. While all scholars consider the vanity theme to be Enlil's speech to Namzitarra, we are of the opinion that it is actually Namzitarra who delivers them (Cohen 2010a). What use have I of your material gifts, says Namzitarra, if the days of mankind are short; to where, he asks rhetorically, can I take them, meaning to say that they are useless in the place he is going to—in other words, to the Netherworld (see above). Having Namzitarra speak out these lines fits well indeed with other articulations of similar themes elsewhere in Mesopotamian wisdom literature. Compare the son's speech to his father in *Šimâ Milka*. He tells him that material wealth is useless upon the day of death (ll. 133′–139′).

Let us recall indeed that the shortness or futility of human life is always expressed, if not by the poet, then by human figures and not by the gods. Archetypical figures, such as a father instructing his son (as represented in *Šimâ Milka* or The Instructions of Šuruppak), out of which the figure of the wise man, such as Ziusudra, emerged, or the barmaid Siduri in The Epic of Gilgameš, are the ones to offer advice on the attainment of a good or proper life in spite of its difficulties and eventual death. Gods determine the fates, as Enlil does, but they do not impart reflective attitudes concerned with the limit or futility of human life.

In our story then it is Namzitarra who presents his reflections on the nature of human life but he is not so much concerned with the overall futility of life, as was the poet of The Ballad of Early Rulers who urged of his readers to seize the day. Namzitarra speaks about the very shortness of life which renders material wealth insignificant. And not only are the days of mankind decreasing with the passage of time—they are limited. Here we find a precise limit to mankind's day, which in The Ballad of Early Rulers is determined by Ea. Let us quote again lines 23′–24′ of this composition:

> mu 2 *šu-ši* mu-meš nam-lú-u$_{18}$-lu níg-gig-bi ḫi-a
> 2 *šūši šanātu lū ikkib amēlutti ba-la/šu*$^{!}$*-ša*$^{?}$
>
> 120 years—such is the limit of mankind's life, *this is its term/this is its existence.*

There are two issues of concern here. The first issue is how are we to understand the semantically loaded word níg-gig (Sumerian) or *ikkibu* (Akkadian); the second is what are we to make of the limit of 120 years assigned to mankind.

Klein (1990) and Alster (2005: 338) translate níg-gig or *ikkibu* as "abomination" or "bane," but the meaning of the word can have a more neutral sense in this case. It can be understood as "taboo," in the sense of "something reserved or cut off," hence simply "reserved" or "limited" (Cooper 2011) or simply "not allowed." The idea that mankind's time is limited is expressed elsewhere in Mesopotamia literature (Klein 1990: 64; Alster 2005: 338). In the Sumerian poem The Death of Gilgameš, the hero is told that Enlil has granted him kingship, but not eternal life, hence he like other humans cannot escape death.

> níg-gig ak nam-lú-u_{18}-lu-ke_4 ne-en de_6-a ma-ra-dug_4
>
> You must have been told that this is what the limit of mankind's existence brings about.
>
> (The Death of Gilgameš; Cavigneaux and Al-Rawi 2000: 16 and 61; ETCSL 1.8.1.3, Segment E, l. 17; George 1999: 195–208)

A similar idea is expressed by Siduri when she tells Gilgameš that

> *balāṭam ša tasaḫḫuru la tutta*
> *inūma ilū ibnû awīlūtam*
> *mūtam iškunū ana awīlūtim*
> *balāṭam ina qātīšunu iṣṣabtū*
>
> The life which you seek you will not find.
> When the gods created mankind,
> Death they allotted to mankind,
> Life they held fast in their grasp.
>
> (The Epic of Gilgameš, Old Babylonian Version, The Sippar Tablet, iii 2–5; George 2003: 278–279).

With that, however, the composition from Emar stands unique for it specifies the number of years set to be the limit of mankind's life—not over one-hundred and twenty years. This absolute limit was rightly compared by Klein (1990) with Gen 6:3:

> והיו ימיו מאה ועשרים שנה
> And his day will be one-hundred and twenty years.

Klein (1990: 62) understood in light of the composition from Emar that the 120 years in Gen 6:3, "must refer to the lifespan of the individual human at large, and not to a specific time in history." Although the number by itself is without parallel in other Mesopotamian wisdom compositions, it stems from a Mesopotamian tradition which speaks about the limit set by the gods to man's life, as we have seen above. Likewise, the choice of the figure, based on multiplication of the base number of 60, implies a Mesopotamian tradition, especially as it is written 2 *šūši* "twice-sixty," a writing convention found elsewhere in Mesopotamian sources. Hence, the tradition of "120 years" as a limit to man's life does not seem to be an innovation of the Emar scribes, appealing as this idea may seem at first glance. It probably arrived at Emar, as it did at Ugarit, part and parcel of the whole of the bilingual version of the composition from Babylonia.

Sources

Section A = *Emar* 773 (+) *Emar* 592; Section B = *Emar* 771 (+) *Emar* 774 // RS 22.341 + RS 28.53a (Arnaud 1985–1987; Arnaud 2007: 140, no. 47; see also Civil 1989: 7 and Cohen 2010a).

The Old Babylonian Sumerian Version: Civil 1974–1977; Alster 2005: 327–35; ETCSL 5.7.1

Editions and Discussions

Alster 2005, 3.5; 2008: 59–60; Arnaud 1985–1987, no. 771; 2007, no. 47; Civil 1974–1977; Cohen 2010a; Cooper 2011; Klein 1990; Lambert 1989; Vanstiphout 1980. For additional discussions concerning the meaning of níg-gig/*ikkibu*, apart from those appearing in the cited studies, see Cohen 2002 and Geller 1990.

2.4

The Righteous Sufferer or A Hymn to Marduk from Ugarit

The partly broken tablet RS 25.460 found at Ugarit is a hymn to the god Marduk. Unsurprisingly it does not comfortably sit within the definition of wisdom literature; perhaps it would have found a better slot under the category of hymns or prayers dedicated to Marduk and other Mesopotamian gods. Although not as plentiful as in Mesopotamia, such hymns are not unknown from Late Bronze Age sites. There are hymns from Ugarit dedicated to Šamaš and other gods (Arnaud 2007, nos. 28–33; Dietrich 1988 and 1993). And from the archives of Ḫattuša several hymns were retrieved—dedicated to godheads such as Ištar, Adad, and Šamaš. It was argued that this type of composition influenced the genre of prayers written in Hittite and found in the Hittite capital (Singer 2002; Archi 2007; Klinger 2010).

Why therefore should RS 25.460 be included in this book? As was already recognized on its initial publication in 1968 by Nougayrol, it shares its basic structure and content with the composition *Ludlul Bēl Nēmeqi* "I will Praise the Lord of Wisdom," one of the first great wisdom literature works from Mesopotamia to be published (at the end of the nineteenth century C.E.), and often compared since then with the book of Job. Although this work can be defined as a hymn to Marduk, its complex approach and development of the subject of divine retribution has guaranteed that *Ludlul Bēl Nēmeqi* be considered a piece of wisdom literature. It occupies a prominent place in Lambert's *Babylonian Wisdom Literature*; and recently it has been the subject of an updated edition including additional materials (Annus and Lenzi 2010).

What *Ludlul Bēl Nēmeqi* and RS 25.460 from Ugarit share is that both introduce the theme of the "righteous sufferer" (sometimes called the "Babylonian Job")—a person who inexplicably suffers horrible physical and mental punishments at the hands of the gods whom he himself worships. He like Job seeks to understand why such punishment is visited upon him. Eventually Marduk relents and saves the sufferer. While the short Ugarit piece only briefly touches upon these issues, the much longer and more sophisticated *Ludlul Bēl Nēmeqi* takes over several hundred lines to develop these ideas.

The present edition relies on the studies of previous scholars, taking into special consideration Arnaud's (2007) edition, although not all of his suggestions are adopted here. The poor condition of some lines of the tablet, textual corruptions, and the nonstandard orthography, perhaps the result of dictation

---

Text

Obverse

1′ *šunāt lumni ittaškanānim ina m*[*ūši*]
2′ *šīrūa īta'dara īmâ kīma* [...]
3′ *ul iparras*! *bārû purussâya*
4′ *itta ul inaddin*! *dayyānu*
5′ *dalḫā*! *têrētu šutābulū šīrū*
6′ *muššakku šā'ilu bārû puḫādī*
7′ *igdamrū ummânū ša-ar-šu-ba-ša-a-a*
8′ *uštāmû ul iqbû adān*! *murṣiya*
9′ *paḫrat*! *kimti ana quddudi lām*! *adanni*
10′ *qerub salāti ana itkulimma izzaz*
11′ *aḫḫūa kīma maḫḫê dāmīšunu ramkū*
12′ *aḫḫātua šamna ḫilṣā*! *uraḫḫâni*
13′ *adi bēlu iššû rēšī*
14′ *mīta uballiṭa yâši*
15′ *adi Marduk bēlu iššû rēšī*
16′ *mīta uballiṭa yâši*
17′ *ātakal muṭṭâ akala*
18′ [*aštati maš*]*tītam dāmam ṭābūti*
19′ [*mušīta*]*mma ul iṣabbatanni šittu*
20′ [*adalli*]*p kala mūšiya*
21′ [...]x-*da-an-ni libbī beri karāšī*!
22′ [*aššum mu*]*ruṣ*! *amraṣu anāku ar-ra-su*

or misunderstandings of the copyist (whether at Ugarit or perhaps elsewhere previous to the transmission of the text to the city), still, in spite of numerous editions, hamper our full and proper understanding of the text. We set out here what we judge to represent scholarship's best efforts of reading and making sense of this difficult composition, but note that we include in our line-by-line commentary, following the presentation of the text, only the most essential readings and suggestions, hence the reader is advised to consult the bibliography for additional details.

Translation

Obverse

1′	Bad dreams kept besetting me at night,
2′	My omens became ever more troubling, changing like […],
3′	The diviner could not determine the meaning of my oracular prognosis,
4′	The Judge (i.e., the god Šamaš) does not hand out (my) omen,
5′	(My) omens are confused, (my) extispicy totally senseless,
6′–7′	The interpreter used up the incense (for smoke omens), the diviner—the lambs,
7′–8′	The experts debated about my *tablets concerned with the situation*, but they did not say when my illness will end,
9′	The family has assembled in order *to mourn* (over me) before (my) time,
10′	The kin by marriage were standing *as gloom was imposed*,
11′	My brothers (were mournful) like the *maḫḫû* personnel bathed in their own blood,
12′	My sisters were pouring *fine oil*,
13′	Until the lord lifted my head,
14′	Reviving me from the dead,
15′	Until Marduk the lord lifted my head,
16′	Reviving me from the dead,
17′	I ate scarce bread,
18′	[(I drank) as dri]nk blood and *brine*,
19′	And [at nigh]t, sleep would not overcome me,
20′	[I was sleep]less my entire night,
21′	…(corrupt line)… My heart … *My belly was starved.*
22′	[Because] I was so sick, I am *wasting away.*

Reverse

23′ [...]-*ti ša šudlupann*[*i*...]
24′ [... *dīm*]*ātiya kī kurummātiya*
25′ [*ša l*]*a mašê Marduk ša dalāli Marduk*
26′ [*in*]*a la Marduk šāru ina pîya ittaṣima*
27′ [...]-*en-tu*$_4$ *ḫu*-x *ul iltasi-maku*
28′ [*ad*]*allal adallal ša* [*b*]*ēli*
29′ [*ša*] *Marduk adallal*
30′ [*ša il*]*i šabsi adallal*
31′ [*ša*] *Ištar zenīti adallal*
32′ [*dul*]*la dulla la taba'aš dulla*
33′ [*an*]*a Marduk anāku utnēnšu*! *utnēnšu*!
34′ [*š*]*a imḫaṣanni u irēmanni*!
35′ [*u*]*kīlanni u irkusanni*
36′ [*i*]*ḫpânni u išmuṭanni*
37′ *uparriranni u utabbikanni*
38′ *itbukanni u īsipanni*
39′ *iddânni u ušaqqânni*
40′ *ultu pî mūti īkimanni*
41′ *ultu erṣēti ušēlânni*
42′ *išbir*! *kakkī māhiṣiya*
43′ *ina qāt qēberiya marra īkim*
44′ *iptâ īnīya katimāti*
45′ [*ṣī*]*t pîya ultetēšer*
46′ [...*u*]*znīya*

Break

Notes on Individual Lines

1′–2′: Reading and translation after ARG; see also von Soden 1990: 141 but cf. Arnaud 2007: 110 and 112. *Šīrūa* literally means "my exta," referring to the inner parts of the sacrificial animal (usually a lamb) according to which an individual's future is divined.

4′: The verbal form is corrupt, although all editors agree it is some form of *nadānu*, "to give," hence the restoration here. The "Judge" (Akkadian *dayyānu*) probably refers here to the divine judge—Šamaš.

Reverse

23′ […]…which troubled me…,
24′ My [*tea*]*rs* are like my food rations.
25′ Marduk must not be forgotten! Marduk is to be praised!
26′ [Wit]hout Marduk, the breath of my mouth would have departed,
27′ Would not the […] cried out …
28′ I praise, I praise the deeds of my lord,
29′ [the deeds of] Marduk I praise,
30′ [the deeds of] (even) an angry god I praise,
31′ [the deeds of] (even) an offended goddess I praise,
32′ Praise! Praise! So that you will not come to shame, praise!
33′ [*To*] Marduk—I *pray* to him, I *pray* to him,
34′ [*The one wh*]*o* struck me but then was merciful to me,
35′ He held me back and bound me,
36′ He broke me and *tore* me,
37′ He shattered me and rendered me limp,
38′ He cast me aside but picked me up again,
39′ He threw me down but raised me up,
40′ He saved me from death's mouth,
41′ He raised me from the Netherworld,
42′ He broke the weapons of my smiter,
43′ He took the spade from the hand of the one who wished to bury me,
44′ He opened my covered eyes,
45′ He set right [*the speech of*] my mouth,
46′ [*He*…] … my ears …

Break

6′–7′: Compare here Etana's words when wishing to demonstrate his piousness towards the gods: *ilāni ukabbit eṭemmē aplaḫ // igdamrā maššakkīya šā'ilātu // aslīya ina ṭubbuḫi ilānu igdamrū*, "I revered the gods, I worshiped the spirits of the dead. The dream-interpreters used up all my incense (used for smoke omens), upon sacrifice the gods used up all my sacrificial lambs." (The Epic of Etana, ii 134–136; Haul 2000: 187–89).

7′–8′: See *CAD* Š/2, 125 under *šaršubbû* ("meaning uncertain"); and consider also Dietrich 1993: 63, n. 130.

9′–12′: These lines apparently describe the sufferer's funerary rites: he is considered dead but then revived by Marduk. Cf. *Ludlul Bēl Nēmeqi*, ii 114–120 and iv 29–38.

9′: *quddudi* "to bow down."

10′: Dictated by context.

11′: The brothers are to be understood performing funerary rites in mourning like the *maḫḫû* or *muḫḫû* prophets or cult functionaries in the service of Ištar. Ištar's cultic personnel, such as the *kurgarrû* or the *assinnu*, are sometime considered, although this is a controversial point in scholarship, to perform acts of mutilation in cultic rites.

12′: Following ARG's reading; see also Arnaud 2007: 113 for a different suggestion.

18′: Thus most translations, including *CAD* Ṭ, 42, although as Arnaud notes, there is hardly any room for the verb, so perhaps it is to be supplied *ad sensum*; see Arnaud 2007: 111, l. 18′ for a different suggestion; he reads here *damām ṭābūti* as "le gémissement de l'amitié."

19′: Translation after ARG.

21′: The line is possibly corrupt and resists elucidation; following here ARG's suggestion.

22′: Following *CAD* R, 183; see also von Soden 1969: 191. The verb has been considered a Canaanite or West Semitic form meaning "to thin, pine away" (from the root *rz'*), but there is no proof of that. A learned composition, such as the one before us, certainly could have included rare items of vocabulary. Compare the many obscure items in *Ludlul Bēl Nēmeqi*; see Annus and Lenzi 2010: xxvi–xxvii. The translation offered here is *ad sensum*; ARG suggests possibly to read here *ar-ṣú-*⸢*un*$^{!}$⸣, "I yelled out loud."

27′: There have been various suggestions for the interpretation of this broken line, and although a consensual opinion has not been reached, it seems to be that someone is crying out some utterance—perhaps a priestess lamenting over the speaker. Most commentators take the signs *ma-ku* suffixed to the verb as an irrealis particle, *-maku*, although see Arnaud 2007: 111 and 114.

32′: Arnaud 2007: 111 and 114 reads differently. For the present translation, see Oshima 2011: 179, and cf. *CAD* B, 5–6.

33′; The verbal form is written *at-na-ni-šu* usually taken as a corrupt form of *utnēnšu* "I pray for him," although see Dietrich 1993: 64, n. 145.

34′–38′: Following *CAD* R, 264, P, 162, and T, 6–7. Compare this section with *Ludlul Bēl Nēmeqi*, iv 1–17.

35′: See von Soden 1990: 142 for a different suggestion.

37′: It has been suggested to read the second verbal form as *ú-dáb-bi-qa-an-ni* as "he joined me" from an allegedly West Semitic root *dbq*. There is no need to recourse to such an option as the Akkadian verb *tabāku* in the D Stem fits very well the sense here. See *CAD* T, 8. As ARG brings to my attention, the metaphoric language used in this passage is partly taken from the handling and storage of barley.

Discussion

Synopsis

The beginning and the end of the Ugarit tablet are lost, but enough remains for us to understand the general structure and content of the composition. We find the speaker suffering—he is sick and seeks the help of professional diviners and experts. They, however, cannot assist him in resolving his problem. It seems that the god Šamaš refuses to divulge the speaker's omens or portent signs. Being sick and without knowledge of the cause of his sickness because his omens are obscure, hence not armed with the necessary expiatory rites, the speaker stands on the edge of death. He offers Marduk praise, not forgetting to thank his own personal gods. He is only saved, as in *Ludlul Bēl Nēmeqi*, when Marduk intervenes.

The Righteous Sufferer from Ugarit, Ludlul Bēl Nēmeqi and Other Compositions

This composition was found only at Ugarit and presently remains unknown elsewhere. As mentioned, however, it shares its structure and content with the wisdom composition *Ludlul Bēl Nēmeqi*. This invites us to discuss the origin of RS 25.460 and its relationship to *Ludlul Bēl Nēmeqi*. We begin by examining more closely the dating of the two compositions.

The composition *Ludlul Bēl Nēmeqi* is a lengthy exposition on the theme of the "righteous sufferer" delivered in the first person by somebody called Šubši-mešrê-Šakkan, who possibly was active as a government official in the time of the Kassite king Nazimurutaš (ca. the beginning of the thirteenth century). It is generally thought that Šubši-mešrê-Šakkan himself was the author of the poem, but this assumption is far from certain. At any rate, under king Nazimurutaš' reign intense intellectual activities took place (as attested to in literary texts celebrating the king's military activities and in a later colophon; see Brinkman 1999: 191 and Lambert 1957: 8). These allow the dating of *Ludlul Bēl Nēmeqi* to a comfortable historical timeframe. It certainly can be imagined that a reign known for the compilation of literary pieces as well as works of the science of divination (specifically hemerologies), is a suitable time for a piece of literature like *Ludlul Bēl Nēmeqi*, with plentiful allusions to the Mesopotamian world of learning, to be written (see 1.2; also Beaulieu 2007).

It is not yet fully established how long the composition originally was, but it is assumed that it ran between 600 to 800 lines. It is also not known over how many tablets it extended, but most likely either four or five. These unknowns remain despite the many manuscripts at hand—as yet the piece cannot be fully reconstructed. On account of some of the manuscripts' formats, it is clear that *Ludlul Bēl Nēmeqi* served as a school text studied in the scribal schools of the first millennium.

Although *Ludlul Bēl Nēmeqi* is known exclusively from first-millennium manuscripts, it is generally agreed that it was written during the late-second millennium, in the Kassite period, as discussed above. The manuscript from Ugarit, roughly contemporary, is dated to the thirteenth century. However, because the piece from Ugarit contains linguistic features and orthographic traits associated with literary Babylonian compositions of the Late or post-Old Babylonian period (from around the seventeenth century and later), it is quite certain that the composition itself was committed to writing earlier than the actual date of the Ugarit manuscript. This suggests that RS 25.460, perhaps with additional compositions, served as a precursor to the more developed *Ludlul Bēl Nēmeqi*. Hence it may have inspired *Ludlul Bēl Nēmeqi* but this is not to imply that it is its direct antecedent.

When coming to compare the content of both compositions in greater detail it can be demonstrated that they go beyond sharing the general theme of the "righteous sufferer." For example, they have in common specific expressions concerning the sufferer's unsuccessful consultation with the professionals of Mesopotamian divination sciences. Compare the following passages from *Ludlul Bēl Nēmeqi* with lines 1′–8′ of the Ugarit manuscript.

bārû ina bīr arkat ul iprus
ina maššakki šā'ilu ul ušāpi dīnī

The diviner could not determine by divination (my) condition,
The interpreter could not explain my case by the help of smoke omens.
(*Ludlul Bēl Nēmeqi*, ii 6–7; Annus and Lenzi 2010: 19 and 35)

dalḫā têrētua nuppuḫū uddakam
itti bārî u šā'ili alaktī ul parsat

My omens were confused, contradictory every single day,
My condition remaining un-deciphered either by diviner or interpreter.
(*Ludlul Bēl Nēmeqi*, i 51–52; Annus and Lenzi 2010: 16 and 32)

sakikkîya išḫuṭ mašmaššu
u têrētiya bārû ūtešši
ul ušāpi āšipu šikin murṣiya
u adanna sili'tiya bārû ul iddin

The exorcist priest *avoided* my illness,
And the diviner became confused over my omens,
The incantation priest could not discover the nature of my disease,
And the diviner could not determine the end of my sickness.
(*Ludlul Bēl Nēmeqi*, ii 108–111; Annus and Lenzi 2010: 22 and 37)

It has been suggested that the lack of success in divulging the sufferer's condition by means of divination implicitly criticized the practice of this medium. As Lenzi (2012) argues, the author of *Ludlul Bēl Nēmeqi* (and by implication of RS 25.460) recognized that the science of omens may have failed an inquiring patient of an inquisitive and critical mind. In our opinion, it is doubtful, however, given the prominence omens occupied in Mesopotamian scholarly thought that such a secular critique could have been articulated. The view expressed by the sufferer is not a critique of the system itself or the professionals in its service but rather that his god, because of the severity of the sufferer's sin, refuses to manifest himself in the sufferer's dreams or send signs to his worshipper through divination. Another possibility, discussed by Schwemer (2010) is that the patient may be bewitched and his omens are intentionally obscured by an evil force, preventing their interpretation and as a consequence, finding the cause of punishment and the appropriate rites of expiation.

Whatever the case, it can be seen from the lines quoted above that a rather detailed and specific knowledge of Mesopotamian divination practices is displayed by both compositions, put to use in order to advance the main theme. On this ground, the case for a relationship between the older Ugarit composition and the later composition *Ludlul Bēl Nēmeqi* can be strengthened. This may indeed be so but caution in assuming a direct dependence of *Ludlul Bēl Nēmeqi* on the Ugarit composition is advised since we know so little about the literary history of these compositions. The study of similar articulations about the failure of divination, found elsewhere in Mesopotamian literature (e.g., Schwemer 2010; Oshima 2011: 354–62), or of the genre of "šuilla-prayers," the so-called incantation prayers, can demonstrate how compositions like RS 25.460 and *Ludlul Bēl Nēmeqi* were woven out of different strands of literary traditions (Annus and Lenzi 2010: xxviii–xxiv and xxxv; Beaulieu 2007: 10–11). These were all put together when the theme of the "righteous sufferer" had begun to be seriously explored in literary compositions during the Late or post-Old Babylonian period and into the Kassite period. Consider in this respect The Babylonian Theodicy (*BWL*, 63–89). It is known from first-millennium manuscripts, although probably composed, like *Ludlul Bēl Nēmeqi*, at the end of the second millennium. And it too deals with a theme similar to the one under discussion—the misfortune of a man in spite of his piety.

The relationship between *Ludlul Bēl Nēmeqi* and RS 25.460, although still not fully understood, can teach us something else. It shows us that the origin of the Ugarit composition lies in Mesopotamia. It was not therefore the product of Ugaritic scribes, but rather transmitted from Mesopotamian scribal centers to the city, like other learned compositions. RS 25.460, like other hymns and prayers found at Ugarit and Ḫattuša, is best considered as a component of the scribal curriculum. Although we lack concrete evidence to understand exactly how it fitted in the training of scribes, it is quite obvious that at Ugarit the composition was not utilized in ritual or cultic contexts (Dietrich 1993: 63 and 1988). With that said, one may cautiously assume that RS 25.460 bore some religious significance for its copyists at Ugarit, although unlike at Ḫattuša this work and other hymns did not play a significant role in the formation of expressions of worship in the city, as far as can be judged.

As with other compositions we have been discussing, it needs to be asked whether this composition underwent any local editorial changes or modifications at all upon its reception in Ugarit. As far as can be judged, apart from a few orthographic features and a small number of rather arguable West Semitic or Ugaritic lexical items (Oshima 2011: 205–15 [P 4]; and above the commentary of individual lines), there is nothing remarkably out of place to suggest an interfering hand of a local scribe or editor, whether at Ugarit or elsewhere outside of Mesopotamia. A wider investigation into the genre of prayers and hymns during the Late Bronze Age is required in order to settle this question more precisely.

SOURCE AND EDITIONS

Source: RS 25.460 (= *Ugaritica* 5 no. 162).

Editions, Translations and Discussions: Nougayrol 1968: 265–73; von Soden 1969: 191–93; von Soden 1990; Arnaud 2007: 110–14; Dietrich 1988; Dietrich 1993: 62–67; Kämmerer 1998: 160–163; Oshima 2011, no. P 4; Foster 1997 and 2005: 410–11.

Editions of *Ludul Bēl Nēmeqi*: Annus and Lenzi 2010; see also Annus and Lenzi 2011. The previous standard and classic edition still of worth is found in *BWL*.

For the theme of the righteous sufferer in *Ludlul Bēl Nēmeqi* and elsewhere in Mesopotamian literature and its relation to the book of Job, see the bibliography provided by Annus and Lenzi 2010.

For an introduction to the genre of hymns and prayers, including an updated bibliography, see Lenzi, Frechette and Zernecke 2011.

2.5

THE DATE PALM AND THE TAMARISK

The composition The Date Palm and the Tamarisk belongs to a subgenre of Mesopotamian wisdom literature—the debate or disputation poem. This type of wisdom composition is known chiefly from Sumerian compositions dating to the Old Babylonian period and from a few Akkadian pieces attested by manuscripts of a mostly later date. There are about ten Sumerian compositions and only about six known Akkadian compositions, which, so it is assumed, relied either wholly or partly on now-lost Sumerian antecedents (see below). The Akkadian compositions are usually shorter and less elaborate than the Sumerian debates. They are also represented by fewer manuscripts, most obviously incomplete, hence their reconstruction is severely limited.

On the whole, the genre of disputation literature is poorly represented in the Late Bronze Age. Apart from The Date Palm and the Tamarisk debate poem found at Emar, at Ugarit a few pieces belonging to a rather poorly known cycle of stories about the fox have been recovered (Arnaud 2007, nos. 52 and 53; see 1.1).

At the core of the disputation or debate poem are two protagonists, one pitted against the another, each trying to outwit the other by declaring through alternating perorations its superiority. The pairs include observable phenomena such as "winter" versus "summer" or, more commonly, animals, plants, and various agricultural implements competing against each other. The pairs, although standing in opposition to one another, may share a biological (types of trees or animal species) and/or an economic domain (e.g., sheep versus grain). The main thrust of the arguments throughout the debate poem is concerned with the evaluation of each of the contestants' usefulness to mankind. The debate ends when both contestants are brought to the judgment of the god. In the present composition, however, the end is missing so we are not in a position to know which of the two contestants won—whether it was the date palm or the tamarisk.

The aim of the debate poems, as discussed in detail by Vanstiphout in several studies, was not to generate knowledge about the world, but to engage in the art of the dispute itself, involving the exposition of folklore or common knowledge, and the ostentation of erudition and wit, informed through the curriculum of the scribal schools. Hence the debates, like other compositions collected here, are the products of the scribal school, although unlike other wisdom compositions, they do not explicitly impart morals or serve a straightforward didactic purpose.

For a thoroughly comprehensive introduction to the genre of the Mesopotamian debate poems, see in particular the studies of Vanstiphout (1990, 1991, 1992a, and 1992b).

The Sources

The composition The Date Palm and the Tamarisk is known from a few sources dating to different periods. In Emar we find it represented by one badly broken manuscript written in Akkadian (another fragment duplicates a few lines, hence there may have been another manuscript present in Emar). It can be dated to the thirteenth century on account of its so-called Syro-Hittite script. The obverse of the tablet contains at least forty-four lines, and the reverse has around twenty-five incomplete lines after which comes a break. This means that the conclusion of the composition is gone. The colophon, like the whole of the reverse side of the tablet, is very badly preserved: the scribe's name and his affiliation are broken away. Given that the tablet was written in the Syro-Hittite script, it stands to reason that it was produced by one of the Zū-Ba'la family members. Perhaps it was the work of Šaggar-abu, who also copied The Ballad of Early Rulers.

Apart from the Emar manuscript, there are three additional Akkadian sources and one Sumerian source. The oldest Akkadian source is represented by two very fragmentary and incomplete Old Babylonian pieces (of the same tablet) from Šaddupûm (Tell Harmal, near modern-day Bagdhad). They are considered to represent an eastern (probably originally from Ešnunna) dialect of Old Babylonian. Thus they provide us with the evidence of the transmission changes the work had already undergone since the days of its composition in one of the sites of (most likely) southern Babylonia.

Two Assyrian manuscripts, none of which is complete, come from Assur. One source (KAR 324) is written in an atypical tablet format, containing only the beginning of the composition; it is dated on the basis of its script and language to the Middle Assyrian period. The other Assyrian source (KAR 145) is likewise not fully preserved although it is much better written; it is likely to be of a somewhat later date.

The Sumerian source is written in an exercise or excerpt-tablet format from Susa; it is dated to the Old Babylonian or post-Old Babylonian period. It has been argued that it is a translation of the Akkadian version of this composition (Cavigneaux 2003; see also George 2009: 107). This is to say that the Sumerian source from Susa does not represent the earliest stage of the composition. It offers us but a translation of one of the Akkadian versions of The Date Palm and the Tamarisk, just as the Sumerian of the Late Bronze Age Akkadian recension of The Ballad of Early Rulers probably is a translation of the Akkadian.

The contribution of the Emar fragment is twofold. First, in spite of its state of preservation, it allows us to restore with the help of the other Akkadian manuscripts almost the entire composition. Thus we gain a stronger grip than previously of the structure and contents of The Date Palm and the Tamarisk. Secondly, it also allows us to achieve a better understanding of the composition's development from its Old Babylonian Sumerian and Akkadian recensions to its later recensions. This issue will be explored in greater detail in the discussion below, but for now it can briefly be noted how the introduction of the debate poem changed through time, as it can be observed how some of its lines were abandoned in later versions. It can also be seen how the Assur and Emar manuscripts, although similar in their overall contents, have situated particular perorations differently. This demonstrates how building blocks of the work could be moved around while its narrative frame remained the same. This flexibility is also seen among the versions of The Ballad of Early Rulers, where the opening lines and the end of the work framed various proverbs.

The canonical, or to use a more appropriate term, standardized, form of this composition might be represented by the manuscript KAR 145 from Assur, the latest of all versions, dated to perhaps the early Neo-Assyrian period. This, however, cannot be verified, because we lack the final stage of the transmission and standardization of the debate poem. The end product of Babylonian literary compositions is generally assumed to be represented by Neo-Assyrian manuscripts (generally from Nineveh) or Neo-Babylonian manuscripts dated to the first millennium, at a time when cuneiform literature enjoyed a certain standardization. In spite of a lack of clear first-millennium manuscripts, there is no doubt that The Date Palm and the Tamarisk was known, if not also copied and studied, during this period. A Nineveh library catalogue mentions (albeit in a corrupt form) the title of the work (*BWL*, 151). The Date Palm and the Tamarisk was not the only debate poem in circulation, for other works in this genre are known from this period and extant in fragmentary Neo-Assyrian manuscripts.

The basic text that allows us to reconstruct the work is the Emar manuscript. Where there are lacunae, I have supplemented it from the Middle

Assyrian and sometimes from the Old Babylonian versions, to the best of my understanding. The gender distinction between the two trees—the date palm as feminine and the tamarisk as masculine—evident in the Akkadian text cannot be maintained in English; I have however, capitalized the designations of the two protagonists to assist the reader in their immediate recognition in the debate.

The edition and translation of the piece given below follow Wilcke (1989), who rearranged into a single and coherent tablet the many fragments first

---

Text

Obverse

Introduction

1 *ina ūmē ellûti ina m[ūšī el]lûti ina šanāti [rūqēti]*
2 *enūma ilū [u]kinnū māta [u] ālāni ēpušū [ana] nišī rūqēti*
3 *enūma uš[ta]ppikū šadê [u] nārāti iḫ[rû napšat] māti*
4 *puḫra iškunū ilū ša māti [Anu Enlil Ea iltē]niš*
5 *imtalkūma ina birišunu ašib Šamaš [u Ay]a ušbat*$^{!}$

6 *ina panāma šarruttu ina māti ul ibbašši u [bēluttu ana ilī] šarkat*
7 *ilū irāmūma nišī ṣalmāt qaqqadi it[tadnū šarra]*
8 *ša māt Kiš u[g]ammirūniššu ana ⸢naṣāri*$^{?}$*⸣ [šarru ina ekallišu izzaqap gišimmara]*
9 *idātišu umalli*$^{?}$ *bīnī*$^{!}$ *[ina] ṣilli bīni [...]*
10 *una[qqi*$^{?}$*] ina ⸢ṣilli⸣ gišimmari urt[aṣṣan*$^{?}$ *uppu…]*
11 *[…] ummānumma irâš ekallum*

12 *[iṣṣū a]ḫû ištannū kilallū b[īnu u gišimmaru]*
13 *[ṣalta kila]llū ētepšūma eppušū [… umma bīnuma]*

14 *[magal rabâk]u anāku šumma gišimmaruma šūturāku*$^{!}$ *[elika]*

published by Arnaud (1985–1987 as nos. 783 and 784). Thus he provided an edition of the composition from its beginning to its final preserved lines, near its original end. Wilcke also included a comparison of all known Akkadian versions, so the reader is advised to consult his edition to see in detail how one version relates to the other. Extremely helpful to my translation and discussion of the work is also the study of Streck 2004, who offers additional comments and suggestions to Wilcke's edition and includes information based on other sources regarding the economic, religious, and symbolic value of the date palm and the tamarisk.

Translation

Obverse

Introduction

1 In far-away days, in [far-aw]ay ni[ghts], in [distant] years,
2 When the gods established the land [and] created cities [for] the ancient folk,
3 When they poured out the mountains [and] dug out rivers, [life of] the land,
4 The gods of the land set up council, [Anu, Enlil and Ea toge]ther
5 deliberated and among them sat Šamaš [and (his consort) Ay]a sat.

6 Once there was no kingship in the land and [rulership] was assigned (only) to the gods,
7 But the gods loved the black-headed folk and they g[*ave them a king*]
8 *to whom they delivered the protection of the land of Kiš*. [The king planted in his palace the Date Palm],
9 All around he planted Tamarisk(s). [In] the shade of the Tamarisk [*a libation*]
10 *He lib*[*ated*]. In the shadow of the Date Palm [the drum] *thundered…*
11 The crowd [was…] and the palace was joyous.

12 [The trees] were enemies—the Ta[marisk and the Date Palm] became rivals,
13 and started [a quarrel. The Tamarisk said:]

14 "I am [much bigger (than you)]." The Date Palm responded, "I am superior to [you],"

EXCHANGE I

15 [*atta*] *bīnu iṣu la ḫašiḫti mī*[*nu larûka*]
16 [*bīnu l*]*a inbi niûti inbū ana paššuri* [*ša šarri*]
17 [*šarru ikka*]*l ummānumma ṭātī iqabbi*

18 [*…nu*]*karibbu nēmela ušarša ušaḫḫa*[*z bēlta*]
19 [*urabb*]*a ummašu šerra ṭāt emūqīya* [*ikkal irabbi*]
20 [(*inbūa*$^?$) *kayyānam*]*ma ana maḫar šarrutti*

21 [*bīnu pîšu ēpuš ītapal utter pîšu ša*]*rḫa* [*ma'diš*]
22 [*attūya šērū ana šērī…*] / [su-mu su-dingir-re-e-ne-ke$_4$ gá-⸢ke$_4$$^?$⸣]

(Restored from the Assyrian tablet KAR 145, l. 4′ and the Sumerian version l. 3)

23 [*mim*]*mâki banâ* [*kīma amti ša ana bēltiša*] *ubba*[*lamma…*] *uṭaḫḫa iškārša*
24 [*aqri d*]*amqima tubbal*[*ī ana ṣē*]*riya*

EXCHANGE II

25 [*utte*]*r pîša ī*[*tapal gišimmaru issaqqara ana*] *aḫiša bīni*
26 [*umma*] *ina ūrini*[*ma ittadi parakka…*]
27 …
28 [*šumma ilamma nisaqqar ana ṭīdima šērī* (*ilāni taqbi*)…]
29 …

(Restored according to KAR 145, ll. 8′–9′; KAR 324, l. 41; and the Sumerian version)

11 súr-ra-a-ni-ta gišnimbar mu-un-na-ni-ib-gi$_4$-gi$_4$
12 inim bí-in-dug$_4$ ^{giš}šinig šeš-bi-šè
13 tukum-bi ugu ùr-ra barag al-dù-dù-ne
14 NI.I.NI in-sa$_6$-sa$_6$-ne
15 dingir mu-un-pàd-dè-ne im-ma-e-še
16 su dingir-re-e-ne ab-bi-zé-en

Exchange I

15 "[You]—Tamarisk—are a tree of no use. W[hy are your branches]
16 [O Tamarisk—] fruitless? Our fruits are fit for the [royal] table!,
17 [The king eat]s and the crowd says "(they are) my gift."

18 "Thanks to me the orchard cultivator gains a profit and he provides (it) [to the queen].
19 The mother [raise]s (her) baby, the gift of my resources [it eats and grows up].
20 [(*My fruit*) *is always present*] before royalty."

21 [The Tamarisk spoke out, proudly responded, with] much [pride].
22 "[M]y flesh is for/to the flesh of …[…]" / Sumerian: "My flesh is the flesh of the gods"… (Restored from other sources)
23 Your excellent assets—[like a maid] who brings and presents her finished product [to her mistress]—
24 [what is worthy and g]ood you will bring to me."

Exchange II

25 [The Date Palm] proudly replied, [speaking out] to its brother, the Tamarisk.
26 ["You say,] *upon our roof* [*a dais will be built…*]
27 …
28 [Should we dare evoke the god: "*It will come to nothing*!" (You say you are) the flesh (of the gods)].
29 …

These fragmentary lines are understood somewhat better thanks to the Sumerian version.

11 The Date Palm answered it in its anger,
12 It spoke to the Tamarisk, its brother,
13 "You say, *if upon the roof they build a dais for me*
14 *And they beautify all around,*
15 *They evoke the gods:* "*It will come to nothing*!,"
16 "You may say that (you are) "flesh of the gods,"

17 barag dingir-re-e-ne mu-bi íb-sa$_4$-sa$_4$-ne
18 kug-babbar su dingir-re-e-ne dul$_9$-a
19 taka$_4$-ma-ab níg-dingir-ra níg-sa$_6$-ga-zu dug$_4$-ga-ab

30 [*ul ide bīnu dumuq ilāni dumuq…*]…[…]…*ili balṭū*
31 …
32′ [*d*]*umuqka maḫ*[*ar… bīnu pîšu ēpuš ītapal utter pîšu šarḫ*]*a ma'diš*
33′ *ḫassāku muttallika* [*ina ekal šarri mīnuya šakin ina ekal šarri ina paššuriya šarru*] *ikkal*
34′ *ina mallati*[*ya bēltu išatti ina itqūriya ikkalū qarrādū ina buginniya*] *nuḫatimmu qēmī ilâš*
35′ *išparākuma qê a*[*maḫḫaṣ*$^{!}$ *ulabbaš u*]*mmānamma unammar šarra*
36′ *mašmašākuma bīt* [*ili uddaš/ullal etellēku utter p*]*îyama šānina ul i*[*šu*]

Exchange III

37′ *utter pîša īta*[*pal gišimarru issa*]*qqara ana aḫiša bīni*
38′ *ina gizinakki ina n*[*iqî Sîn rub*]*ê balu anāku izuzzi*$^{!}$
39′ *ul inaqqi šarru ina* [*šāri e*]*rbetta sulluḫā šulu˹ḫḫātuya˺*
40′ *tabkū erūya ina* [*qaqqa*]*rimma eppašū isinna*

41′ *ina ūmišu bīnu* [*ana qāt*] *sīrāšî iradduma*
42′ *tuḫḫū kīma* [*kamari eli*]*šu*$^{!}$ *kamrū*

43′ [*bīnu pîšu īpuš ītapal utter pî*]*šu šarḫa ma'diš*
44′ [*alkī i nillika anāku u kâši ana āl ki*]*škattêka āl šipri*

Reverse

45′ [*umma itâtuya la mala* (*ṣu*)*mb*(*abî*)]
46′ [*la mala qatrini qadištu mê bīni*]

17 However, it is the dais of the gods which is given this term,
18 And it is silver which coats the flesh of the gods,
19 Leave to me all things divine and tell me what you are worth!"

30 [The Tamarisk does not understand the beauty of the gods, the beauty…]…of the god…are alive.
31 …
32′ Your beauty in front…[…" The Tamarisk spoke out, proudly responded] with much pride.
33′ "I am thinking of the furniture [in the king's palace. What is mine in the king's palace? The king] eats [upon my table],
34′ Out of my cup [the queen drinks, with my spoon the warriors eat, in my trough] the baker kneads the dough,
35′ I am a weaver, I s[pin] thread, [I clothe the c]rowd, and make the king all bright,
36′ I am an exorcist priest, [I renew/purify] the tem[ple, I am supreme; I proudly pro]claim I have no rival."

Exchange III

37′ The [Date Palm] proudly replied, speaking out to its brother, the Tamarisk.
38′ "In the offering place, when o[ffering to Sîn the prin]ce, without myself being present,
39′ The king cannot perform libation. My purification rites are performed through all corners of the world,
40′ My fronds are dropped to [the ground] and a festival is celebrated.

41′ Whereas, the Tamarisk is (only) suitable for the brewer's [usage],
42′ The spent grain like [piled-up dates/earth-works] are piled [upon] it!"

43′ [The Tamarisk spoke out, proudly respond]ed, with much pride.
44′ "[Come, let us go you and I to the district] of my[!] workshops, the craftsmen's quarter!"

Reverse

45′ [Behold: isn't my surroundings full of *resin*?]
46′ [Isn't it full of incense? The *qadištu* priestess collects the water of the Tamarisk,]

47′ [*ilaqqema idallalūma ippašū isinna*]

(Restored according to the Assyrian Tablet KAR 145, rev. 6–8)

48′ *ina ūmišu gišimmaru ina qā*[*t ṭābiḫi bašima*]
49′ *erūša ina parši u dāmē* [...]

EXCHANGE IV

50′ *utter pîša ītapal gi*[*šimmaru issaqqara*] *a*[*na aḫiša bīni*]
51′ *alka i nillik anāku u kâ*[*ši ana āl isinniya ašar ḫidāti ē*]*piška b*[*īnu nagāra*]
52′ *ana zinîya anaddi u* [...*ipal*]*laḫa nagaru* [*ūmišamma una"adanni*]

53′ *bīnu pîšu īpuš ī*[*tapal utter*] *pîšu šarḫa ma'diš*
54′ [*ana*] *ummâni nē*[*mel*]*a kalašu išu ana ikkari* [*nēmela*]
55′ ⌜*malašu*⌝ *išu i*[*kkaru ina*] *papallīya ittakis*! [*ina*...]
56′ *ina utliya marrašu ultēli ina marriya uḫta*[*rri* (*palga*)]
57′ [*ipet*]*te namgara*[*ma*] *išatti eqlu*
58′ [*assanqa*] *qaqqara* [...]x *ana* ‹*nu*›*rrubi erṣ*[*ēti Ašnan*...]
59′ [...] *šarrutta udd*[*aš u*] *Nisaba šummuḫat* [...]

EXCHANGE V

60′ [...*utt*]*er pîša īt*[*apal giš*]*immaru issaqqara ana aḫiša* [*bīni*]
61′ [*anāku*] *elika ana ummân*[*i nēmel*]*a kalašu išu ana ikkari nēm*[*ela malašu išu*]
62′ [*šumm*]*annī tamšāra*! *eb*[*il na*]*ṣmadi ebil ebēḫi isiḫ*[*ti* ...]
63′ [*še'et*] *ereqqi* [...*ša unūt*] *ikkari mimma mala ibaššû* [*elik*]*a atrāku*

64′–66′ Very fragmentary; basically the Emar source ends here—there is a gap after which comes a fragmentary colophon. The parallel lines of the dispute containing the reply of the Tamarisk are also poorly preserved in the Assyrian tablet KAR 145, hence not given here. However, the following part of dispute in the same source, which contains the response

47′ [and then praise is given and a festival performed.]

48′ When at the same time the Date Palm [is (only) suitable] for the butcher's use.

49′ Its fronds *are found* in gore and blood…"

EXCHANGE IV

50′ The D[ate palm] proudly replied, [speaking out to its brother, the Tamarisk].

51′ "Come, let us go, you and I [to my festival city, place of joy.]

52′ I will lay down upon my (bed of) palm fronds 51′ your (wood)maker—[O Tamarisk—the carpenter], and […] the carpenter will re[vere me and take care of me daily]."

53′ The Tamarisk spoke out, proudly responded, with much pride.

54′ "I have everything for the craftsman's benefit,

55′ I have as much as needed for the farmer's [benefit. The farmer] cut down my saplings [in order to…],

56′ The farmer had his spade produced from my inner part, with my spade he du[g irrigation ditches],

57′ [(Thus) he open]s the irrigation canal so that the field can drink.

58′ [I inspected] the soil…[*I planted* grain] *in the moistness* of the ear[th].

59′ […] I renew kingship and Nisaba (the grain-goddess) is very plentiful […]."

EXCHANGE V

60′ [The Da]te Palm proudly replied, speaking out to its brother [the Tamarisk].

61′ ["I] am of more [benefit] to the craftsman than you are, [I am of more] benefit to the farmer.

62′ [Tet]hering ropes, whips, ropes for the harness, rope(s) for girdles, mater[ials for…]

63′ [bolsters] for wagons, whatever there is [among *the utensils of*] the farmer. I am by far superior [than] you."

64′–66′ The Tamarisk's reply is almost totally lost. The reply of the Date Palm given below is restored on the basis of the parallel section in the of the Date Palm, is in a better condition, until it breaks away as well. The Tamarisk's answer is missing.

EXCHANGE VI

(Assyrian Tablet KAR 145, rev. 18–23 [= Wilcke's edition, ll. 67′–71′])

18 ki.min *anāku elukka šeššīšu mutturāku sebîšu*...[...]
19 *ana Nisaba tēnû anāku šalāšat arḫī*...[...]
20 *ekūtu almattu eṭlu lapnu*...[...]
21 *ekkalū akala la maṭâ ṭābū suluppū*⸢*ya*⸣ [...]
22 $^{\textit{ḫepi}}$ *šer šerrī* [...]
23 *liblibbīya edallalū* [...]
24 ...
25 ...

(Assyrian Tablet KAR 145 breaks off)

NOTES ON INDIVIDUAL LINES

1: The form *ellûti* is for *ullûti* > *ullû*, "distant." For the opening lines, which are also found in additional Mesopotamian compositions, see Dietrich 1995.

5: The end of line is restored according to Arnaud's suggestion (1985–1987: 391). The form *ušbat* is Assyrian for Babylonian *ašbat*.

7–8: The reading and interpretation of these two lines are not secure.

10–11: The reading of these lines in all versions follows Streck 2004: 259.

12–13: Translation after ARG.

14: The Emar version reads ^{giš}gišimmar *mu-uš-šu-ra-ku*, which is probably corrupt (ARG), hence the Assyrian version (KAR 324 , l. 21) is followed here.

17: Reading and translation after ARG.

21: For the formulation *bīnu pîšu ēpuš ītapal utter pîšu šarḫa ma'diš*, see Wilcke 1989: 185–87.

26: Restored following Streck 2004: 261.

28: Restored from KAR 145 obv. 9: *a-na ṭé-di* = *ana ṭīdi* "to, before clay," supported also by the Sumerian version, l. 15, although the meaning of "swearing or evoking the god before or to clay" remains unclear. Perhaps it means "this will come to nothing," hence worthless.

Assyrian tablet KAR 145, rev. 18–23.

EXCHANGE VI

18 (The Date Palm proudly replied, speaking out to its brother the Tamarisk). "I am six times more important than you, seven times [more… than you].
19 I am considered a replacement for grain (lit., Nisaba, the grain-goddess) for a period of three months…[…],
20 The orphan, the widow, the pauper…[…],
21 They eat food which never diminishes. My dates are good…[…],
22 broken (scribal comment) *My offspring* … […],
23 They praise my shoots/offspring…[…]."
24 …
25 …

(Assyrian manuscript breaks)

30: This line is made up to two sources but it is not sure that both indeed meet at this place.

38′: Wr. *iz-zi-iz-zu* perhaps for the infinitive *izuzzi*, as Babylonian grammar dictates (ARG).

41′: Babylonian *iredduma*.

42′: For this line, see the remarks of Wilcke 1989: 181 and Streck 2004: 261.

44′: The text has "your workshops," but surely, "my" is intended. See Wilcke 1989: 181.

55′–57′: For the verb forms in these lines, see Wilcke 1989: 190 and Streck 2004: 262.

56′: *utliya*, lit. "my lap" refers here to the core or inner flanks of the tree trunk.

58′: The meaning of the form *ru-ú-bi* is not clear; consider perhaps emending to ‹*nu*›-*ru-ú-bi* > *nurrubu* "moist." Cf. the Assyrian version KAR 145, obv. 15′: *ana nurbi ša erṣēti* "to the *moisture* of the soil."

59′: Cf. the Assyrian tablet KAR 145, obv. 16′: *u* ^{d}*Nisaba šumuḫ nišī udda*[*š*] "And Nisaba (the grain-goddess) renew[ed] the people's growth."

61′: Translation after ARG.

62′: The reading *tam*$^{!}$*-ša-ra* in the Emar version on the basis of the Assyrian manuscript is not certain. See additional suggestions by Wilcke 1989: 190.

64′–66′: The Assyrian tablet KAR 145, rev. 22 inserts the scribal remark *ḫepi* "broken," indicating that the scribe, when copying the composition onto his tablet, was faced with a broken or fragmentary original. Exchange VI of this tablet is read a bit differently by Wilcke (1989: 183).

Exchange VI, 18: The form *e-lu-ka* is in the locative; see *CAD* E, 89.

Exchange VI, 22: Following Streck 2004: 262 and cf. *CAD* Š/2, 308.

Discussion

The Date Palm and the Tamarisk is structured very much in the same fashion as other compositions belonging to the debate-poem genre. It includes a mythological introduction, the setting of the debate in a royal banquet, the introduction of the contenders—the Date Palm and the Tamarisk—and the debate itself. As has been suggested, the setting of the debate in a royal banquet hints as to the original audience for which the debate poems were intended: before being committed to writing the debates were perhaps performed orally for the entertainment of the upper echelons of society, royalty and nobility included.

The core of the debate poem is the debate itself. It consists of almost equal-length alternating perorations that create a balanced if not somewhat monotonous composition, moving from one contestant to the next. The outcome of the debate or the verdict, which in the Sumerian compositions is usually declared by a god, is missing from our composition. Whether The Date Palm and the Tamarisk included such a verdict at all is not known because the end of the composition is lost from all our sources.

I will focus first on the so-called mythological introduction of the composition, following which I will discuss in some detail the contents of the piece in order to explicate some of its more opaque passages. I will end with an evaluation of the setting and role of this debate poem in Emar and will briefly consider the genre of disputation wisdom literature in noncuneiform sources.

The Mythological Introduction

Like many compositions of this genre, The Date Palm and the Tamarisk begins with the so-called mythological introduction. In the Sumerian compositions the mythological introduction may stretch for over a third of the entire poem (in some cases over one-hundred lines). In the present composition, however, the introduction is relatively short, placing the debate in long-gone days, when the gods created the world. The intention of the mythological introduction in this composition as in others was however not to supply the reader with Mesopotamian beliefs about cosmogony, but to set the stage for the ensuing debate between the protagonists (Vanstiphout 1990: 289–95). We learn that after establishing the land and opening the rivers—the source of livelihood of the land, the gods bestow kingship on mankind. The first king rules over Kiš, a city associated in Mesopotamian traditions with the first seat of kingship after the deluge (as related in The Sumerian King List). There the king plants in his garden the first or prototypical date palm and tamarisk (Bottéro 1991: 14). It can be implied, unlike the case in some Sumerian compositions where it is explicitly stated, that the contenders were the creation of the gods. In the garden, a royal banquet is celebrated, as in other debate poems (Vanstiphout 1992b), at which point the debate begins. The setting of a banquet in the royal garden supplies the background against which the protagonists will contend, as both will mention time and time again their use of wood or yield within a royal context in order to emphasis without doubt their importance and high standing.

Having three sources containing the mythological introduction, we are in a good position to compare the versions. First is the Old Babylonian version from Tel Harmal, ancient Šaddupûm, followed by the Middle Assyrian version (KAR 324); the other Assyrian tablet does not preserve the introduction. Both are to be compared with the Emar introduction.

The Old Babylonian Introduction

1 *[in]a ūmī! ullûtim ina šanātim rūqātim inūma*
2 *⸢Igigu⸣? ukinnū mātam ītanḫū ilū ana a[wī]lūtim*
3 *[p]uḫrum ipšahū u‹šē›redūšim nuḫšam ina pani*
4 *[an]a šutēšir mātim guššur nišī ibbû šarram*
5 *[āla]m Kiši ana šapārim ṣalmāt qaqqadi nišī mādātim*
6 *[šarru]m ina ki[sa]llišu izzaqap gišimmaram itâtušša*
7 *[umalla] bīnam ina ṣil⸢li bīnim! na⸣ptanam*
8 *[iškunū ina ṣi]lli gi[šimmarim…] ⸢uppum⸣? lapit*

1 [I]n distant days, in far-away years, when
2 The *Igigi gods* established the lands, the gods toiled instead of mankind.
3 They took rest in the assembly, allowing abundance to reach it (mankind). Then
4 They named a king to govern correctly the land and strengthen the people,
5 To administer [the cit]y of Kiš, the multitudinous black-headed folk.
6 [The kin]g planted in his courtyard the Date Palm and around it

7 [He filled it] with Tamarisk (trees). In the shade of the Tamarisk a banquet
8 [was set. In the sh]ade of the Da[te Palm…] the drum was played.
(The rest is very fragmentary)

(The Date Palm and the Tamarisk, Old Babylonian Version; *BWL*, 155–56; Wilcke 1989)

The Middle Assyrian Introduction (KAR 324)

Obverse
1 *ina ūmē ellûte nišē nesûte* (wr. *na-šu-u-te*)
2 *nārāte iḫreū napšāt mātāte*
3 *puḫra iškunū ilānu mātāte Anu Enlil Ea*
4 *i[št]ēniš*! *iddalgū*
5 *ina berišunu*! *ašib*! *Šamaš*
6 *berīt bēlat ilāni rabûte ušbat*
7 *ina pana šarrūtu ina mātāte ul baši*
8 *u bēlūtu ana ilāni šarkat*
9 (unclear sign)… *šarra ilānu rāmū nišū*
10 *ṣalam qaqqadi iqbūniššu*
11 *šarru ina ekallišu*
12 *ezzaqap gišimmarē*
13 *edātešu* ki.min (*šarru ezzaqap*) *mali bīnu*

Lower edge
14 *ina ṣilli bīni naptu*[*nu*]
15 *šakin*!*ma ina ṣilli gišimmari*
16 *urtaṣṣ‹an›*! *uppu* […]*tu uppu*

Reverse
17 *‹la›pit ina* … (the rest is unclear or corrupt)

Obverse
1 In distant days, (in the times of) ancient folk,
2 (The gods) dug the rivers, life of the lands.
3 The gods of the lands, Anu, Enlil and Ea, convened an assembly,
4 Together they deliberated,
5 Among them sat Šamaš,
6 (and) the lady of the great gods sat.
7 Formerly, there was no kingship in the lands,

8 And rulership was assigned (only) to the gods,
9 ... *The gods loved the black-headed*
10 *folk and they named (for them)*[9] *a king.*
11 The king in his palace
12 Planted Date Palms,
13 All around *ditto* (the king planted) the same number of Tamarisk(s).
Lower Edge
14 In the shade of the Tamarisk a banquet
15 was held[!]. In the shade of the Date Palm
16 The drum thundered...[...] The drum

Rev.
17 *was played* in...(unclear)...

(The Date Palm and the Tamarisk, Middle Assyrian Version, KAR 324; *BWL* 162–63; Wilcke 1989)

What are the marked differences between all three introductions? The Old Babylonian recension includes an allusion to the myth of Atraḫasis, when it relates how the gods toiled instead of mankind (l. 2), but this line disappears from the later recensions. The later recensions compensate for this lack by including a few additional details about the creation of the inhabited world. The Middle Assyrian manuscript KAR 324, although similar to the Emar version, transmits a somewhat truncated version of the introduction, corrupt at times. It also displays a deep influence of the Middle Assyrian dialect in the introduction as in its remaining lines, implying perhaps an oral transmission of the piece.

THE EXCHANGES

With the banquet set, the two trees commence their debate through a series of exchanges. At the core of the debate is the degree of usefulness of each tree to mankind. Each contender provides a short peroration in order to make its point. There are six preserved exchanges (Exchange VI is missing the Date Palm's response to the Tamarisk's speech, itself barely preserved). We follow the order of the exchanges according to the Emar manuscript, although note that their order was not fixed. The Old Babylonian manuscript includes Exchanges I, II (the Date Palm's speech is very fragmentary; see Streck 2004: 261), and III, before breaking off. The Emar manuscript seems to follow the order given in the Old Babylonian manuscript, as far as can be seen, containing Exchanges I–VI. The Middle Assyrian manuscript KAR 324 includes after the introduction Exchange I (but only the Date Palm's speech), which is followed by Exchange II; the tablet then ends. The Assyrian manuscript KAR 145, lacking the introduction, includes the following exchanges in this order: Exchanges I (only the Tamarisk's response is preserved), II (only the Date Palm's speech), IV (as the Tamarisk's response to II), V (only the Date Palm's speech), II (as the Tamarisk's response to V), III, IV (only the Date Palm's speech), V (as the Tamarisk's response to IV), and VI (only the Date Palm's speech is preserved; the rest is broken).

Exchange I (ll. 15–24). The first to speak is the Date Palm. It points out how the Tamarisk's branches are bare of fruit while it itself bears plentiful fruit fit for royalty. It also provides nourishment for growing babies.

On the basis of the Sumerian source, because the Akkadian is heavily broken in this place, it can be understood that the Tamarisk responds to the Date Palm's accusations by saying that its wood is the flesh of the gods, informing us that it was from this tree's wood that the statues of the gods were fashioned (Streck 2004: 277–78; Livingstone 1986: 92–112). Intending to humiliate the Date Palm and to establish a degree of superiority over it, the Tamarisk as "the flesh of the gods" regards the dates of the palm as offerings placed at its feet.

Exchange II (ll. 25–36'). The Date Palm disputes the Tamarisk's claim to be the flesh to the gods contending that it is silver that coats or decorates the flesh of the gods and that therefore the Tamarisk has no claim to such high status. This is understood on the basis of the Sumerian version (of which a few lines in this passage remain unclear).

The Tamarisk responds by enumerating all the utensils in the king's palace that are made out of its wood: tables, cups, spoons, and a mixing trough. The Tamarisk is also the weaver—implying by way of metonymy that the tamarisk's wood provides part of the loom that is responsible for spinning thread to clothe people and royalty alike. By calling itself a *mašmaššu* priest or purification priest, again by metonymy, the Tamarisk alludes to the well-attested role of the tree in purification rituals, as known from other sources (Streck 2004: 282–84).

Exchange III (ll. 37'–49'). The Date Palm responds by boasting of its place in the cult on three different occasions: upon the celebration of the *gizinakku* offering to Sîn, during the performance of the purification rites (*šuluḫḫu*), and in rituals for eradicating evil (Streck 2004: 272–73). The Tamarisk, on the other hand, the Date Palm continues, is covered with the waste products of beer production, perhaps alluding to an occasion when wooden sieve-like implements made out of tamarisk wood were used in beer-brewing processes to filter the beverage (Streck 2004: 276–77).

The Tamarisk does not remain silent and replies to the Date Palm. From its speech we learn that its wood contains *ṣumbabû* (*ṣubbabû* in the Old Babylonian version). This rare word was considered by Wilcke (1989: 188–89) to refer to the *manna*, which some scholars had sought in the past to associate with the secretion of honeydew by insects living on tamarisk, eponymously named the *tamarix mannifera*. However, Streck (2004: 279–82) contested Wilcke's idea on the grounds that the *tamarix mannifera* was not native to ancient Mesopotamia and neither is it found in present-day Iraq. He thought therefore that the *ṣumbabû* refers to the salt secretion of the tree, which was perhaps considered to be the tree's resin.

Apart from *ṣumbabû,* the Tamarisk also boasts of producing *materia magica*: incense, which was used in magical rituals, and "water," employed by a *qadištu* priestess, probably alluding to performances of purification rituals in which tamarisk branches were used in conjunction with purifying water (Streck 2004: 284–85). Whereas, the Tamarisk continues to explain, the Date Palm is suitable for the butcher's use: its fronds serve, so Streck (2004: 264–66) imagines, as a broomstick for clearing away gore and blood from the butcher's floor.

Exchange IV (ll. 50′–59′). The Date Palm urges the Tamarisk to follow it to the city of cultic festivals where the Tamarisk's maker, the carpenter will be induced to lie down on a bed constructed of the Date Palm's mid-rib branches, and then will sing praise to the tree (Streck 2004: 266–67).

The Tamarisk's response consists of asserting his usefulness in the fabrication of various tools. As an example the Tamarisk brings a spade made of its wood. With it the farmer opened irrigation canals and the earth was dug in order to plant crops.

Exchange V (ll. 60′–66′). The Date Palm considers its own benefit to the craftsman and farmer. From its fibrous bark ropes of various kinds are produced—for harnesses, girdles, and wagons (Streck 2004: 268–70). Note that the listing of various types of rope, like other utensils in this debate, may indicate the learned background of the composition. It is possible that the inspiration for such a collection of terms may have been the lexical lists, like the encyclopedic ḪAR-ra=*ḫubullu*, which provides entries for many household utensils and agricultural tools. The twenty-second tablet of ḪAR-ra=*ḫubullu* lists types of ropes, some of which are mentioned in our composition (see MSL 11, 31–33; cf. Vanstiphout 1991: 32–33; Veldhuis 2004: 99).

At this point of the debate, the Tamarisk's reply is almost totally lost and neither is the response of the Date Palm (*Exchange VI*) well preserved.

Exchange VI (KAR 145, ll. 18–23). The Date Palm declares its dates to be an important source of food. They can replace grain for a period of three months and can feed the needy and the poor (Streck 2004: 264, 270–71).

The Tamarisk's reply is lost in the break and in the end it is not known which of the two wins. However, if we follow Vanstiphout's (1990: 280–81; 1991: 41–44) argument that the one who wins is the contender who holds the higher moral ground, then surely the Date Palm may be considered the winner, for it provides nourishment for the poor, the orphan, and the widow, as well as providing food fit for royalty.

A Mesopotamian Debate Poem in Emar

With this overview of the debate poem at hand, we can evaluate The Date Palm and the Tamarisk at Emar and try to explain its role and appeal.

The protagonists of the debate poem represent two specific species of the plant kingdom, the date palm and the tamarisk, whose roles in the economy of Mesopotamia were central and whose cultural and symbolic values were paramount in this society. The date palm yielded dates, an important source of nourishment as well as of offerings to the gods and the wood of both trees was extensively exploited in the manufacture of household goods and agricultural and industrial implements (Moorey 1994: 355–60). This debate and other literary sources and economic documents inform us that both trees played an important part in the cult and in a variety of rituals. On these grounds it is doubtful therefore that the cultural-specific references spread throughout this poem meant much to the Emar scribes whose physical environment and cultural milieu were different from those of their counterparts living in Mesopotamia. Perhaps for this reason the poem has not been recovered at Ḫattuša, where the date palm does not grow. Indeed, this line of thought leads one to suggest that the low yield of debate poems from sites outside of Mesopotamia was the result of their highly culturally specific contents, which would have rendered them largely incomprehensible to anybody not intimately acquainted with Mesopotamian civilization. As much as one is tempted to accept this explanation, one needs to remember that such culture-specific details also occur in other compositions that were widespread at Late Bronze Age sites, such as the lexical lists. Many fauna and flora items listed in the lexical lists are specific to lower Mesopotamia and nowhere else. Some lexical lists included details of topography, such as canal-names or cities from the

Old Babylonian period, defunct or long abandoned when copied. These items would have yielded little sense not only to scribes from Emar or Ugarit but also to Mesopotamian scribes who continued copying such lists throughout the second millennium and into the first.

This example can be applied to other genres known from the curriculum, such as hymns, prayers, and incantations: the contents of many probably remained obscure to their copyists, definitely so to those who were educated outside of Mesopotamia. Hence we can conclude that the reason compositions such as debate poems were copied was because of their pedagogical value and not because of their content. Like other wisdom compositions found in Emar's scribal school, the debate poem The Date Palm and the Tamarisk was copied and studied as part of the final stages of education of the scribal arts (Vanstiphout 1991). We can only guess to what degree this piece pleased the aesthetic sensibilities of the Emar scribes.

Debate Poems Elsewhere

All in all, as various scholars have commented, the genre of dispute per se is not found in the biblical wisdom books, although some of the sayings found in Proverbs are concerned with animals and plants. For example, the ways of the ant are to be studied in order to gain wisdom (Prov 6:6–11; and the Septuagint adds to it a parable about the bee); and so are the behavioral patterns of the smaller animals—the ant, the rock hyrax, the locust, and the gecko (Prov 30:24–28). Other animals, such as the lion or the pig, are also found to demonstrate one moral point or the other; for all these see the study of Forti 2008 and 2.8. That is the role of such animals in these moral parables, unlike in the genre under study here, where the animals or plants are not intended to demonstrate ethical values. In addition, the main trait of the disputation genre, where one species is placed in comparison with the other is missing from these proverbs.

Nonetheless, there are brief stories or sayings that share some features with the Mesopotamian disputation poem. The famous fable of Jotham (Judges 9) sees the participation of various plants. Each plant—the olive tree, the fig, and the vine—speaking in the first person, highlights its beneficial qualities to mankind but refuses kingship. Only the thorn (thus the common translation of אטד) agrees to govern over the plant kingdom (Tatu 2006). Another disputation-like episode is found in 2 Kgs 14:9 whose participants are the thorn or thistle and the cedar. The fable is perhaps a quote from a longer debate between the two trees, now of course lost.

More direct echoes of the composition we have been studying are found in other extra-cuneiform sources. A debate between the two trees seems to have been transmitted—in what means and fashions remains unclear—to a Pahlavi story, although there the Tamarisk is replaced by a goat. The goat echoes the Tamarisk, by proclaiming its centrality to Zoroastrian rites. It is the contender who eventually won the dispute (Brunner 1980). Likewise, the Date Palm and the Tamarisk is argued to have been transmitted to the Hellenistic world, where Callimachus speaks of two trees disputing—the olive and the laurel. While the first yields fruits, the other is put to use in the cult by the Pythian priestess (and cf. here line 46′). (This story is also found in Aesop; see West 1969: 118–19). The fact that in these later sources one contender emphasizes its fruitfulness and the other its participation in the cult demonstrates their dependence, though of course not direct, on the Akkadian debate poem. The Sayings of Ahiqar include a short debate between the bramble and pomegranate (Lindenberger 1983: 167, no. 73; Porten and Yardeni 1993: 38–39, ll. 101–102; Weigl 2001: 66–68), showing us a route by which such wisdom works could have traversed the gap between the cuneiform cultural sphere and the Greek-speaking world—through the translations and adaptations of Mesopotamian works to Aramaic.

On the longevity of the genre in Near Eastern literature up to modern times (where one finds, e.g., a disputation between the telegraph pole and the train as to which is faster), see the studies collected by Reinink and Vanstiphout 1991.

SOURCES AND EDITIONS

Emar: Arnaud 1985–1987, nos. 783 and 784; Wilcke 1989.
Middle Assyrian: *BWL*, 158–64; Wilcke 1989.
Old Babylonian: *BWL*, 155–57; Wilcke 1989.
Sumerian: Cavigneaux 2003; ETCSL 5.3.7.

Translations and discussions: Wilcke 1989, Streck 2004, Dietrich 1995, Krämmer 1998: 230–51; Foster 2005: 927–29; Ponchia 1996 (note that editions and translations of The Date Palm and the Tamarisk before Arnaud 1985–1987 and Wilcke 1989 are now outdated, hence not included here).

General discussions of debate poems: Bottéro 1991; Vanstiphout 1990, 1991, 1992a, 1992b, Vogelzang 1991.

Translations of other debate poems: Vanstiphout 1997; ETCSL 5.3.1–5.3.7.

2.6

PROVERB COLLECTIONS FROM ḪATTUŠA

This chapter introduces two partly preserved proverb collections from Ḫattuša, the Hittite capital. These proverbs cannot be assigned to a larger work or attributed to some clear source. Because of the condition of the tablets it is also not clear if the proverbs stand here independently or were framed within a narrative like The Ballad of Early Rulers. The first collection, Text A, consists of proverbs written in Akkadian. The second collection, Text B, has only the Hittite translation of Akkadian proverbs, now almost entirely broken away.

TEXT A

INTRODUCTION

The fragmentary tablet published as KUB 4.40 contains a collection of Akkadian proverbs written over eighteen incomplete lines. The fragment is but one face of what was originally a four-sided prism. Another face of the prism is very poorly preserved and hence its contents obscure. The other sides of the prism are lost. It is not clear whether proverbs covered all sides of the prism, for it might have included additional works. A comparison with similar prism tablet formats from Ḫattuša shows that prisms include collections of Mesopotamian compositions: KBo 19.98 and 19.99 consist of *narû* literature about the Sargonic kings (Westenholz 1997: 280–93); KUB 4.39 is an Edubba composition in the genre of learned Sumerian "school letters" (Civil 2000); KBo 26.2 is an unidentified god list (Weeden 2011a: 108, n. 516); and KBo 26.5+6 is a prism of the great ḪAR-ra=*ḫubullu* lexical list (Weeden 2011a: 112–25; see in addition Klinger 2005: 111; Beckman 1982: 102).

The Mesopotamian origin of texts written on prisms at Ḫattuša leads us to surmise that the proverbs contained in the KUB 4.40 prism did not include a translation into Hittite. On the basis of the other prism pieces, it is likely that the proverbs served an educational role in the training of scribes in the Akkadian language at Ḫattuša. Generally, prisms are considered to be scribal exercises, when students finished studying extracts and moved to produce (probably by memory) full compositions (see 1.3 and 1.5).

Obviously, what we gain from the remains of the prism is only a fraction of the original, more extensive compilation. In spite of the meager remains

---

Text

(ll. 1′–3′ are not well preserved)

4′ *šuplī ul ēneḫma ṣūmī ul at*[*ru*]
5′ *muššur šētu ul išêṭ bir*[*tu*]
6′ *alteqe qātāta ibissû ul iq*[*atti*?]

7′ *tallik mīnu tušib mī*[*nu*]
8′ *tazziz mīnu tatūram mī*[*nu*]

9′ *šummaman la allika idāya mannumma ā*[*lik*…]

(lines 10′–13′ not given)

14′ [*ib*]*rīmi la nāṣir pirištiya nakru lu* [*māru*]
15′ ⸢*u*⸣? *lu mārtu ibrīmi nāṣir piri*[*štiya*]

(lines 16′–18′ not given)

Notes to Individual Lines

6′: Reading with *BWL*, 278; cf. *CAD* Q, 170–71. Compare here the following proverb:

> "Don't act as a guarantor; that man will have a hold on you."
>
> (The Instructions of Šuruppak, ll. 19–20; Alster 2005: 60)

7′–8′: See here *BWL*, 278.

14′: "Enemy," *nakru* is written here kúr.ra, a writing attested in the lexical tradition.

available to us, the tablet demonstrates yet again the circulation of Mesopotamian wisdom compositions to the western regions, Ḫattuša included, during the Late Bronze Age. It also provides us with a few additional wisdom sayings, which, it is important to note, are not known from other sources.

I present here only the more intelligible parts of the tablet. My edition and translation are based on previous studies by Ebeling (1928–1929), Pfeiffer (1969), and *BWL*, 277–78.

TRANSLATION

4′ "The depth (of) my (well) is not exhausted (in giving water), (hence) my thirst does not grow."
5′ "The net is loosened, but the fetter is not remiss/negligent."
6′ "I have become a guarantor—hence (my) losses will be never *e*[*nding*?]."

7′ "You went, so what? You sat, so wh[at]?,
8′ You stood, so what? You returned, so what?"

9′ "If I myself had not come, who would [*have been*] my [*helper*]?

(lines 10′–13′ are incomplete and difficult to understand)

14′ "My friend—the person who does not keeps my secrets is the enemy;
15′ It is either (my) [son] *or* (my) daughter, my friend, who keeps [my] secr[ets]."

(lines 16′–18′ are not in good condition)

TEXT B

Another collection of proverbs from Ḫattuša is contained in the tablet fragment published as KBo 12.128. Only the Hittite column is preserved, however, as the Akkadian column is lost, but for a few signs. Some rubrics of the Hittite column are left blank, as was seen also in the Ḫattuša version of *Šimâ Milka*, leaving the Akkadian without a translation. The text edition follows here Beckman (1986) and Archi (2007).

TEXT

(lines 1′–4′ are very fragmentary)

5′ *ḫantezzin paḫḫuenanza*[!] *karapi*

6′ *nukku karušten nu ištamašten*
7′ *nu* DUMU.LÚ.U_{19}.LU^{LI} *kue ūttar*
8′ *piyan maḫḫan* GAR-*ri*
9′ *n=at=za=kan ḫaddanaza*
10′ *arḫa aušten*
11′ *n=at išḫiulaza ḫarten*
12′ *n=at kardit šekten*
13′ *n=at tuliyaza punušten*
14′ *n=at* GIŠ.ḪUR-*za aušten*
15′ *nu* ˹*anda*˺ *daruppten*[!]
16′ *n=at=za=kan šumedaza*
17′ …X.MEŠ-*za šekten*
18′ …x…

Break

NOTES TO INDIVIDUAL LINES

5′: This is the first complete line of the tablet; ll. 1′–4′ are poorly preserved, but they appear to translate only parts of the lost Akkadian column. Indeed, one rubric was left completely blank; in other words, the Akkadian part was left untranslated; see *CHD* P, 13 and the discussion below for a interpretation of this proverb and its meaning.

7′: Possibly understand as DUMU.LÚ.U_{19}.LU-*li* for the genitive syntagm *dandukišnaš* dumu-*li*, "child of mortality" (following Melchert 1983: 145, n. 31).

14′: Generally in Hittite texts GIŠ.ḪUR refers to a wooden writing board (recently, Weeden 2011a: 234–37; Waal 2011), but here we suggest that its meaning is "ordinances," under influence of the Akkadian version. Indeed, although for the most part lost, in the parallel Akkadian section, just enough is preserved to allow us to read [gi]š.ḫur, no doubt intending, as on many occasions, *uṣurtu* "ordinances." Therefore, perhaps the usual translation of this sentence, "Look them up on the wooden tablets" (Beckman 1986: 29), or "read them from the tablet" (*CHD* Š, 24) is to be reconsidered. With this new sug-

TRANSLATION

5′ "The fire consumes the first one."

6′ "Be quiet now and listen!
7′–10′ Observe with wisdom the matters which are placed in front of mankind,
11′ Maintain them according to the rule,
12′ And know them by heart.
13′ Inquire about them by means of an assembly,
14′ And observe them according to the ordinances.
15′ *Collect* (*them*) *together*,
16′–17′ And know them *for/by yourselves* according to the …-s.
18′ …

Break

---

gestion, note that GIŠ.ḪUR (l. 14′) parallels Hittite *išḫiul* "regulations" (l. 11). For *uṣurtu*, see The Ballad of Early Rulers, ll. 1–2 and further in the following section.

16′: The Akkadian column perhaps reads [*kīma/ša ti*]-*du-ú*, "[as/which you will k]now."

DISCUSSION

It has been suggested that the fragment KBo 12.128 belongs to the composition *Šimâ Milka*, which as we have seen, was known in Ḫattuša and also supplied with a Hittite translation. There is, however, no correspondence of the fragment to known parts of this composition. The Hittite fragment seems to be the end of the composition, but there is no mention of son or father. The speaker of KBo 12.128 seems to address directly the readers or listeners rather than a specific person or persons. Hence, the fragment is not part of *Šimâ Milka* but probably represents another compilation of wisdom sayings, held perhaps within a narrative frame of which we have only the end.

As in the Hittite translation of *Šimâ Milka*, line 5′ (and probably 4′ as well) of the Hittite column provides only the partial translation of a now lost Akkadian proverb. Let us consider if we can recover in full the Akkadian proverb that the Hittite translates. First the Hittite proverb again:

5′ *ḫantezzin paḫḫuenanza*[!] *karapi*
The fire consumes the first one.

And now what can be considered to have been the full Akkadian proverb. Although lost in our source, it is preserved in a bilingual version (Sumerian and Akkadian). It runs as follows:

[lú] dub-sag-gá	*maḫrâ*
[i]zi an-gu$_7$-e	*išātu ik*[*kal*]
nu-ub-bé	*ul iqab*[*bi*]
lú egir.ra	*arkû*
me-a lú dub-sag-gá-e-še	*ali ša maḫ*[*rî*]

When fire consumes the first one, the next in line doesn't ask "Where is the first one?"

(Bilingual Proverbs, ll. 3′–7′; *BWL*, 254; *CAD* M/1, 108–9)

There is an earlier parallel on which the bilingual version relies. It appears in the Sumerian Proverb Collection:

lú dub-sag-e izi al-gu$_7$-e
nu-ub-bé lú-egir-ra me-a lú dub-sag-e

If the foremost is devoured by fire, those behind do not ask, "Where is the foremost?"

(Sumerian Proverb Collection, 3.188; Alster 1997: 111)

All these versions can be compared with a proverb found in the Mari letters, where a similar sense is intended (see 2.8, no. 9):

kīma ša tēltim ša šuppatam išātum ikkalma u tappātāša iqullā

> As in the saying, "When a fire devours a reed—do its two companions stay silent?"

We now understand what the Hittite truncated translation wished to convey: when there is danger and the first in line perishes, others grow wary, wanting to escape.

The rest of the Hittite column continues, so one can assume, with a full translation of the lost Akkadian passage, which cannot, however, be identified in other sources. The speaker of the passage, unknown, apparently addresses his audience, requesting that they take to heart words of wisdom. The passage is of importance, because it is one of the few instances in which the reason for the study and collection of wisdom is stated.

The speaker first requests silence and attention from his audience, as if in a live presentation of his oration. He wishes that his hearers learn with wisdom, Hittite *ḫattatar* (the translation of presumably Akkadian *nēmequ*) what concerns humanity—issues presumably articulated at the beginning of the composition, now obviously lost. Issues of concern are to be held according to *išḫiul*, "rule" or "regulation" (the Hittite word perhaps translating Akkadian *riksu*, *rikistu* "rule, regulation") and are to be learnt by heart. They should be sought after in the *tuliya*, the Hittite "assembly." "You should observe these (concerns) according to the ordinances," the speaker continues (and see my notes to l. 14′).

Matters of concern for humanity, the speaker comes to conclude, are to be collected together (l. 15′) so that they can be studied by those who listen. The end of the composition is not well preserved (it is obvious that it ends here because the reverse side of the tablet is blank) and breaks rather abruptly for us to understand the full implications of this injunction. Care should be taken before we reach conclusions especially when the Akkadian version is broken (and, as mentioned, without parallel) and with the likelihood that the Hittite scribe might have had difficulty in understanding the text in front of him. But could it be imagined that the speaker is requesting that wisdom injunctions be collected as texts, such as the ones we have been studying in our book, to serve future generations of scholars? A more comprehensive study is required to investigate this question seriously. (See also 1.5).

Source and Discussions

Text A

Source: KUB 4.40.

Editions and discussions: Ebeling 1928–1929; Pfeiffer 1969; *BWL*, 277–78 and pl. 72; Klinger 2005.

TEXT B

Source: KBo 12.128.

Editions and discussions: Beckman 1986; Archi 1995; Lebrun 1980: 399–401.

2.7

An Akkadian-Hurrian Bilingual Proverb Extract

Wisdom literature was not only translated or adapted into Hittite as we previously saw (2.1 and 2.6 A) but also into Hurrian. Two compositions attest to this. The first work is a bilingual two-column fragment of The Instructions of Šurrupak. Although its provenance is unknown because it derives from the antiquity market, its origin is to be sought perhaps in Ugarit, Emar, or elsewhere in Syria. It is not included in our survey, however, for the reasons given in 1.1.

The second piece is apparently an excerpt from a larger composition, containing two wisdom sayings, each no longer than a few lines; each saying is first given in Akkadian and then provided with a Hurrian translation. As with the bilingual manuscript of *Šimâ Milka*, we can assume that the purpose of providing a Hurrian translation was instructional.

The tablet is completely preserved. The text is arranged along the longer axis of the tablet, in the so-called landscape format. Hence, it does not follow the usual tablet format of wisdom compositions we have been examining so far where the text is inscribed along the shorter axis, usually in two columns, two on each side. Another remarkable feature is the tablet's size: approximately 10 × 5 cm, certainly smaller than the other tablets we are concerned with here. For these two reasons, it looks like an exercise tablet. Similar tablet formats have been found at Ugarit and Emar, although they do not contain literary compositions. They are inscribed with several or more lines extracted from lexical lists, clearly representing student drills in the context of scribal education. It is very likely that the tablet from Ugarit was likewise especially formed for educational purposes. Worth comparing are two examples of similar-looking tablets (both dated to the Middle Babylonian period) containing proverbs in Alster 2007: 29–30 and 52–53. These are also scribal exercises: the first includes syllabic Sumerian, Sumerian, and Akkadian proverbs, each separated by a dividing line; the second includes bilingual Sumerian and Akkadian proverbs arranged interlinearly.

This circumstantial evidence leads us to conclude that the proverbs on the tablet from Ugarit were extracted from a longer work unknown to us today. It is also possible that although the proverbs themselves remain only attested in the present source, originally they were embedded in one of the popular wisdom compositions of the day, such as The Instructions of Šuruppak or The Ballad of Early Rulers (of which two manuscripts included various proverbs).

Text

1 *šukun kaspī ša māmīti itti ili teleqqe*
2 *māmīta pilaḫma*! *pagarka šullim*
3 *tāmê ana nāri kālî apilti*!
4 *dūriš marḫītašu māra ul išu*

10 *la mudû arna ana ilišu ḫemuṭ*
11 *la imtallak*! *ḫamṭiš ana ili inašši qātīšu*
12 *la mādū arnūšu al pîka*? *šaqâta⸢ma⸣*
13 *la idema amēlu ana ilišu ḫemuṭ*

Notes to Individual Lines

1. Although written with the plural determinative, dingir.meš ("gods") is to be understood as a singular; see Wilhelm 2003.

3. Reading here with Wilhelm 2003.

10 and 13: *ḫemuṭ* (wr. *ḫé-mu-uṭ*) for Babylonian *ḫamuṭ* "is in a hurry"; ARG suggests reading *ḫé=iḫ* > *iḫmuṭ* (preterite).

11. Following *BWL*, 116.

12. The reading of this line is very conjectural and hinges on the reading of the second sign. Read either as TIR (by Nougayrol) or UN (by Arnaud), the sign however according to the photograph is clearly MAḪ, a Sumerogram for *mā'du* "great," phonetically complemented with –*du* resulting in a Plural Stative *mādū* that agrees with *arnūšu*. The reading of the sequence (which is nonstandard), also concurs with the Hurrian translation (l. 17: *te-a-la-an ar-ni*

Either way, the Akkadian-Hurrian proverbs of this extract tablet could have been transmitted from memory by the teacher and might not have necessarily depended on a manuscript to which the copyist had access in Ugarit itself.

The presentation below provides the Akkadian; the Hurrian, which lies outside of the expertise of this author, still awaits a definitive edition and the reader is referred to the bibliography for previous studies.

Translation

1 “Place the silver for (the payment of) the oath ceremony! You will receive it back from the god.
2 Respect the oath and so keep yourself safe!
3 He who swears by the river(-god) (but) holds on to the payment—
4 His wife will not bear him a son for ever and ever.”

(ll. 5–9, Hurrian translation of the above; not given here)

10 “Ignorant of (his) sin, he rushes to his god,
11 He does not consider (his deeds), in haste he lifts his hands (in prayer) to his god,
12 Are his sins no more numerous than…*You are elevated…*,
13 The ignorant person rushes to his god.”
(ll. 14–19, Hurrian translation of the above; not given here)

“many sins”). That this is what is written here was already the suspicion of Speiser (1955), although he read the Akkadian incorrectly. The rest of the sentence is obscure, but some kind of comparison is intended. ARG considers reading *al pîka šaqâta,* “you are taller than your speech (suggests).”

Discussion

Although the two proverbs found in this extract are not known from elsewhere, by their content it is obvious that they are related to the type of sayings we have encountered in *Šimâ Milka*. The first proverb warns of the consequences of holding on to the payment that is due for the ceremony of oath-taking. Not paying the money for the oath ceremony will result in a lack of sons. The second proverb, not perfectly preserved and hence less-well understood, is concerned with the fault that lies in the ignorance of sin, implying that prayer and supplication will not help the sinner if he does not atone for his deeds (and see also Dijkstra 1993). This interpretation, due to the condition of line 12, is far from certain.

We have already discussed in our introduction to this text its apparent educational purpose. Now that we are more familiar with its contents, it is worth pointing out that the four lines of the second proverb all open with the sign *la*, meaning in Akkadian "not"—which if intentional is a good mnemonic device for retrieving the contents of the proverbs from the mind of one responsible for their transmission.

Although the overall content and formulation of the proverbs speak for their Mesopotamian origin, as far as one can argue, an interesting cultural or religious transposition, rarely sighted in our corpus, occurs in this text. In the first proverb, while the Akkadian of line 3 reads *tāmê ana nāri* "he who swears by the river(-god)," the Hurrian translation (not given here) mentions the god Kušuḫ. The Hurrian translator replaced the Mesopotamian river(god) of the oath with the moon-god Kušuḫ, who in the Hurro-Hittite milieu was considered the god of the oaths (Wilhelm 2003: 344). Such religious and cultural transpositions are known elsewhere in the Mesopotamian-Hurrian interface (e.g., see *Ugaritica* 5, no. 137 [=S^a Vocabulary] and below), but this is a good example of a translation that goes beyond the literal into the cultural (Compare *Šimâ Milka*, Hittite Parallel Text H, where the Fate Goddesses (^{d}Gulšaš) translate Akkadian *ūmi ša šīmtika* "the day of your fate"). This proves that not only did the translator understand the language of the text, but that he was also able to offer a cultural commentary on it by bringing into play his knowledge of the syncretistic world he inhabited. Thus whether the translator was the teacher or student—he imparted his knowledge beyond vocabulary and grammar. This is just one example of course, but it neatly demonstrates to us the intellectual milieu and international spirit of the scribal schools of the period located outside the core area of Mesopotamia.

Seen in its wider perspective, the Hurrian translation of the piece is rare but not unique and should not come as a surprise when viewed as part of a phenomenon of Hurrian translations within the larger context of the transmission and reception of Mesopotamian scholarly materials to regions outside of Babylonia. Other compositions were translated into Hurrian, most notably lexical lists found at Ugarit. One list provides a Hurrian translation of the Sumerian column (a type of vocabulary); others supply a Hurrian column (followed in most cases also by a syllabically written Ugaritic column) to translate entries of the Sumerian-Akkadian S^a Vocabulary. A god list appended to the lexical list S^a Vocabulary includes a Hurrian column as commentary rather than a straightforward translation of the Mesopotamian entries. Hurrian-only compositions are also known from Ugarit and they include the famous "musical notation" text and ritual texts (Dietrich and Mayer 1999; Vita 2009).

From Ḫattuša also derives a Hurrian translation or adaptation of The Epic of Gilgameš, as well as Hurrian adaptations of Mesopotamian scholarly materials, such as omens. There is also evidence of independent wisdom creations in Hurrian, notably the set of animal parables in the Hittite-Hurrian bilingual The Song of Release. This composition, found in Ḫattuša, was probably first written in Hurrian and later provided with a Hittite translation (Hoffner 1998, no. 18a; Neu 1996; Wilhelm 2001).

Sources and Discussions

Source: RS 15.10 (*PRU* III, 311–12 and pl. 106; photo: *Ugaritica* 4, fig. 119)

Editions and discussions: Nougayrol and Laroche 1955; *BWL*, 116; Dijkstra 1993; Wilhelm 2003; Arnaud 2007: 139–40, no. 46.

2.8

Proverbs and Proverbial Sayings in Letters: The Mari Letters and Late Bronze Age Correspondence

The objective of this chapter is to supplement our knowledge about the expression of wisdom by venturing beyond the strict confines of the learned environments of scribal schools, its teachers and students. The chapter brings a collection of proverbs and proverbial sayings found in letters dating to the Old Babylonian period and to the Late Bronze Age.

Old Babylonian proverbs and proverbial sayings found in this chapter are collected from the Mari letters. The proverbs that occur in the Mari correspondence provide us with an understanding of the type of wisdom circulating, either oral or written, during the Old Babylonian period, the approximate time when many of the wisdom compositions we have met were written in Babylonia. Like Emar, Mari is located in the Middle Euphrates region amidst a West Semitic seminomadic population that interacted with the city representatives, the king, the royal family, and the bureaucracy, who were acculturated, even if not fully, into Mesopotamian culture. Hence Mari falls under the geographic as well as the cultural zone under our investigation, even if properly speaking its textual finds—letters and administrative documents as well as cultic texts—are dated earlier than the Late Bronze Age.

Proverbs from the Late Bronze Age are mainly found in letters belonging to the famous El Amarna archive. Other scribal centers we are already acquainted with, Ugarit and Ḫattuša, have yielded a considerable number of letters, but apparently, by this time, the practice of embellishing letters with learned sayings or proverbs had become less common.

One of the chapter's chief concerns is to ask whether the proverbs cited in these letters report oral traditions that were not part of the world of learning, or whether they ultimately reflect the world of the Edubba because, for the most part, letters were written by professional scribes. There is no clear-cut answer to this question, since the boundary between written wisdom and oral wisdom, is ill-defined; thus both possibilities must be considered.

On one hand, the evidence seems to indicate that many of the proverbs encountered in letters are not known from elsewhere. For example, they are not found in the great Sumerian Proverb Collection or other compilations, hence they may not be considered as part of the scribal curriculum. On some occasions when a proverb is cited in a letter, it is defined by its reporter as a *tēltum*, "saying" (see nos. 1, 9, and 23). It is generally assumed that *tēltum* specifically designates an oral utterance rather than a written dictum. Note indeed that the word *tēltum* is never used to define a proverb in wisdom compositions, including proverb compilations (Alster 1996: 6–7; Durand 2006; Hallo 2010a[=1990]: 611–12).

On the other hand, as we will see below, some of the proverbs, while not cited verbatim in other sources, have a long history of written transmission. Variations on the proverbs given here can be found at times in the cuneiform record, and occasionally in later alphabetic sources (Aramaic or Greek; e.g., Rahman 2006). The alphabetic sources themselves may have depended on now-lost Akkadian originals. This may then speak for the learned background of these proverbs, regardless of their origin.

Both of these options are to be kept in mind as we proceed to examine more closely, proverbs from first the Mari letters and then Late Bronze Age letters. We may eventually reach the conclusion (advocated by Alster 1996, for example) that since the written or oral origin of sayings and proverbs in letters cannot be securely determined, this phenomenon should be considered simply the result of a growing literacy within society. With the advent of the Old Babylonian period, as the written use of the vernacular Akkadian grew, and Sumerian became only a learned language studied in the scribal schools, people either by themselves or with the help of professional scribes may have felt more comfortable in communicating their own experiences and expressing their acquired knowledge, including articulations of wisdom (Charpin 2010).

The Mari Letters

The proverbs presented in this section are all imbedded in letters recovered from the royal palace of the city of Mari. Approximately 25,000 documents have been found at this site, out of which several thousand are letters. To date, some 2,500 letters have been published. Many of the letters were found in Room 115 of the palace and prior to the destruction of the city were carefully organized and stored in containers (Charpin 2012: 66).

The Mari letters are dated from the early to mid-eighteenth century B.C.E. They mainly represent the correspondence of Yasmaḫ-Addu, son of the emperor of upper Mesopotamia, Samsi-Addu, and later, of Zimri-Lim, scion of the Lim dynasty. With the conquest of the city by Hammurapi (in ca. 1760 B.C.E.) and it subsequent abandonment, the documentation from Mari ends.

The vast corpus of letters from Mari opens to us the Old Babylonian world of the Middle Euphrates region. We learn of the competition between multiple kingdoms, each attempting to control both urban centers and their hinterland, populated by seminomadic tribes, in the literature often called "Amorites," although in reality composed of different clans.

Within this unique corpus, a number of letters incorporate proverbs and common sayings. The language of the proverbs seems to be colloquial and can even be judged to be dialectical, closer to the spoken language(s) of the region than the standard Old Babylonian employed in the written correspondence. Let us explain: the syntax of the proverbs as well as the choice of words do not follow the rules of proper Akkadian. The result is a sort of mixed language alternating between the spoken West Semitic dialect(s) of the Middle Euphrates (never officially recorded in writing) and the Akkadian common among the urban or higher levels of society (Durand 2006: 4–10; Charpin 2010: 117–53). Nonetheless, some proverbs found in the Mari letters are documented in other sources from later periods and different locations. Hence, as discussed above, their oral origin cannot be automatically assumed.

The reader is advised to consult the definitive collection of over forty Mari proverbs and locutions by Durand (2006) from which all citations here are taken and upon which much of the translation and commentary depends. Out of Durand's collection, we have chosen a small but representative number of proverbs whose meaning is apparent without full recourse to the letters themselves. Marzal 1976 is now outdated because of the publication of many additional letters and joins, which since the 1980s have been commented upon extensively by the Mari philological team in Paris. Therefore Marzal's study is not referred to, although it contains a few locutions that are not included here. The same can be said of the study by Finet (1974), which, although still valuable to specialists, must be used with caution.

Proverbs and Proverbial Sayings in the Mari Letters

1.

assurrē kīma tēltim ullītim ša ummāmi kalbatum ina šutēpuriša ḫuppudūtim ulid

May it (not) be perchance like that old saying which goes so, "A bitch in her haste gives birth to blind puppies."

(ARM 1 5; Moran 1977, 1978; Durand 2006, no. 23)

This proverb was quoted by Samsi-Addu, emperor of upper Mesopotamia, to his sons. He advised them to combine forces cleverly and decisively against the enemy in order to prevent a coming attack. Otherwise, Samsi-Addu seems to warn, a hasty plan will surely fail.

This proverb has a long history. It can be traced, as demonstrated (Moran 1978; Alster 1979), from its ancient Near Eastern Mari source to a Greek proverb, and hence evidently to Europe, where versions in Italian, German, and English survive. It has not yet been recovered in collections of Akkadian proverbs or other wisdom compositions.

2.

Animal imagery is frequently found in the Mari proverbs. The next example, like the first, finds in a dog's behavior an appropriate mirror of human weaknesses. King Zimri-Lim reminds his minister Bannum of what Bannum had advised him in the past—neither to follow slanderers nor listen to slanders. But now Bannum himself behaves contrary to his own advice. A proverb is recalled to reinforce the king's criticisms of his minister.

kalbatum mārīša usannaq ummāmi ana mimma qattukkunu la tubbalā u šī ibûma maškam ina kurrim ušēlīma irtup akālam

A bitch would discipline her puppies saying "Don't place your paws where they don't belong" but then she herself went and pulled a (piece of) skin out of a (burning) brazier and began eating."

(ARMT 26 6; Heimpel 2003: 178–179; Durand 2006, no. 41-bis)

As Durand points out, a double irony is intended here for not only did the bitch risk burning itself, it gained a mere piece of skin.

A dog's behavior in and about ovens was a topos that informed at least two more sayings. Compare the Neo-Assyrian proverb (repeated also in The Sayings of Ahiqar) of a dog who entered the potter's kiln to warm up and barked at the potter as his only show of gratitude.

ina tēlte ša pî nišī šakin umma kalbu ša paḫāri ina libbi utūni kī īrubu ana libbi paḫāri unambaḫ

According to the popular proverb: "The potter's dog, when it entered the kiln, started barking at the potter."

(ABL 403 = SAA 18 1; *BWL*, 281)

The Hurrian-Hittite Bilingual (The Song of Release) tells of the dog who grabbed a loaf of bread from the oven, dipped it into oil and commenced eating it. The story is a parable of a crooked administrator who embezzles the city under his charge; see Hoffner 1998: 71.

3.

Describing a state of confusion in the midst of a military emergency, Kibri-Dagan, Zimri-Lim's governor at Terqa says that an inciter of rebel troops is seeking his own escape, behaving—

kīma kalbim šagê[m] ašar inaššaku ul ide

Like a rabid dog who doesn't know where it bites.

(ARM 3 18 ; Durand 2006, no. 3)

4.

A traitor or rebel pretender deserves to be treated as a rabid dog, probably to be captured and put to death.

inann[a awīlam šêti kīma ka]lbim līpušū[šuma ana imittim u] šumēlim la [inaššak]

Now [that man] should be treated [like a d]og [so that he] won't [bite right and] left.

(ARMT 28 32 = Durand 2006, no. 2)

The topos of a rabid dog, foaming at the mouth and biting whoever it encounters (see above, no. 3) is widespread, appearing in several magico-medical incantations. Its dripping salvia was likened to semen, which transfers the dog's disease to man; the disease itself was likened to the dog's puppies.

In its (i.e., the dog's) mouth its semen is carried.
Wherever it bit, it left behind its child.
(Finkel 1999: 214–15, with slight revisions)

To counter the spread of rabies, the rabid dog is to be captured and put to death:

A dog bit a man—
Speak to the blowing wind:
"May the dog's bite not produce offspring,
Take the dog into custody,
Let the dog die so that the man will live!"
(Finkel 1999: 214–15, with slight revisions)

Compare how King David in the presence of Achish of Gath likens his behavior to a rabid dog:

וישנו את־טעמו בעיניהם ויתהלל בידם ויתו על־דלתות השער ויורד רירו
אל־זקנו: ויאמר אכיש אל־עבדיו הנה תראו איש משתגע למה תביאו אתו אלי:
חסר משגעים אני כי־הבאתם את־זה להשתגע עלי הזה יבוא אל־ביתי

He became rabid in their eyes and grew mad at their hands; he marked the gate-posts (with his bites) and dripped his saliva on to his beard. Achish said to his servants "Behold a rabid man—why have you brought him to me? Am I lacking in mad men that you brought him to be rabid in my presence? Shall this one come to my house?" (1 Sam 22:14–16 [13–15])

Not surprisingly, many of the proverbs and proverbial sayings reflect to a close degree the daily concerns of the Middle Euphrates pastoralists tending their livestock, the main source of their livelihood. The following proverbs, hence, concentrate on the ox or bull, expressing the common metaphors associated with the animal, such as its strength and vitality, but also its stubbornness or even stupidity, as in the next proverbial saying.

5.
A time of hardship has fallen on the city of Zalluḫan: locusts have devoured the crops and as a consequence the population is driven to forage in the neighboring land. However, far from understanding the plight of the population, the people of the neighboring land promptly imprison thirty of the pillagers along with some livestock. What kind of people are those then who instead of helping

behave in such a way? Complaining to King Zimri-Lim, King Zakura-abu from Zalluḫan writes as follows:

> *kīma alpim ša ikullâm šebûma [aḫa/tappa]šu unakkapu awīlū šunu*
>
> Those people are like an ox, who having satiated itself with fodder, gores its [own brother/friend].
> (ARMT 28 79; Durand 2006, no. 29)

Durand's restoration "[its own brother/friend]" follows the context, but instead perhaps restore [*bēl*]*šu*, yielding the following—"an ox, in spite of having satiated itself with fodder, gores its [own owner]," and compare Isa 1:3:

> ידע שור קנהו וחמור אבוס בעליו
>
> The ox recognizes its master and a donkey the manger of its owner.

The ox and donkey recognize who is in charge of feeding them, but not Israel, who spurns God. The English parallel to all these proverbs is "don't bite the hand that feeds you."

6.

> *tēzibma qaran rīmim ša ṣabtāta u uzun šēlibim taṣbat*
>
> Having grasped a bull's horn you let go of it in order to grasp a fox's ear.
> (A.1017; Durand 2006, no. 33; Charpin 1989–1990: 98)

The interpretation of this proverb depends on our understanding of the imagery conveyed by the animals mentioned: a bull on the one hand and a fox on the other. The first possesses positive qualities such as strength, vigour, and virility, the second—cunningness, craftiness, and lying. So the speaker says that it is foolish to abandon a source of strength in favor of someone who's far from reliable.

A very similar sentiment is expressed by a proverb in *Perkei Avot* 4:15:

> הוי זנב לאריות ואל תהי ראש לשועלים
>
> (Better) be a tail to lions than a head to foxes.

A variation of this proverb is cited in a Neo-Assyrian letter that provides, however, a twist to the positive and negative images associated with the lion and the fox respectively.

> *eṭlu ša sibbat nēši iṣbatuni ina nāri iṭṭubu ša sibbat šēlebi iṣbatuni ussēzib*
>
> The guy who seized a lion's tail was drowned in the river, but (the guy) who seized a fox's tail was saved.
>
> (ABL 555 = SAA 13 45; *BWL*, 281; Alster 1989)

Indeed, sometimes in order to be saved craftiness is better than brute strength.

The proverb had a widespread popularity, for a close echo occurs in a letter sent by a Hittite king to his vassal; see no. 22 below. For Greek and later European parallels, see Alster 1989.

Additional sapiential sayings and locutions reflect life on the steppe among the herds.

7.

> *ištu anāku muḫḫam amazzaqu šū kursīnātim linakkis*
>
> Let him hack away at the fetlocks, while I suck the marrow.
>
> (A.111; Durand 2006, no. 34)

One man's easy gain of the juicy part is contrasted with another's toil of hacking at the lower legs of an ox carcass. Many popular fables employ the theme of easy gain in the face of another's hard toil.

8.

> *ammīnim itti sugāgī la illik kursinātum īteliāma qaqqadātum uštaplā*
>
> Why didn't he go with the sheiks? Fetlocks above and heads below!
>
> (A.4285; Durand 2006, no. 32; Charpin 1989–1990: 96)

More a locution than a proverb, it is interesting to observe how imagery at home with pastoralists is employed for rendering the expression "It's a topsy-turvy world."

9.

kīma ša tēltim ša šuppatam išātum ikkalma u tappātāša iqullā

As in the saying, "When a fire devours a reed—do its two companions stay silent?"

(ARM 10 150; Durand 2006, no. 24; *CAD* Q, 73 and T, 181)

Some menial workers broke out of their workhouse and escaped but they were captured. Care should be taken, so writes king Zimri-Lim to the queen mother, Adda-duri, that such cases not repeat themselves. The proverb illustrates his point that once a single reed catches fire it can easily spread far and wide. As Durand points out, fire advancing across the plain as it burns patch after patch of vegetation must have been a familiar sight to the pastoralists. The moral of this proverb is that trouble is quick to spread. Indeed very similar proverbs were discussed previously (2.6 Text B). This leads us to consider the spread of such topical ideas: as stated in the introduction to this chapter, was the transmission of the proverbs into the letters due to the scholarly erudition of their writers, hence accomplished scribes, or does this demonstrate the oral transmission of such wisdom?

Army life was central in the world of shifting alliances between the pastoralists and the city-states of the Middle Euphrates and beyond. As such it dominated a large part of the Mari correspondence, generating a collection of locutions about the character of a fighting force as well as the individual warrior.

10.

atlak ina ištēn zūkim ištēn awīlam leqe šinā līm šalāšat līmi ṣābum ul ipaḫḫur

Go ahead, pick out some guy for some infantry regiment—a two-thousand, three-thousand strong army will not amass!

(ARM 5 17+A.1882; Durand 2006, no. 19)

This sarcastic statement was delivered to Yasmaḫ-Addu, son of Samsi-Addu who ruled over Mari, by the king of Qatna, Išḫi-Addu. The latter mocks the inability of Samsi-Addu's Upper Mesopotamian Empire to gather up a serious military force to assist him. "A drop in the sea" may be a good English equivalent of this saying. The step parallelism poetically marks out this sentence as a locution, bringing to mind similar constructions in Ugaritic and biblical poetry and prose. Another step or numerical parallelism is seen in The Date Palm and the Tamarisk, Exchange VI 18.

11.

rēdû ana gerri la kušīrim abnum ina nārim iltanassum

Soldiers on a profitless campaign—a rolling stone without direction in the river.

(A.2707; Durand 2006, no. 40)

An army may be set on campaign, but without a clear gain of booty, or purpose, it fails in its task, so in a message relayed to the king of Mari. The image of a rolling stone (literally, "running about here and there") remains familiar to modern readers.

12.

All the following locutions or sapiential sayings derive from a single long letter (A.1146; Marello 1992; Durand 2006, nos. 13–18) in which the writer commends the addressee (probably Yasmaḫ-Addu, Samsi-Addu's son) to leave his idle city life in favor of the life of a warrior on the plain. The writer extols the life of pastoralists and young warriors in comparison to bourgeoisie city life and lauds life outdoors, which the addressee had so far never experienced.

ula matima šārum emmum u kaṣûm panīka ul imḫaṣma

Never did a wind—hot or cold—strike upon your face.

(Marello 1992, ll. 32–33)

Inactivity is not a hallmark of the true man, who should be out in the elements, his skin burned by the scorching sun.

wašābum u ṣalālum ul iṣarrapka

Lounging about or sleeping won't get you a tan!

(Marello 1992, l. 16)

Gender and class distinctions are marked by one's color: a male warrior supports a dark complexion, while women who stay indoors are pale. Such distinctions are also echoed in Song of Songs. The young girl wishes to be rather thought of as possessing a white skin like a lily than that of a menial worker scorched black by the sun (1:6): "Don't think of me as a darkie, tanned by the sun" אל־תראוני שאני שחרחרת ששזפתני השמש and (2:1): "I am the lily of the Sharon, the rose of the valleys" אני חבצלת השרון שושנת העמקים.

Indeed, life indoors among women is scorned, in contrast to life among warriors.

> *u ašar abu u ummum panīka ittaplasū u ištu biṣṣurim tamqutamma annānum biṣṣurum imḫurka u pan mimma ul tide*
>
> Dad and mum gazed down at your face as you fell out of (your mother's) c*** and yet still the c*** is still in your face! You don't understand anything!
>
> (Marello 1992, ll. 35–37)

Manhood has not been reached, since the addressee is still a child, kept close to his maternal home. A real man is Dumuzi (Marello 1992, l. 42), the king-god of the pastoralists.

Expressions of wisdom in the Mari letters sometimes occur not as proverbs, but as short anecdotes, serving as *exempla*. Thus this *exemplum*:

13.

> *matima awīlum ša ina ṣūmim imūtu ina nārim iddûšuma ibluṭ ištu qātam ba-i-tam ippešū warkānum mītum ul iballuṭ*
>
> Did ever a man who was dying of thirst come back to life after being thrown into the river (i.e., the Euphrates)? In spite of the nice try—being dead he couldn't be brought to life.
>
> (ARMT 26 171; Durand 2006, no. 26; Heimpel 2003: 241)

This proverb is embedded in a letter sent to the king from the representatives of the city of Mišlan. The letter warns that the fields need attention and the city and its inhabitants are under threat. Unless proper reinforcement arrives it will be too late to help Mišlan. An *exemplum* is provided to illustrate: help, even if offered with good intentions, is of no use if it arrives too late.

14.
The final example to consider is not so much as a proverb or anecdote but a prophetic utterance quoted in three letters. The utterance, which has garnered countless interpretations, goes as follows:

šapal tibnim mû illakū

Beneath straw runs water.

(ARMT 26 197, 199 and 202; Nissinen 2003, nos. 7, 9 and 12; Heimpel 2003: 251–252 and 255)

This sentence was pronounced by a prophetess, a *qammātum*-woman, speaking in the name of Dagan. It was reported to Zimri-Lim by his officials, each quoting verbatim this oral statement within a different message, although each warning the king about the intentions of the kingdom of Ešnunna. The utterance seems to convey some warning about false appearances, but how the imagery is deployed here remains unclear. Perhaps, as suggested by Sasson (1995), it was intentionally opaque, left to the interpretation of its hearers. Heimpel (2003: 252) suggests that "the image is of water whose surface is hidden under a cover of chaff, as happens in the time of winnowing."

Late Bronze Age Correspondence: The Amarna Letters and Other Sources

The famous Amarna letters were recovered at El Amarna, ancient Akhetaten, the capital of Amenhotep IV, better known as Akhenaten. The letters cover the later part of the reign of Akhenaten's father, Amenhotep III, and the reign of Akhenaten himself, up to his death, when Akhetaten was abandoned, in the mid-fourteenth century B.C.E. After this period and towards the close of the Late Bronze Age, from the thirteenth to the early-twelfth centuries, our sources regarding the vassal kingdoms of Canaan and the Lebanon (apart from Ugarit and its environs) dwindle significantly.

The Amarna letters can be divided roughly into two groups: letters sent to the Pharaoh from the great powers of the day—Babylonia, Assyria, Mitanni, and Hatti, and letters sent from the Pharaoh's vassal kings in the Lebanon and Canaan. Most of the Amarna vassal correspondence is concerned with interregional politics. Local rulers appointed by the Egyptians write to the Pharaoh to request his (usually) military intervention against other rulers or other hostile elements, such the *ḫabiru* bands.

It is interesting to note that proverbs and proverbial sayings are only typical of the correspondence of the vassal kings to the Pharaoh—never do we find such in the correspondence of the great kings. Naturally these are the letters that will be at the center of our discussion. Moreover, it is important to note, the vassal letters, especially in their greeting formulae, are studded with a verbose rhetoric, typical of the epistolary genre of the Old Babylonian period (e.g., Sallaberger 1999). Hence, we may suggest that the embellishment of letters with proverbs may have been part of the scribal legacy of the Old Babylonian period (see for a summary Wasserman 2011), abandoned by contemporary sophisticated urban centers, but still maintained by peripheral places, like the city-states of the Lebanon and Canaan.

Much has been written on the Amarna letters sent from Canaan and the Lebanon, but scholars are yet to arrive at an agreed definition of the particular language and writing system put to use in the vassal letters. The very least that can be said is that a sort of mixed language (or writing) is encountered in them, somewhere between Akkadian and the local Canaanite dialect(s). As in the Mari letters, the case can be made that some of the proverbs, written in this mixed style, reflect the common wisdom of the region rather than knowledge transmitted by the scribal schools. Further research into this question is required. For now we note that due to this mixed language or writing system, the proverbs are normalized as elsewhere in our study but for the occurrence of clear non-Akkadian forms and Canaanite glosses (marked on the tablet itself with the so-called *Glossenkeil*, a single diagonal wedge, which is here indicated by a colon): these forms and glosses are given in transliteration.

The choice of proverbs from the Amarna vassal letters given here is not comprehensive but selective. The order of the proverbs more or less starts from the north, from Gubla (Byblos), down to the cities of Canaan, such as Gezer, Jerusalem, and Shechem. The translation usually follows Moran (1992) and the Akkadian text is based on Shlomo Izreel's electronic edition kindly put on the web (see http://oracc.museum.upenn.edu/contrib/amarna/corpus).

The proverbs in the Amarna letters definitely stand out as a unique collection, for such a concentration of wisdom sayings is not found outside this corpus. Later correspondence from the region (not from Canaan, but from more northerly regions, i.e., Ugarit and Ḫattuša) does not display such a richness, hence what is on offer is much thinner.

15.

eqliya aššata ša la muta mašil aššum bali erēšim

My field is like a woman without a husband because it lacks plowing.
(EA 74:17–19; Moran 1992: 142–43; Marcus 1973)

Thus the most loquacious of all Amarna age rulers, Rib-Adda from Byblos, pronounces. (There are more than sixty letters sent from this ruler). Given the many nonstandard Akkadian forms in this saying it is generally thought, like some other Amarna proverbs we will meet, to reflect a popular saying current in Byblos at that time. Indeed there is no exact parallel to this proverb in other cuneiform sources, although a very similar saying is found in the Bilingual Proverbs.

erín nu-bàn-da nu-me-a	*ṣābu [ša la lap]uttê*
a.šà engar-ra in-nu	*eq[lu ša l]a ikkari*
é en-bi nu-nam	*bītu ša la bēli*
munus nitá nu-tuku	*sinništu ša la muti*

A workforce without a foreman—a field without a farmer,
A house without its owner—a woman without a husband.
(Bilingual Proverbs, ll. 18–21; *BWL*, 229 and 232)

There are also parallels outside of the cuneiform world, for which see Marcus 1973 and Moran 1992: 144, n. 6.

16.

kīma iṣṣūri[!] *ša ina libbi ḫuḫāri :ki-lu-bi šaknat kišūma anāku ina Gubla*

Like a bird which is caught in a trap (gloss: cage), thus am I in Byblos.
(EA 74:45–49 [and six additional occurrences, all in the Byblos corpus]; Moran 1992: 142–43)

Again from the mouth of the ruler of Byblos—or his scribe. Note that the word for trap *ḫuḫāru* is glossed by a Canaanite word *ki-lu-bi* "cage." Akkadian *ḫuḫāru* is otherwise, as far as the dictionaries show us, not attested outside of Babylonia in nonlearned texts. This may point to the foreign origin of this proverb. There exists the possibility that, even if the proverb is local, the word itself may have been picked up by the Byblos scribe during his scribal training because *ḫuḫāru* features in the lexical list tradition. In the western regions, it is found in the Emar bilingual recension of ḪAR-ra=*ḫubullu*, Tablet "VI," 314′ (Arnaud 1985–1987: 74).

17.

ti-na-mu-šu libittu :la-bi-tu ištu šupal tappātiši u anāku la i-na-mu-šu ištu šupal šēpē šarri bēliya

(Sooner would) a brick move from under its companion (brick) than I would move away from under the king's feet, my lord.
(EA 296:17–22; Moran 1992: 338)

This proverb is found in the opening of three letters: from the governor of Gezer (EA 292), from Tagi, the ruler of Gath (EA 266), and from a ruler called Yaḫtiru, writing from an unknown location, possibly Ashdod (EA 296). Its aim is to convince the Pharaoh of the vassal kings' loyalty by recourse to imagery. Again, the key word of the proverb "brick" (written logographically as sig_4) is glossed by its Canaanite rendering, as in no. 16. Because the proverb is found in three letters, each attributed to a different ruler from a different location, it can be argued that either the proverb was well-known among scribal circles in southwest Canaan, or more likely, all letters were written by the same scribe (Vita 2010). This is a clear demonstration that at least some of the proverbs of the Amarna letters were not the expression of individual rulers but rather elaborate articulations of wisdom utilized by professional scribes to achieve a maximum rhetorical effect.

18.

en-né-ep-ša-te kīma riqqi erî :sí-ri ḫubulli ištu qāt amēlī māt Sute

I have become like a copper cauldron (gloss: pot) in pledge because of the Suteans.
(EA 297:12–16; Moran 1992: 339)

The letter is sent from Yapaḫu of Gezer. The same saying appears also in EA 292 from a different ruler, probably also from Gezer. Hence, it stands to reason that both EA 292 and EA 297 were written by the same scribe; see also no. 17.

19.

ša-ak-na-ti enūma elippu ina libbi tâmti

I am situated like a boat in the midst of the sea.
(EA 288:32–33; Moran 1992: 331).

Thus says the governor Abdi-Ḫeba(t) (or his scribe) from Jerusalem, 2,500 feet above sea-level! The saying may have struck a cord with the Pharaoh to whom the letter is addressed, in view of the Egyptians' well-known fear of the sea.

20.

> *amur anāku la abiya u la ummiya ša-ak-na-ni ina ašri annê zu-ru-uḫ šarri* kalag.ga *ušēribanni ana bīt abiya*
>
> Behold! As for myself—neither my father nor my mother installed me in this place but the strong arm of the king had me enter my father's house.
>
> (EA 286:9–13; Moran 1992: 326–27; cf. EA 287:25–28 and EA 288:13–15)

More a locution than a proverb, this expression is found in three letters, again from Jerusalem. Given the many linguistic and orthographic peculiarities in the letters attributed to the Jerusalem scribe (Moran 1975), there is some reason to suspect that he himself was responsible for these two sayings rather than the ruler of Jerusalem, Abdi-Ḫeba(t).

21.

> *ki-i na-am-lu tu-um-ḫa-ṣú la-a ti-qà-pí-lu ù ta-an-šu-ku qà-ti* lú-*lì ša yi-ma-ḫa-aš-ši*
>
> "When an ant is smitten, does it not fight back and bite the hand of the person who smote it?'
>
> (EA 252:16–19; Moran 1992: 305–6; Halpern and Huehnergard 1982; Hess 1993)

This remarkable proverb was quoted by Labayu ruler of Shechem, or his scribe. Because of its astute observance of the ant's typical behavior, it has been compared on numerous occasions with Prov 6:6–8 and 30:25. Proverbs, as expected, serves however didactic purposes. Nonetheless, a point of comparison with Labayu's proverb and Prov 30:25 is worth pointing out: both proverbs (as is typical of many proverbs) intentionally choose a minor or insignificant animal to prove their point—the ant.

ארבעה הם קטני־ארץ והמה חכמים מחכמים:
הנמלים עם לא־עז ויכינו בקיץ לחמם

> "Four things there are which are smallest on earth, yet wise beyond wisest.
> Ants, a people with no strength, they prepare their store of food in the summer."

Two additional saying from letters are added to our selection; they derive from the Hittite sphere. The first letter is dated to the end of the Old Babylonian period, the other letter to the close of the thirteenth century.

22.

This proverb is preserved in one of the few letters dating to the formative period of the Hittite kingdom, the so-called Tikunani Letter (the tablet comes from the antiquity market and is without provenance). The speaker here is the Hittite king, most probably Ḫattušili I, addressing the king of Tikunani and demanding loyalty from him as his vassal.

> *sarrāti ša idabbub la tašamme qarnī*[!] *rīmi uṣur u sibbat nēši uṣur sibbat šēlabi la taṣbat*

> Don't listen to the lies he (i.e., the enemy) utters: heed the bull's horns and heed the lion's tail!; don't grasp the fox's tail!
>
> (Salvini 1994 and 1996; Hoffner 2009: 75–80; Durand and Charpin 2006)

The allusion to the bull may point to the Storm God, whose symbol this animal is; the lion probably metaphorically refers to the Hittite king, who elsewhere is compared to the royal beast, while the fox obviously refers to the nameless enemy, who speaks lies.

From a later period and more explicit in spelling out these animal metaphors is another Hittite letter, KBo 1.14, written to the king of Assyria. There is no doubt that lines 18′–19′ of the letter allude to one or another version of the proverb above. The speaker is the Hittite king, probably Ḫattušili III, here identified with the lion whereas the aggravating men of Turira are represented by the fox:

> *ammīni ana yâši nēši amēlū Turira šēlebu uzzannûninni*

> Why have the people of Turira—the fox!—aggravated me, the lion?
>
> (KBo 1.14 = Mora and Giorgieri 2004: 57–75)

Both these sources are to be compared with no. 6 above.

23.

> *tēltum ša amēlī māt Ḫatti mā ištēn amēlu ḫamiš šanāti ina bīt kīli kalimi u kīme iqta[bûšu] mā ina šērti umaššarūka u ittaḫnaq*
>
> There is a saying among the people of Ḫatti so: "A certain man was imprisoned in jail for five years. When he was told, 'Tomorrow you will be released,' he strangled himself."
>
> (RS 20.216; *Ugaritica* 5, no. 35; Beckman 1999, no. 38C)

This proverb is quoted by the king of Carchemish, the Hittite viceroy, writing to his vassal, the king of Ugarit, probably Ammurapi. The meaning of the proverb is not clear, as the letter itself is in very poor condition, and scholars have come up with various suggestions regarding its translation and meaning. The letter is concerned with the famous divorce case of the Hittite princess, Eḫli-Nikkal, which involved many well-known figures of the ancient world. Perhaps the proverb illustrates an act of irrationality of which the king of Carchemish accuses the king of Ugarit in his behavior over the affair. For the divorce affair, see Singer (1999:701–2) and Lackenbacher (2002: 126–30).

Notes (Numbered according to the Proverbs)

1. For the meaning of the particle *assurē*, see Wasserman 2012.

2. *qattukkunu* should probably be analyzed as *qātum=kunu* in the locative case but with an instrumental sense, as if **ina qātikunu* "don't carry (yourselves) to anywhere with/upon your paw(s)"; cf. Ps 61:6: הפך ים ליבשה בנהר יעברו ברגל "Sea turned into land, in the river they passed by foot"; *kurrum* = *kūru*(*m*) "kiln, brazier"; see Durand 2006: 31, whose interpretation settles previous disputes regarding the meaning of the proverb (see lastly Heimpel 2003: 179 with literature).

3. *šagû* = *šegû* "mad, rabid"; cf. Hebrew שגעון and see no. 4.

4. Translation after ARG. Kupper in ARMT 28 32 restored [*i-sa-ḫu-ur*], translating "who doesn't [stop turning to the right] or to the left."

5. *ikullûm* = *ukullûm*, "fodder."

7. *muḫḫum* in Akkadian means "skull" or "forehead," but also "brain," and in this case "marrow"; see Westenholz and Sigrist 2006, and esp. p. 4, for the marrow of the fetlock or lower ankle; and cf. אחד עצם שיש בו מוח ואחד עצם שאין בו מוח "a bone which contains the 'brain,' a bone which doesn't

contain 'brain.'" (Babylonian Talmud, *Mo'ed, Masechet Pesachim*). Compare *kursinnu* to Hebrew קרסל "lower part of the leg, ankle."

8. Perhaps take as a question: "Have fetlocks exchanged places with heads?" (ARG).

9. Translation after ARG. The form *uštaplā* (as cited by Charpin 1989–1990: 96) in Babylonian would possibly be *ištaplā* or *uštappilā*.

12. The choice of the word *biṣṣurum* in the letter was no doubt intentional, because it is surely the most derogatory word for the female genitalia in the Akkadian language; see Civil 2006. It was meant to either humiliate or embarrass its hearer. In a lexical list from Emar the word is glossed over by *ṭannapu*, "dirty, soiled'; see Cohen 2010b. (Dr. Ahuva Ashman suggested the comparison with Song of Songs to me.) The positive qualities of life on the go rather than that of an idle city dweller are reflected also in The Epic of Erra, i 46–60; see Marello 1992: 121.

13. See also Ziegler and Wasserman 1994 and Heimpel 1997.

18. *riqqu* = *ruqqu* "kettle, cauldron."

22. See also Durand 2006: 26 and 35–36. For animal imagery in Old Hittite sources, see Collins 1998; Miller (2001) provides a discussion regarding the geopolitical setting of the letter and its historical implications. The Tikunani Letter, ll. 34–35: understand the writing *ši-pa-at* as *sibbat* (or *zibbat*) from *s/zibbatum* "tail," following Durand and Charpin (2006); *qa-ni* is for *qannī*, a variant of *qarnī*, "horns" (ARG).

23. Beckman, among others, translates *ittaḫnaq* "he was annoyed." See also the comments by Durand (2006: 19).

Bibliography

Alaura, Silvia. 1998. Die Identifizierung der im "Gebäude E" von Büyükkale-Boğazköy gefundenen Tontafelfragmente aus der Grabung von 1933. *AoF* 25:193–214.

———. 2001. Archive und Bibliotheken in Ḫattuša. Pages 12–26 in *Akten des IV. Internationalen Kongresses für Hethitologie, Würzburg, 4.–8. Oktober 1999*. StBoT 45. Edited by Gernot Wilhelm. Wiesbaden: Harrassowitz.

Alster, Bendt. 1979. An Akkadian and a Greek Proverb. *WO* 10:1–5.

———. 1989. An Akkadian Animal Proverb and the Assyrian Letter ABL 555. *JCS* 41:187–93.

———. 1991. Väterliche Weisheit in Mesopotamien. Pages 103–15 in *Weisheit*. Edited by Aleida Assmann. Archäologie der literarischen Kommunikation 3. Munich: Wilhelm Fink.

———. 1996. Literary Aspects of Sumerian and Akkadian Proverbs. Pages 1–18 in *Mesopotamian Poetic Language: Sumerian and Akkadian*. Edited by Marianna E. Vogelzang and Herman L. J. Vanstiphout. CM 6. Groningen: Styx.

———. 1997. *Proverbs of Ancient Sumer*. Bethesda, Md.: CDL.

———. 2005. *Wisdom of Ancient Sumer*. Bethesda, Md.: CDL.

———. 2007. *Sumerian Proverbs in the Schøyen Collection*. CUSAS 2. Bethesda, Md.: CDL.

———. 2008. Scribes and Wisdom in Ancient Mesopotamia. Pages 47–63 in *Scribes, Sages, and Seers: The Sage in the Eastern Mediterranean World*. Edited by Leo G. Perdue. FRLANT 219. Göttingen: Vandenhoeck and Ruprecht.

Alster, Bendt and Takayoshi Oshima. 2006. A Sumerian Proverb Tablet in Geneva with Some Thoughts on Sumerian Proverb Collections. *Or* 75:31–72.

Annus, Amar and Alan Lenzi. 2010. *Ludlul bēl nēmeqi: The Standard Babylonian Poem of the Righteous Sufferer*. SAACT 7. Winona Lake, Ind.: Eisenbrauns.

———. 2011. A Six-Column Babylonian Tablet of *Ludlul Bēl Nēmeqi* and the Reconstruction of Tablet IV. *JNES* 70:181–205.

Archi, Alfonso. 1995. "Pensavano" gli ittiti? *SEL* 12:13–19.

———. 2007. Transmission of Recitative Literature of the Hittites. *AoF* 34:185–203.

Arnaud, Daniel. 1982. Les textes suméro-accadien: un florilège. Pages 43–51 in *Meskéné-Emar: Dix ans de travaux 1972–1982*. Edited by Dominique Beyer. Paris: ERC.

———. 1985–1987. *Recherches au pays d'Aštata: Emar VI: Les textes sumériens et accadiens*. Paris: ERC.

———. 2007. *Corpus des textes de bibliothèque de Ras Shamra-Ougarit (1936–2000) en sumérien, babylonien et assyrien.* AuOrSup 23. Barcelona: Ausa.

Beaulieu, Paul-Alain. 2007. The Social and Intellectual Setting of Babylonian Wisdom Literature. Pages 3–19 in *Wisdom Literature in Mesopotamia and Israel*. Edited by Richard J. Clifford. SBLSymS 38. Atlanta: Society of Biblical Literature.

Beckman, Gary. 1982. The Hittite Assembly. *JAOS* 102:435–42.

———. 1983. Mesopotamians and Mesopotamian Learning at Ḫattuša. *JCS* 35:97–115.

———. 1986. Proverbs and Proverbial Allusions in Hittite. *JNES* 45:19–30.

———. 1999. *Hittite Diplomatic Texts*. SBLWAW 7. Atlanta: Society of Biblical Literature.

Beyer, Dominique, ed., 1982. *Meskéné-Emar: Dix ans de travaux 1972–1982*. Paris: ERC.

———. 2001. *Emar IV. Les sceaux. Mission archéologique de Meskéne-Emar. Recherches au pays d'Aštata*. OBO Series Archaeologica 20. Göttingen: Vandenhoeck and Ruprecht.

Bottéro, Jean. 1991. La "tenson" et la réflexion sur les choses en Mésopotamie. Pages 7–22 in *Dispute Poems and Dialogues in the Ancient and Mediaeval Near East: Forms and Types of Literary Debates in Semitic and Related Literatures*. Edited by Gerrit J. Reinink and Herman L. J. Vanstiphout. OLA 42. Leuven: Peeters.

Brinkman, John A. 1999. Nazi-Maruttaš. *RlA* 9:190–91.

Brunner, Christopher J. 1980. The Fable of the Babylonian Tree. *JNES* 39:191–202 and 291–302.

Bryce, Trevor R. 2003. *Letters of the Great Kings of the Ancient Near East. The Royal Correspondence of the Late Bronze Age*. London: Routledge.

———. 2005. *The Kingdom of the Hittites*. New ed. Oxford: Oxford University Press.

Buccellati, Giorgio. 1981. Wisdom or Not: The Case of Mesopotamia. *JAOS* 101:35–47.

Cavigneaux, Antoine. 2003. Fragments littéraires susiens. Pages 53–62 in *Literatur, Politik und Recht in Mesopotamien: Festschrift für Claus Wilcke*. Edited by Walther Sallaberger, Konrad Volk, and Annette Zgoll. Orientalia Biblica et Christiana 14. Wiesbaden: Harrassowitz.

Cavigneaux, Antoine and Farouk N. H. Al-Rawi. 2000. *Gilgameš et la Mort. Texts de Tell Haddad VI, avec un appendice sur les textes funéraires sumériens*. CM 19. Groningen: Styx.

Charpin, Dominique. 1989–1990. Compte rendu du CAD volume Q (1982). *AfO* 36–37: 92–106.

———. 2010. *Reading and Writing in Babylon*. Translated by Jane Marie Todd. Cambridge, Mass.: Harvard University Press.

———. 2012. *Hammurabi of Babylon*. London: I.B. Tauris.

Chavalas, Mark W. 2002. Assyriology and Biblical Studies: A Century and a Half of Tension. Pages 21–67 in *Mesopotamia and the Bible: Comparative Explorations*. Edited by Mark W. Chavalas and K. Lawson Younger, Jr. JSOTSup 341. London: Sheffield Academic Press.

Civil, Miguel. 1974–1977. Enlil and Namzitarra. *AfO* 25:65–71.

———. 1989. The Texts from Meskene-Emar. *AuOr* 7:5–25.

———. 1992. Education in Mesopotamia. Pages 301–5 in *The Anchor Bible Dictionary*.

Edited by David Noel Freedman. New York: Doubleday.

———. 1994. *The Farmer's Instructions: A Sumerian Agricultural Manual*. AuOrSup 5. Barcelona: Ausa.

———. 1995. Ancient Mesopotamian Lexicography. Pages 2305–14 in *Civilizations of the Ancient Near East*. Edited by Jack M. Sasson. New York: Scribner.

———. 2000. From the Epistolary of the Edubba. Pages 105–18 in *Wisdom, Gods and Literature. Studies in Assyriology in Honour of W.G. Lambert*. Edited by Irving L. Finkel and Andrew R. George. Winona Lake, Ind.: Eisenbrauns.

———. 2006. be_5/pe-en-zé-er = *biṣṣuru*. Pages 55–62 in *If A Man Builds a Joyful House: Assyriological Studies in Honor of Erle Verdun Leichty*. Edited by Ann K. Guinan et al. CM 31. Leiden: Brill.

Clifford, Richard J. 2007. Introduction. Pages xi–xiii in *Wisdom Literature in Mesopotamia and Israel*. Edited by Richard J. Clifford. SBLSymS 38. Atlanta: Society of Biblical Literature.

Cohen, Yoram. 2002. *Taboos and Prohibitions in Hittite Society: A Study of the Hittite Expression* natta āra. THeth 24. Heidelberg: Carl Winter.

———. 2009. *The Scribes and Scholars of the City of Emar in the Late Bronze Age*. HSS 59. Winona Lake, Ind.: Eisenbrauns.

———. 2010a. Enlil and Namzitarra: The Emar and Ugarit Manuscripts and a New Understanding of the "Vanity Theme" Speech. *RA* 104:87–97.

———. 2010b. The Glosses of the Emar Lexical Lists: Akkadian or West Semitic? Pages 813–39 in *Proceedings of the 53rd Rencontre Assyriologique Internationale*. Vol. 1: *Language in the Ancient Near East*. Edited by Leonid Kogan. Winona Lake, Ind.: Eisenbrauns.

———. 2012. Where is Bazi? Where is Zizi? *The Ballad of Early Rulers* and the Mari Rulers in the Sumerian King List. *Iraq* 74:137–52.

Cohen, Yoram and Lorenzo d'Alfonso. 2008. The Duration of the Emar Archives and the Relative and Absolute Chronology of the City. Pages 3–25 in *The City of Emar among the Late Bronze Age Empires. History, Landscape, and Society. Proceedings of the Konstanz Emar Conference*. Edited by Lorenzo d'Alfonso, Yoram Cohen, and Dietrich Sürenhagen. AOAT 349. Münster: Ugarit-Verlag.

Collins, Billie Jean. 1998. Hattušili I, The Lion King. *JCS* 50:15–20.

Cooper, Jerrold S. 2011. Puns and Prebends: The Tale of Enlil and Namzitarra. Pages 39–43 in *Strings and Threads: A Celebration of the Work of Anne Draffkorn Kilmer*. Edited by Wolfgang Heimpel and Gabriella Frantz-Szabó. Winona Lake, Ind.: Eisenbrauns.

Delnero, Paul. 2010a. Sumerian Extract Tablets and Scribal Education. *JCS* 62:53–69.

———. 2010b. Sumerian Literary Catalogues and the Scribal Curriculum. *ZA* 100:32–55.

Dietrich, Manfried. 1988. Marduk in Ugarit. *SEL* 5:79–101.

———. 1991. Der Dialog zwischen Šūpē-amēli und seinem "Vater": die Tradition babylonischer Weisheitgesprüche im Westen. *UF* 23:33–68.

———. 1992. "Ein Leben ohne Freude…" Studie über eine Weisheitkomposition aus den Gelehrtenbibliotheken von Emar und Ugarit. *UF* 24:9–29.

———. 1993. Babylonian Literary Texts from Western Libraries. Pages 41–67 in *Verse in Ancient Near Eastern Prose*. Edited by Johannes C. de Moor and Wilfred G. E.

Watson. AOAT 43. Neukirchen-Vluyn: Neukirchener Verlag.

———. 1995. *ina ūmī ullûti* "An jenen (fernen) Tagen": Ein sumerisches kosmogonisches Mythologem in babylonischer Tradition. Pages 57–72 in *Vom Alten Orient zum Alten Testament: Festschrift für Wolfram Freiherrn von Soden zum 85. Geburtstag am 19. Juni 1993*. Edited by Manfried Dietrich and Oswald Loretz. AOAT 240. Neukirchen-Vluyn: Butzon & Bercker Kevelaer.

———. 1996. Aspects of the Babylonian Impact on Ugaritic Literature and Religion. Pages 33–47 in *Ugarit, Religion and Culture: Proceedings of the International Colloquium on Ugarit, Religion and Culture*. Edited by Nicolas Wyatt, Wilfred G. E. Watson, and Jeffery B. Lloyd. Münster: Ugarit-Verlag.

Dietrich, Manfried and Walter Mayer. 1999. The Hurrian and Hittite Texts. Pages 58–75 in *Handbook of Ugaritic Studies*. Edited by Wilfred G. E. Watson and Nicolas Wyatt. HO 39. Leiden: Brill.

Dijk, Johannes J. A. van. 1953. *La sagesse suméro-accadienne: Recherches sur les genres littéraires des textes sapientiaux*. Leiden: Brill.

Dijkstra, Meindert. 1993. The Akkado-Hurrian Bilingual Wisdom-Text RS 15.010 Reconsidered. *UF* 25:157–62.

Durand, Jean-Marie. 1998. *Les documents épistolaires du palais de Mari, Tome II*. LAPO 17. Paris: Cerf.

———. 2006. Dictons et proverbes à l'époque amorrite. *Journal Asiatique* 294:3–38.

Durand, Jean-Marie and Dominique Charpin. 2006. La lettre de Labarna au roi de Tigunânum, un réexamen. Pages 219–27 in *Šapal tibnim mû illakū: Studies Presented to Joaquín Sanmartín on the Occasion of His 65th Birthday*. Edited by Gregorio del Olmo Lete, Lluís Feliu, and Adelina Millet Albà. AuOrSup 22. Barcelona: Ausa.

Ebeling, Erich. 1928–1929. Reste akkadischer Weisheitsliteratur. Pages 21–29 in *Altorientalische Studien Bruno Meissner zum sechzigsten Geburtstag am 25. April 1928 gewidmet von Freunden, Kollegen und Schülern*. MAOG 4. Leipzig: Harrassowitz.

Filippo, Francesco, di. 2004. Notes on the Chronology of Emar Legal Texts. *SMEA* 46:175–214.

Finet, André. 1974. Citations littéraires dans la correspondence de Mari. *RA* 68:35–47.

Finkel, Irving L. 1986. On the Series of Sidu. *ZA* 76:250–53.

———. 1988. Adad-apla-iddina, Esagil-kīn-apli and the Series SA.GIG. Pages 143–60 in *A Scientific Humanist: Studies in Memory of Abraham Sachs*. Edited by Erle Leichty, Maria deJong Ellis, and Pamela Gerardi. Philadelphia: The University Museum.

———. 1999. On Some Dog, Snake and Scorpion Incantations. Pages 213–50 in *Mesopotamian Magic: Textual, Historical, and Interpretative Perspectives*. Edited by Tzvi Abusch and Karel van der Toorn. Ancient Magic and Divination 1. Groningen: Styx.

Fleming, Daniel E. 2000. *Time at Emar. The Cultic Calendar and the Rituals from the Diviner's House*. MC 11. Winona Lake, Ind.: Eisenbrauns.

Forti, Tova L. 2008. *Animal Imagery in the Book of Proverbs*. VTSup 118. Leiden: Brill.

Foster, Benjamin R. 1997. The Poem of the Righteous Sufferer. Page 486 in *The Context of Scripture: Canonical Compositions from the Biblical World*. Edited by William W. Hallo and K. Lawson Younger, Jr. Leiden: Brill.

———. 2005. *Before the Muses: An Anthology of Akkadian Literature*. 3rd ed. Bethesda, Md.: CDL.

———. 2007. *Akkadian Literature of the Late Period*. GMTR 2. Münster: Ugarit-Verlag.

Fox, Michael V. 2011. Ancient Near Eastern Wisdom Literature (Didactic). *Religion Compass* 5:1–11.

Frahm, Eckart. 2010. The Latest Sumerian Proverbs. Pages 155–84 in *Opening the Tablet Box: Near Eastern Studies in Honor of Benjamin R. Foster*. Edited by Sarah C. Melville and Alice L. Slotsky. CHANE 42. Leiden: Brill.

———. 2011. *Babylonian and Assyrian Text Commentaries: Origins of Interpretation*. GMTR 5. Münster: Ugarit-Verlag.

Gabbay, Uri. 2011. Lamentful Proverbs or Proverbial Laments. *JCS* 63:51–64.

Geller, Markham J. 1990. Taboo in Mesopotamia: A Review Article. *JCS* 42:105–17.

George, Andrew R. 1999. *The Epic of Gilgamesh: The Babylonian Epic Poem and other Texts in Akkadian and Sumerian*. London: Allen Lane.

———. 2003. *The Babylonian Gilgamesh Epic: Introduction, Critical Edition, and Cuneiform Texts*. Oxford: Oxford University Press.

———. 2005. In Search of the É.DUB.BA.A: The Ancient Mesopotamian School in Literature and Reality. Pages 127–37 in *"An Experienced Scribe Who Neglects Nothing": Ancient Near Eastern Studies in Honor of Jacob Klein*. Edited by Yitschak Sefati et al. Bethesda, Md.: CDL.

———. 2007a. The Epic of Gilgamesh: Thoughts on Genre and Meaning. Pages 37–66 in *Gilgamesh and the World of Assyria. Proceedings of the Conference Held at the Mandelbaum House, the University of Sydney, 21–23 July 2004*. Edited by Joseph Azize and Noel Weeks. ANESSup 21. Leuven: Peeters.

———. 2007b. The Gilgameš Epic at Ugarit. *AuOr* 25: 237–254.

———. 2009. *Babylonian Literary Texts in the Schøyen Collection*. CUSAS 10. Bethesda, Md.: CDL.

George, Andrew R. and Junko Taniguchi. 2010. The Dogs of Ninkilim, Part Two: Babylonian Rituals to Counter Field Pests. *Iraq* 72:79–148.

Gesche, Petra D. 2001. *Schulunterricht in Babylonien im ersten Jahrtausend v. Chr.* AOAT 275. Münster: Ugarit-Verlag.

Gianto, Augustinus. 1998. Human Destiny in Emar and Qohelet. Pages 73–79 in *Qohelet in the Context of Wisdom*. Edited by Antoon Schoors. BETL 136. Leuven: Leuven University.

Glassner, Jean-Jacques. 2004. *Mesopotamian Chronicles*. SBLWAW 19. Atlanta: Society of Biblical Literature.

Gordin, Shai. 2011. The Tablet and Its Scribe: Between Archival and Scribal Spaces in Late Empire Period Ḫattusa. *AoF* 38:177–98.

———. in press. *The Scribal Circles and Writing Habits of Late Empire Period Ḫattuša*. StBoT. Wiesbaden: Harrassowitz.

Gressmann, Hugo, ed., 1909. *Altorientalische Texte zum alten Testament*. Tübingen: de Gruyter.

Hallo, William W. 1992. The Syrian Contribution to Cuneiform Literature and Learning.

Pages 69–88 in *New Horizons in the Study of Ancient Syria*. Edited by Mark W. Chavalas and John L. Hayes. Malibu: Undena.

———. 2010a (1990). Proverbs Quoted in Epic. Pages 607–23 in *The World's Oldest Literature: Studies in Sumerian Belles-Lettres*. CHANE 35. Leiden: Brill.

———. 2010b (1991). The Concept of Canonicity in Cuneiform and Biblical Literature: A Comparative Appraisal. Pages 699–716 in *The World's Oldest Literature: Studies in Sumerian Belles Lettres*. CHANE 35. Leiden: Brill.

Hallo, William W. and K. Lawson Younger, Jr. (eds.). 1997–2003. *The Context of Scripture*. Leiden: Brill.

Halpern, Baruch and John Huehnergard. 1982. El-Amarna Letter 252. *Or* 51:227–30.

Haul, Michael. 2000. *Das Etana-Epos*. Göttinger Arbeitshefte zur altorientalischen Literatur. Göttingen: Seminar für Keilschriftforschung.

Hawley, Robert. 2008a. On the Alphabetic Scribal Curriculum at Ugarit. Pages 57–67 in *Proceedings of the 51st Rencontre Assyriologique Internationale Held at the Oriental Institute of the University of Chicago, July 18–22, 2005*. Edited by Robert D. Biggs, Jennie Myers, and Martha T. Roth. SAOC 62. Chicago: Oriental Institute of the University of Chicago.

———. 2008b. Apprendre à écrire à Ougarit: une typologie des abécédaires. Pages 215–32 in *D'Ougarit à Jérusalem: recueil d'études épigraphiques et archéologiques offert à Pierre Bordreuil*. Edited by Carole Roche. Orient & Méditerranée 2. Paris: De Boccard.

Heeßel, Nils, P. 2009. The Babylonian Physician Rabâ-ša-Marduk. Another Look at Physicians and Exorcists in the Ancient Near East. Pages 13–28 in *Advances in Mesopotamian Medicine from Hammurapi to Hipprocrates*. Edited by Annie Attia, Gilles Buisson, and Markham J. Geller. CM 37. Leiden: Brill.

———. 2011. "Sieben Tafeln aus sieben Städten." Überlegungen zum Prozess der Serialisierung von Texten in Babylonien in der zweiten Hälfte des zweiten Jahrtausends v. Chr. Pages 171–95 in *Babylon: Wissenskultur in Orient und Okzident*. Edited by Eva Cancik-Kirschbaum, Margarete van Ess, and Joachim Marzahn. Topoi: Berlin Studies of the Ancient World 1. Berlin: de Gruyter.

Heimpel, Wolfgang. 1997. Cases of Belated and Premature Initiative. *NABU* 1997 (113):104–05.

———. 2003. *Letters to the King of Mari: A New Textual Translation, with Historical Introduction, Notes, and Discussion*. MC 12. Winona Lake, Ind.: Eisenbrauns.

Hess, Richard S. 1993. Smitten Ant Bites Back: Rhetorical Forms in the Amarna Correspondence from Shechem. Pages 95–111 in *Verse in Ancient Near Eastern Prose*. Edited by Johan de Roos and Wilfred G. E. Watson. AOAT 42. Neukirchen-Vluyn: Neukirchener Verlag.

Hoffner, Harry A., Jr. 1998. *Hittite Myths*. 2nd ed. SBLWAW 2. Atlanta: Society of Biblical Literature.

———. 2009. *Letters from the Hittite Kingdom*. SBLWAW 15. Atlanta: Society of Biblical Literature.

Holloway, Steven W. (ed.) 2006. *Orientalism, Assyriology and the Bible*. Sheffield: Sheffield Phoenix Press.

Horowitz, Wayne, Takayoshi Oshima, and Seth L. Sanders. 2006. *Cuneiform in Canaan:*

Cuneiform Sources from the Land of Israel in Ancient Times. Jerusalem: Israel Exploration Society.

Hout, Theo P. J., van den. 2005. On the Nature of the Tablet Collections at Ḫattuša. *SMEA* 47:277–89.

———. 2006. Administration in the Reign of Tutḫaliya IV and the Later Years of the Hittite Empire. Pages 77–106 in *The Life and Times of Ḫattušili III and Tutḫaliya IV: Proceedings of a Symposium held in Honour of J. de Roos, 12–13 December 2003, Leiden*. Edited by Theo P. J. van den Hout. Leiden: NINO.

———. 2009a. Schreiber. D. Bei den Hethitern. *RlA* 12:273–80.

———. 2009b. Reflections on the Origins and Development of the Hittite Tablet Collections in Hattuša and their Consequences for the Rise of Hittite Literacy. Pages 71–96 in *Central-North Anatolia in the Hittite Period: New Perspectives in Light of Recent Research: Acts of the International Conference held at the University of Florence (7–9 February 2007)*. Edited by Franca Pecchioli-Daddi, Giulia Torri, and Carlo Corti. Studia Asiana 5. Rome: Herder.

Huehnergard, John. 1987. *Ugaritic Vocabulary in Syllabic Transcription*. HSS 32. Atlanta: Scholars Press.

———. 1989. *The Akkadian of Ugarit*. HSS 34. Atlanta: Scholars Press.

———. 1991. More on KI.*erṣetu* at Emar. *NABU* 1991 (2):39.

Hurowitz, Victor A. 1999. Canon, Canonicity and Canonization in Mesopotamia—Scholarly Model or Ancient Reality? Pages *1–*12 in *Proceedings of the Twelfth World Congress of Jewish Studies, Jerusalem, July 29–August 5, 1997. Division A: The Bible and Its World*. Edited by Ron Margolin. Jerusalem: World Union of Jewish Studies.

———. 2007. The Wisdom of Šūpê-amēlī—A Deathbed Debate between a Father and Son. Pages 37–51 in *Wisdom Literature in Mesopotamia and Israel*. Edited by Richard J. Clifford. SBLSymS 38. Atlanta: Society of Biblical Literature.

Izre'el, Shlomo. 1997. *The Amarna Scholarly Tablets*. CM 9. Groningen: Styx.

Jacobsen, Thorkild. 1939. *The Sumerian King List*. AS 11. Chicago: Chicago University Press.

———. 1976. *The Treasures of Darkness: A History of Mesopotamian Religion*. New Haven: Yale University Press.

Kämmerer, Thomas R. 1998. *Šimâ milka: Induktion und Reception der mittelbabylonischen Dichtung von Ugarit, Emar und Tell el-'Amarna*. AOAT 251. Münster: Ugarit-Verlag.

Keydana, G. 1991. Anhang: Die hethitische Version. *UF* 23:69–74.

Khanjian, John. 1975. Wisdom. Pages 373–400 in *Ras Shamra Parallels: The Texts from Ugarit and the Hebrew Bible*. Edited by Duane E. Smith and Stan Rummel. AnOr 50. Rome: Pontifical Biblical Institute.

Kienast, Burkhard. 2003. *Iškar šēlebi: Die Serie vom Fuchs*. FAOS 22. Stuttgart: Franz Steiner.

Klein, Jacob. 1990. The "Bane" of Humanity: A Lifespan of One Hundred Twenty Years. *ASJ* 12:57–70.

———. 1999. "The Ballad about Early Rulers" in Eastern and Western Traditions. Pages 203–16 in *Languages and Cultures in Contact: At the Crossroads of Civi-*

lizations in the Syro-Mesopotamian Realm (CRRAI 42). Edited by Karel van Lerberghe and Gabriella Voet. OLA 96. Leuven: Peeters.

———. 2003. An Old Babylonian Edition of Early Dynastic Insults (BT 9). Pages 136-149 in Literatur, Politik und Recht in Mesopotamien: Festschrift für Claus Wilcke. Edited by Walther Sallaberger, Konrad Volk, and Annette Zgoll. Orientalia Biblica et Christiana 14. Wiesbaden: Harrassowitz.

Kleinerman, Alexandra. 2011. *Education in Early 2nd Millennium BC Babylonia: The Sumerian Epistolary Miscellany*. CM 42. Leiden: Brill.

Klinger, Jörg. 2005. Die hethitische Rezeption mesopotamischer Literatur und die Überlieferung des Gilgameš-Epos in Ḫattuša. Pages 103–27 in *Motivation und Mechanismen des Kulturkontaktes in der Späten Bronzezeit*. Edited by Doris Prechel. Eothen 13. Florence: LoGisma.

———. 2010. Literarische sumerische Texte aus den hethitischen Archiven aus paläographischer Sicht, Teil II. *AoF* 37:306–40.

———. 2012. Literarische sumerische Texte aus den hethitischen Archiven aus paläographischer Sicht – Teil I. Pages 79–93 in *Palaeography and Scribal Practices in Syro-Palestine and Anatolia in the Late Bronze Age. Proceedings of the International Symposium Held in Leiden December 17–18, 2009*. Edited by Elena Devecchi. PIHANS 119. Leiden: NINO.

Kloekhorst, Alwin. 2008. *Etymological Dictionary of the Hittite Inherited Lexicon*. Leiden Indo-European Etymological Dictionary Series 5. Leiden: Brill.

Koppen, Franz, van. 2011. The Scribe of the Flood Story and His Circle. Pages 140–66 in *The Oxford Handbook of Cuneiform Culture*. Edited by Karen Radner and Eleanor Robson. Oxford: Oxford University Press.

Košak, Silvin. 1995. The Palace Library "Building A" on Büyükkale. Pages 173–79 in *Studio historiae ardens: Ancient Near Eastern Studies Presented to Philo H.J. Houwink ten Cate on the Occasion of His 65th Birthday*. Edited by Theo P. J. van den Hout and Johan de Roos. Leiden: NINO.

Krebernik, Manfred. 2004. Wörter und Sprichwörter: der zweisprachige Schultext HS 1461. *ZA* 94:226–49.

Lackenbacher, Sylvie. 2002. *Textes akkadiens d'Ugarit. Textes provenant des vingt-cinq premières campagnes*. LAPO 20. Paris: Cerf.

Lambert, Wilfred G. 1957. Ancestors, Authors and Canonicity. *JCS* 11:1–14.

———. 1960. *Babylonian Wisdom Literature*. Oxford: Clarendon.

———. 1962. A Catalogue of Texts and Authors. *JCS* 16:59–77.

———. 1989. A New Interpretation of Enlil and Namzitarra. *Or* 58:508–9.

———. 1995. Some New Babylonian Wisdom Literature. Pages 30–42 in *Wisdom in Ancient Israel: Essays in Honour of J.A. Emerton*. Edited by John Day, Robert P. Gordon, and Hugh G. M. Williamson. Cambridge: Cambridge University Press.

———. 2003. A New Verb *namû* or a New Meaning? *NABU* 2003 (23):18–19.

Langdon, Stephen Herbert. 1923. *Babylonian Wisdom*. London: Luzac.

Laroche, Emmanuel. 1968. Textes de Ras Shamra en langue hittite. Pages 769–84 in *Ugaritica 5*. Edited by Claude F. A. Schaeffer et al. MRS 16. Paris: P. Geuthner.

Lebrun, René. 1980. *Hymnes et prières hittites*. Homo religiosus 4. Louvain-la-Neuve:

Centre d'histoire des religions.

Lenzi, Alan. 2008. The Uruk List of Kings and Sages and Late Mesopotamian Scholarship. *JANER* 8:137–69.

———. 2012. The Curious Case of Failed Revelation in *Ludlul bel Nemeqi*: A New Suggestion for the Poem's Scholarly Purpose. Pages 36–66 in *Mediating Between Heaven and Earth: Communication with the Divine in the Ancient Near East.* Edited by C. L. Crouch, Jonathan Stökl, and Anna-Elise Zernecke. Library of the Hebrew Bible / Old Testament Studies 566. London: T&T Clark International.

Lenzi, Alan, Christopher Frechette, and Anna-Elise Zernecke. 2011. Introduction. Pages 1–68 in *Reading Akkadian Prayers and Hymns*. Edited by Alan Lenzi. Ancient Near East Monographs/Monografías sobre el antiguo Cercano Oriente 3. Atlanta: Society of Biblical Literature.

Lieberman, Stephen J. 1990. Canonical and Official Cuneiform Texts: Towards an Understanding of Assurbanipal's Personal Tablet Collection. Pages 305–36 in *Lingering over Words: Studies in Ancient Near Eastern Literature in Honor of William L. Moran*. Edited by Tzvi Abusch, John Huehnergard, and Piotr Steinkeller. HSS 37. Atlanta: Scholars Press.

Lindenberger, James M. 1983. *The Aramaic Proverbs of Ahiqar*. Baltimore: Johns Hopkins University Press.

Liverani, Mario. 1990. *Prestige and Interest: International Relations in the Near East ca. 1600–1100 B.C.* Padova: S.A.R.G.O.N.

Livingstone, Alasdair. 1986. *Mystical and Mythological Explanatory Works of Assyrian and Babylonian Scholars*. Oxford: Oxford University Press & Clarendon.

Longman III, Tremper. 1991. *Fictional Akkadian Autobiography: A Generic and Comparative Study*. Winona Lake, Ind.: Eisenbrauns.

Malbran-Labat, Florence. 1995. La découverte épigraphique de 1994 à Ougarit (les textes akkadiens). *SMEA* 36:103–11.

Marchesi, Gianni. 2010. The Sumerian King List and the Early History of Mesopotamia. Pages 231–48 in *ana turri gimilli. Studi dedicati al Padre Werner R. Mayer, S.J. da amici e allievi*. Edited by Maria Giovanna Biga and Mario Liverani. Quaderno di Vicino Oriente 5. Rome: Rome University La Sapienza.

Marcus, David. 1973. A Famous Analogy of Rib-Haddi. *JANES* 5 (Fs Gaster):281–86.

Marello, Pierre. 1992. Vie nomade. Pages 115–25 in *Florilegium marianum: Recueil d'études en l'honneur de Michel Fleury*. Edited by Jean-Marie Durand. Mémoires de N.A.B.U. 1. Paris: Sepoa.

Marzal, Angel. 1976. *Gleanings from the Wisdom of Mari*. Studia Pohl 11. Rome: Biblical Institute Press.

Melchert, H. Craig. 1983. Pudenda hethitica. *JCS* 35:137–45.

Michalowski, Piotr. 2011. *The Correspondence of the Kings of Ur: Epistolary History of an Ancient Mesopotamian Kingdom*. MC 15. Winona Lake, Ind.: Eisenbrauns.

Mieroop, Mark, van de. 2007. *The Eastern Mediterranean in the Age of Ramesses II*. Malden, Mass.: Blackwell.

Miller, Jared. 2001. Ḫattušili's Expansion into Northern Syria in Light of the Tikunani Letter. Pages 410–29 in *Akten des IV. Internationalen Kongresses für Hethi-*

tologie, Würzburg, 4.–8. Oktober 1999. Edited by Gernot Wilhelm. StBoT 45. Wiesbaden: Harrassowitz.

Moorey, P. Roger S. 1994. *Ancient Mesopotamian Materials and Industries*. Oxford: Clarendon.

Mora, Clelia and Mauro Giorgieri. 2004. *Le lettere tra i re ittiti e i re assiri ritrovate a Ḫattuša*. HANE/M 7. Padova: S.A.R.G.O.N.

Moran, William L. 1975. The Syrian Scribe of the Jerusalem Amarna Letters. Pages 146–66 in *Unity and Diversity: Essays in the History, Literature, and Religion of the Ancient Near East*. Edited by Hans Goedicke and Jimmy Jack McBee Roberts. Baltimore: Johns Hopkins University Press.

———. 1977. ARM I 5: 11–13. *RA* 71:191.

———. 1978. Puppies in Proverbs – From Šamši-Adad to Archilochus? *Eretz Israel* 14 (Fs Ginsberg):32–37.

———. 1992. *The Amarna Letters*. Baltimore: Johns Hopkins University Press.

Neu, Erich. 1996. *Das hurritische Epos der Freilassung 1: Untersuchungen zu einem hurritisch-hethitischen Textensemble aus Ḫattuša*. StBoT 32. Wiesbaden: Harrassowitz.

Nissinen, Martti. 2003. *Prophets and Prophecy in the Ancient Near East*. SBLWAW 12. Atlanta: Society of Biblical Literature.

Nougayrol, Jean. 1968. Textes Suméro-accadiens des archives et bibliothêques privées d'Ugarit. Pages 1–446 in *Ugaritica 5*. Edited by Claude F. A. Schaeffer et al. MRS 16. Paris: Geuthner.

Nougayrol, Jean and Emmanuel Laroche. 1955. Tablette bilingue accado-hourrite. Pages 311–24 in *Le Palais Royal d'Ugarit 3: Textes accadiens et hourrites des archives est, ouest et centrales*. Edited by Claude F. A. Schaeffer et al. MRS 6. Paris: Imprimerie Nationale & Klincksieck.

Oshima, Takayoshi. 2011. *Babylonian Prayers to Marduk*. ORA 7. Tübingen: Mohr Siebeck.

Otten, Heinrich. 1963. *Texte Aus Stadtplanquadrat L/18, I. Teil*. Keilschrifttexte aus Boghazköi 12. Berlin: Gebr. Mann.

Otto, Adelheid. 2010. Siegelpraxis. *RlA* 12 (5/6):469–74.

Pedersén, Olof. 1998. *Archives and Libraries in the Ancient Near East 1500–300 B.C.* Bethesda, Md.: CDL.

———. 2005. *Archive und Bibliotheken in Babylon: Die Tontafeln der Grabung Robert Koldeweys 1899–1917*. ADOG 25. Berlin: SDV.

———. 2011. Excavated and Unexcavated Libraries in Babylon. Pages 47–67 in *Babylon: Wissenskultur in Orient und Okzident*. Edited by Eva Cancik-Kirschbaum, Margarete van Ess and Joachim Marzahn. Topoi. Berlin Studies of the Ancient World 1. Berlin: de Gruyter.

Pfeiffer, Robert H. 1969. Akkadian Proverbs and Counsels. Pages 425–27 in *Ancient Near Eastern Texts Relating to the Old Testament*. 3rd ed. Edited by James B. Pritchard. Princeton: Princeton University Press.

Pitard, Wayne. 1999. The Alphabetic Ugaritic Tablets. Pages 46–57 in *Handbook of Ugaritic Studies*. Edited by Wilfred G. E. Watson and Nicolas Wyatt. HO 39. Leiden: Brill.

Ponchia, Simonetta. 1996. *La palma e il tamarisco e altri dialoghi mesopotamici*. Venice: Marsilio.

Porten, Bezalel and Ada Yardeni. 1993. *Textbook of Aramaic Documents from Ancient Egypt 3: Literature, Accounts, Lists*. Jerusalem: Hebrew University, Dept. of the History of the Jewish People.

Pritchard, James B. 1950. *Ancient Near Eastern Texts Relating to the Old Testament*. 1st ed. Princeton: Princeton University Press.

———. 1969. *Ancient Near Eastern Texts Relating to the Old Testament*. 3rd ed. Princeton: Princeton University Press.

Radner, Karen. 2010. Siegelpraxis (sealing practice). A. Philologisch. *RlA* 12 (5/6):466–69.

Rahman, Furat. 2006. "A City does not Approach a City, a Man Approaches a Man": Interpretation of one Old Babylonian Proverb in the Light of a Neo-Aramaic Proverb. *Babel & Bibel* 3:535–39.

Reinink, Gerrit J. and Vanstiphout, Herman L. J., (eds.). 1991. *Dispute Poems and Dialogues in the Ancient and Mediaeval Near East: Forms and Types of Literary Debates in Semitic and Related Literatures*. OLA 42. Leuven: Peeters.

Robson, Eleanor. 2001. The Tablet House: A Scribal School in Old Babylonian Nippur. *RA* 95:39–66.

Rogers, Robert William. 1912. *Cuneiform Parallels to the Old Testament*. London: Oxford University Press.

Rubio, Gonzalo. 2009. Scribal Secrets and Antiquarian Nostalgia: Tradition and Scholarship in Ancient Mesopotamia. Pages 155–82 in *Reconstructing a Distant Past: Ancient Near Eastern Essays in Tribute to Jorge R. Silva Castillo*. Edited by Diego A. Barreyra Fracaroli and Gregorio del Olmo Lete. AuOrSupp 25. Barcelona: Ausa.

Sallaberger, Walther. 1999. *"Wenn du mein Bruder bist, ... ": Interaktion und Textgestaltung in altbabylonischen Alltagsbriefen*. CM 16. Groningen: Styx.

———. 2010. Skepsis gegenüber väterlicher Weisheit: zum altbabylonischen Dialog zwischen Vater und Sohn. Pages 303–17 in *Your Praise is Sweet: A Memorial Volume for Jeremy Black from Students, Colleagues and Friends*. Edited by Heather D. Baker, Eleanor Robson, and Gábor Zólyomi. London: British Institute for the Study of Iraq.

Salvini, Mirjo. 1994. Una lettera di Ḫattušili I relativa alla spedizione contro Ḫaḫḫum. *SMEA* 34:61–80.

———. 1996. *The Ḫabiru Prism of King Tunip-Teššub of Tikunani*. Documenta Asiana 3. Rome: Istituti Editoriali e poligrafici.

Sassmannshausen, Leonhard. 2008. Babylonische Schriftkultur des 2. Jahrtausends v. Chr. in den Nachbarländern und im östlischen Mittelmeerraum. *AuOr* 26:263–93.

Sasson, Jack M. 1995. Water beneath Straw: Adventures of a Prophetic Phrase in the Mari Archives. Pages 599–608 in *Solving Riddles and Untying Knots: Biblical, Epigraphic, and Semitic Studies in Honor of Jonas C. Greenfield*. Edited by Ziony Zevit, Seymour Gitin, and Michael Sokoloff. Winona Lake, Ind.: Eisenbrauns.

Schwemer, Daniel. 2010. Fighting Witchcraft before the Moon and Sun: A Therapeutic Ritual from Neo-Babylonian Sippar. *Or* 79:480–504.

Seminara, Stefano. 1995. Un dilemma della topografia di Emar: kirṣîtu o ki.erṣētu? *UF* 27:467–80.

———. 2000. Le Istruzioni di Šūpē-amēlī. *UF* 32:487–529.

Singer, Itamar. 1999. A Political History of Ugarit. Pages 603–733 in *Handbook of Ugaritic Studies*. Edited by Wilfred G. E. Watson and Nicolas Wyatt. HO 39. Leiden: Brill.

———. 2002. *Hittite Prayers*. SBLWAW 11. Atlanta: Society of Biblical Literature.

———. 2011. *The Calm Before the Storm: Selected Writings of Itamar Singer on the End of the Late Bronze Age in Anatolia and the Levant*. SBLWAWSup 1. Atlanta: Society of Biblical Literature.

Soden, Wolfram, von. 1969. Bemerkungen zu einigen literarischen Texten in akkadischer Sprache aus Ugarit. *UF* 1:189–95.

———. 1990. Klage eines Dulders mit Gebet an Marduk. Pages 140–43 in *Weisheitstexte, Mythen und Epen*. Edited by Willem H. Ph. Römer and Wolfram von Soden. TUAT 3/1. Gütersloh: Gütersloher Verlagshaus Gerd Mohn.

Soldt, Wilfred H., van. 1988. The Title Ṯ'Y. *UF* 20:313–21.

———. 1991. *Studies in the Akkadian of Ugarit: Dating and Grammar*. AOAT 40. Neukirchen-Vluyn: Butzon & Bercker Kevelaer.

———. 1995. Babylonian Lexical, Religious and Literary Texts, and Scribal Education at Ugarit and Its Implications for the Alphabetic Literary Texts. Pages 171–212 in *Ugarit: Ein ostmediterranes Kulturzentrum im Alten Orient: Ergebnisse und Perspektiven der Forschung*. Edited by Manfried Dietrich and Oswald Loretz. Münster: Ugarit-Verlag.

———. 1999. The Written Sources: The Syllabic Akkadian Texts. Pages 28–45 in *Handbook of Ugaritic Studies*. Edited by Wilfred G. E. Watson and Nicolas Wyatt. HO 39. Leiden: Brill.

———. 2001. Naḫiš-šalmu, an Assyrian Scribe Working in the "Southern Palace" at Ugarit. Pages 429–44 in *Veenhof Anniversary Volume: Studies Presented to Klaas R. Veenhof on the Occasion of His Sixty-Fifth Birthday*. Edited by Wilfred H. van Soldt et al. Leiden: NINO.

———. 2011. The Role of Babylon in Western Peripheral Education. Pages 197–211 in *Babylon. Wissenskultur in Orient und Okzident*. Edited by Eva Cancik-Kirschbaum, Margarete van Ess and Joachim Marzahn. Topoi. Berlin Studies of the Ancient World 1. Berlin: de Gruyter.

———. 2012. The Palaeography of Two Ugarit Archives. Pages 171–83 in *Palaeography and Scribal Practices in Syro-Palestine and Anatolia in the Late Bronze Age*. Edited by Elena Devecchi. PIHANS 119. Leiden: NINO.

Speiser, Ephraim Avigdor. 1955. Akkadian Documents from Ras Shamra. *JAOS* 75:154–65.

Streck, Michael P. 2004. Dattelpalme und Tamariske in Mesopotamien nach dem akkadischen Streitgespräch. *ZA* 94:250–90.

Tanret, Michel. 2011. Learned, Rich, Famous and Unhappy: Ur-Utu of Sippar. Pages 270–87 in *The Oxford Handbook of Cuneiform Culture*. Edited by Karen Radner and Eleanor Robson. Oxford: Oxford University Press.

Tatu, Silviu. 2006. Jotham's Fable and the Crux interpretum in Judges ix. *VT* 56:105–24.

Taylor, Jon. 2005. The Sumerian Proverb Collections. *RA* 99:13–38.

Tinney, Steve. 2011. Tablets of Schools and Scholars: A Portrait of the Old Babylonian Corpus. Pages 577–96 in *The Oxford Handbook of Cuneiform Culture*. Edited by Karen Radner and Eleanor Robson. Oxford: Oxford University Press.

Torri, Giulia. 2008. The Scribes of the House on the Slope. Pages 771–82 in *VI Congresso Internazionale di Ittitologia (Roma, 5–9 settembre 2005)*. Edited by Alfonso Archi and Rita Francia. SMEA 50. Rome: CNR.

———. 2009. The Old Hittite Textual Tradition in the "Haus am Hang." Pages 207–22 in *Central-North Anatolia in the Hittite Period: New Perspectives in Light of Recent Research: Acts of the International Conference Held at the University of Florence (7–9 February 2007)*. Edited by Franca Pecchioli-Daddi, Giulia Torri, and Carlo Corti. Studia asiana 5. Rome: Herder.

Vanstiphout, Herman L. J. 1980. Some Notes on "Enlil and Namzitara." *RA* 74:67–71.

———. 1988. The Importance of the "Tale of the Fox." *ASJ* 10:191–227.

———. 1990. The Mesopotamian Debate Poems: A General Presentation (Part I). *ASJ* 12:271–318.

———. 1991. Lore, Learning and Levity in the Sumerian Disputations: A Matter of Form or Substance? Pages 23–46 in *Dispute Poems and Dialogues in the Ancient and Mediaeval Near East: Forms and Types of Literary Debates in Semitic and Related Literatures*. Edited by Gerrit J. Reinink and Herman L. J. Vanstiphout. OLA 42. Leuven: Peeters.

———. 1992a. The Mesopotamian Debate Poems: A General Presentation. Part II: The Subject. *ASJ* 14:339–67.

———. 1992b. The Banquet Scene in the Mesopotamian Debate Poems. Pages 9–21 in *Banquets d'Orient*. Edited by Rika Gyselen. Res Orientales 4. Paris: Groupe pour l'étude de la civilisation du Moyen-Age.

———. 1997. Disputations. Pages 575–88 in *The Context of Scripture: Canonical Compositions from the Biblical World*. Edited by William W. Hallo and K. Lawson Younger, Jr. Leiden: Brill.

———. 1999a. The Use(s) of Genre in Mesopotamian Literature. *Archív Orientální* 67:703–17.

———. 1999b. "I Can Put Anything in Its Right Place": Generic and Typological Studies as Strategies of the Analysis and Evaluation of Mankind's Oldest Literature. Pages 79–100 in *Aspects of Genre and Type in Pre-modern Literary Cultures*. Edited by Bert Roest and Herman L. J. Vanstiphout. Groningen: Styx.

———. 2003. The Old Babylonian Literary Canon. Structure, Function, and Intention. Pages 1–28 in *Cultural Repertoires. Structure, Function and Dynamics*. Edited by Gillis J. Dorleijn and Herman L. J. Vanstiphout. Groningen Studies in Cultural Change 3. Leuven: Peeters.

Veldhuis, Niek. 2000a. Sumerian Proverbs in Their Curricular Context. *JAOS* 120:383–99.

———. 2000b. Kassite Exercises: Literary and Lexical Extracts. *JCS* 52:67–94.

———. 2003. Sumerian Literature. Pages 29–43 in *Cultural Repertoires: Structure, Function and Dynamics*. Edited by Gillis J. Dorleijn and Herman L. J. Vanstiphout. Groningen Studies in Cultural Change 3. Leuven: Peeters.

———. 2004. *Religion, Literature, and Scholarship: The Sumerian Composition Nanše and the Birds*. CM 22. Leiden: Brill.

———. 2011. Levels of Literacy. Pages 68–89 in *The Oxford Handbook of Cuneiform Culture*. Edited by Karen Radner and Eleanor Robson. Oxford: Oxford University Press.

Vincente, Claudine-Adrienne. 1995. The Tall Leilān Recension of the Sumerian King List. *ZA* 85:243–70.

Vita, Juan-Pablo. 2009. Hurrian as a Living Language in Ugaritic Society. Pages 219–31 in *Reconstructing a Distant Past: Ancient Near Eastern Essays in Tribute to Jorge R. Silva Castillo*. Edited by Diego A. Barreyra Fracaroli and Gregorio del Olmo Lete. AuOrSup 25. Barcelona: Ausa.

———. 2010. Scribes and Dialects in Late Bronze Age Canaan. Pages 863–94 in *Proceedings of the 53rd Rencontre Assyriologique Internationale*. Vol. 1: *Language in the Ancient Near East*. Edited by Leonid Kogan. Babel & Bibel 4/2. Winona Lake, Ind.: Eisenbrauns.

Vogelzang, Marianna E. 1991. Some Questions about the Akkadian Disputes. Pages 47–57 in *Dispute Poems and Dialogues in the Ancient and Mediaeval Near East: Forms and Types of Literary Debates in Semitic and Related Literatures*. Edited by Gerrit J. Reinink and Herman L. J. Vanstiphout. OLA 42. Leuven: Peeters.

Volk, Konrad. 2000. Edubba'a und Edubba'a-Literatur: Rätsel und Lösungen. *ZA* 90:1–30.

Waal, Willemijn. 2011. They Wrote on Wood: The Case for a Hieroglyphic Scribal Tradition on Wooden Writing Boards in Hittite Anatolia. *AnSt* 61:21–34.

Waetzoldt, Hartmut and Antoine Cavigneaux. 2009. Schule. *RlA* 12:294–309.

Wagensonner, Klaus. 2011. A Scribal Family and its Orthographic Peculiarities. On the Scientific Work of a Royal Scribe and his Sons. Pages 645–701 in *The Empirical Dimension of Ancient Near Eastern Studies*. Edited by Gebhard J. Selz and Klaus Wagensonner. Wiener Offene Orientalistik 6. Wien: LIT.

Wasserman, Nathan. 2003. *Style and Form in Old Babylonian Literary Texts*. CM 27. Leiden: Styx.

———. 2011. Sprichwort. *RlA* 13:19–23.

———. 2012. *Most Probably: Epistemic Modality in Old Babylonian*. Languages of the Ancient Near East 3. Winona Lake, Ind.: Eisenbrauns.

Watson, Wilfred G. E. and Nicolas Wyatt. 1999. *Handbook of Ugaritic Studies*. HO 39. Leiden: Brill.

Weeden, Mark. 2011a. *Hittite Logograms and Hittite Scholarship*. StBoT 54. Wiesbaden: Harrassowitz.

———. 2011b. Hittite Scribal Schools outside of Hattusa? *AoF* 38:116–34.

Weidner, Ernst F. 1922. *Keilschrifturkunden aus Boghazköi 4*. Berlin: Staatliche Museen, Vorderasiatische Abteilung.

Weigl, Michael. 2001. Compositional Strategies in the Aramaic Sayings of Ahikar: Columns 6–8. Pages 22–82 in *The World of the Aramaeans III: Studies in Language and Literature in Honour of Paul-Eugène Dion*. Edited by P. M. Michèle Daviau, John W. Wevers, and Michael Weigl. JSOTSup 326. Sheffield: Sheffield Academic Press.

West, Martin L. 1969. Near Eastern Material in Hellenistic and Roman Literature. *HSCP* 73:113–34.

Westenholz Goodnick, Joan. 1997. *Legends of the Kings of Akkade: The Texts*. MC 7. Winona Lake, Ind.: Eisenbrauns.

Westenholz Goodnick, Joan and Marcel Sigrist. 2006. The Brain, the Marrow and the Seat of Cognition in Mesopotamian Tradition. *Le Journal des Médicines Cunéiformes* 7:1–10.

Wilcke, Claus. 1988. Die Sumerische Königsliste und erzählte Vergangenheit. Pages 113–40 in *Vergangenheit in mündlicher Überlieferung*. Edited by Jürgen von Ungern-Sternberg and Hansjörg Reinau. Stuttgart: Teubner.

———. 1989. Die Emar-Version von "Dattelpalme und Tamariske"—ein Rekonstruktionversuch. *ZA* 79:161–90.

Wilhelm, Gernot. 2001. Das hurritisch-hethitische "Lied der Freilassung." Pages 82–91 in *TUAT Ergänzungslieferung*. Edited by Otto Kaiser. Gütersloh: Gütersloher Verlagshaus Gerd Mohn.

———. 2003. Bemerkungen zu der akkadisch-hurritischen Bilingue aus Ugarit. Pages 341–45 in *Literatur, Politik und Recht in Mesopotamien: Festschrift für Claus Wilcke*. Edited by Walther Sallaberger, Konrad Volk, and Annette Zgoll. Orientalia Biblica et Christiana 14. Wiesbaden: Harrassowitz.

Woods, Christopher. 2006. Bilingualism, Scribal Learning, and the Death of Sumerian. Pages 91–120 in *Margins of Writing, Origins of Cultures*. Edited by Seth L. Sanders. OIS 2. Chicago: The Oriental Institute of the University of Chicago.

Yon, Marguerite. 1992. Ugarit: History and Archaeology. Pages 695–706 in *The Anchor Bible Dictionary*. Edited by David Noel Freedman. New York: Doubleday.

———. 2006. *The City of Ugarit at Tell Ras Shamra*. Winona Lake, Ind.: Eisenbrauns.

Yon, Marguerite and Daniel Arnaud, (eds.). 2001. *Études Ougaritiques I. Traveaux 1985–1995*. Ras Shamra-Ougarit 14. Paris: ERC.

Ziegler, Nele and Nathan Wasserman. 1994. Qātum ba''ītum – A Check-list. *NABU* 1994 (30):28–29.

Index of Sources

Ancient Near East

Biblical and Post-Biblical Sources

Index of Names

Personal Names (Historical and Fictional)

Divine Names

Place Names

CPSIA information can be obtained at www.ICGtesting.com
Printed in the USA
BVOW08s1543260913

332181BV00003B/9/P

9 781589 837539